INSIGHT PUBLISHING
SEVIERVILLE, TENNESSEE

Published by Insight Publishing Company
P.O. Box 4189
Sevierville, Tennessee 37864

10 9 8 7 6 5 4 3 2

Printed in Canada

ISBN: 1-932863-27-3

Table Of Contents

Rosemary Walter 1

Allen Stam 23

Jay Conrad Levinson 41

Ford Saeks 57

Bette Daoust, Ph.D. 77

Don Benton 95

David G. Edstrom 109

Robert Bly 121

Charles Clarke III 135

Rick Cooper 155

Edward A. Bond, Jr., CCM, FSMPS 171

Merrie Spaeth 189

Kelly McDonald 203

Brian Tracy 215

Jill Lublin 231

Ken Banks, BS, MBA 239

Bob Pritchard 259

Richard Tyler 279

A Message From The Publisher

During staff meetings at our company we discuss ways to grow and prosper. Inevitably, someone quips, "It's all about marketing!" We all laugh, knowing it's not *just* about marketing. We're constantly dealing with production issues, customer service, cash flow, and more. But we have to admit that without the marketing programs that bring us clients, we wouldn't have to worry about production, customer service, and cash flow. So, maybe it is *all about marketing!*

Regardless of what line of work you're in, you need to understand more about marketing, media, and public relations. And you need to learn fast! Your competition is gaining ground and using marketing techniques and programs that you haven't even considered.

You've made a great *first* decision by purchasing this dynamic book, *Marketing Magic!* We reached out into the marketplace and found some of the top media, marketing, and public relations experts in America and asked them to share their most potent strategies. As you read these informational and inspirational interviews, you'll learn powerful ideas to help transform your business. You'll also learn how these professionals can help your business grow even more by inviting them to work one-on-one with your organization. We hope you'll take advantage of this unique opportunity.

Interviews conducted by:

David E. Wright
President, International Speakers Network

Chapter 1

ROSEMARY WALTER

THE INTERVIEW

David E. Wright (Wright)

Today we are talking to Rosemary Walter. Rosemary is a marketing consultant who is an expert at creating customers for her business-to-business (B2B) client companies. She works successfully with marketing and non-marketing folks like engineers, sales, and manufacturing personnel. Her company, Mosaic Marketing Management, has been helping small to large size B2B companies increase their sales and profits for the past six years. Rosemary holds a BS degree in Communications from the University of Illinois in Urbana-Champaign and an MS in integrated marketing communications from Roosevelt University in Chicago. Both degrees were awarded with highest university honors. Rosemary has nearly 30 years' experience in business and marketing management. She has worked for market leaders such as McDonald's, Alberto-Culver, and Illinois Tool Works. She is a professional speaker and contributes articles regularly to national trade publications and newspapers. One of her most noteworthy claims to fame is that she helped introduce Chicken McNuggets to the world. Thank goodness you did! They are one of my all time favorites.

Walter

I'm glad that you appreciate my past efforts.

Wright

I do, Rosemary, and welcome to *Marketing Magic*!

Walter

Well, thank you, David.

Wright

So how long have you been involved with marketing?

Walter

I have been involved professionally for nearly 30 years, but my love for marketing and advertising really started when I was a child. I remember spending hours looking through magazines, reviewing the ads, and studying them very carefully. When I went to college, I searched for a curriculum and degree that tapped into my interests in creative communication. I wanted something that combined business and art and advertising and marketing seemed to provide that perfect blend. Since I graduated college I've had many jobs in the advertising and marketing field, including working with the Alberto-Culver Company on many of their flagship VO5 products, working at the national ad agency for McDonald's and introducing Chicken McNuggets into test markets and, later, into a US roll-out. I've also worked with industrial kinds of companies like Illinois Tool Works where I managed and marketed some of their tool and fastener line for residential construction in one of their divisions. I introduced millions of dollars of new products in consumer and business-to-business industrial markets over the years.

Wright

Those companies couldn't be any more different.

Walter

They sure couldn't, but the bottom line is that marketing principles, like something as simple as market positioning, work equally well across many different kinds of companies and industries. The key is to have a good handle on the principles and then apply them in the most effective way for the industry and market situation at hand whether it is B2B or consumer marketing.

Wright

For some of our readers who may be reading about marketing for the first time, could you explain what you mean when you say B2B or business-to-business?

Walter

Sure. Business-to-business, or B2B, companies sell their products or services to other businesses versus selling them to consumers like you and me. B2B products or services are generally associated with work-related activities. Business-to-consumer companies, like Alberto-Culver, for example, sell health and beauty aid products, among other things, to consumers. I'm sure you've used one or two of their products in the past.

Wright

Oh, most definitely. Give me some examples of some B2B products or services.

Walter

These products could be as small as screws or fasteners that are used in a tool or as large and pricey as a complex painting system that a company needs to produce its final end product, like a car panel or dresser. My clients are those businesses that sell a wide variety of products or services to other businesses.

Wright

Why do you feel so passionate about marketing, especially for business-to-business (B2B) companies?

Walter

There are really two reasons for my passion. The first one goes back to what marketing is – a blend of both art and science. That is very interesting to me. While it is a single discipline it combines concepts and information from other areas like psychology, art and design, creative writing, analysis, and research, to name a few. It also is very professionally satisfying for me to be able to assess a situation and then to offer a correct solution to a particular marketing challenge. It is very exciting to be a part of that process.

The second reason for my special interest in business-to-business marketing is because I've seen marketing have a huge positive impact – greatly increasing sales and profits – for these kinds of companies. You see, David, unlike business-to-consumer companies, business-to-business companies are usually very internally focused. Marketing forces them to look outside themselves to learn about what their end-user customers and prospects want. It also requires them to learn about their competition and overall market trends. This shift in perspective is huge for a lot of my clients, but they realize that the companies that connect and listen to their end-user customers and give them what they want are the ones that win in the marketplace.

We're going to explore this concept of connecting with end-users in this chapter. It's important to know that this is a very powerful concept – especially for B2B companies that haven't connected in that way in the past. They can see some pretty nice results – fairly quickly – by incorporating the marketing discipline into their game plan.

Wright

Earlier you said something as simple as market positioning works well in many industries. Is that what you're going to talk about today?

Walter

Yes, I believe that positioning in the marketplace is one of the first steps any company needs to take to effectively market itself. To me NOT having a clear positioning is the worst mistake any business can make for two reasons. One, if one doesn't provide a position for their company or product the market will create its own – and it likely will not be the most effective one. Second, one loses an extremely important opportunity to influence its chances for success. Positioning is an extremely powerful concept, as we will soon see.

And, David, the best news for our readers is that defining and deciding on the best positioning for your company or product is not an expensive or lengthy process. While it is not a task to be taken lightly – requiring investigation and careful thought – it is not difficult or overwhelming.

As you indicated, I work with marketing and non-marketing people alike so I use everyday ideas and examples that anyone can relate to. That's why I've titled this chapter *Selling Your Sizzle*. I think that everybody has heard that phrase before and understands it very well. We don't buy the steak, we buy the sizzle. And that's what we're going to talk about today.

Wright
So exactly what is sizzle or "positioning?"

Walter
Simply put sizzle is what **other people**, especially customers and prospects, think of when they think about a particular company or product. It's how those precious outsiders known as customers view the company or product in the marketplace relative to competition. It's what immediately comes to mind for them. Let me demonstrate this concept by asking you some questions. When you think of the Swedish car line Volvo, what is the first thing that comes into your mind?

Wright
I think of safe automobiles.

Walter
Right. On the other hand, if you think of Maserati, what do you think about then?

Wright
How I could pick up some women in my fast and cool car!

Walter
Now, David, most people would simply say "fast cars," but you had to elaborate, didn't you? Is it fair to say that when you think about CNN you think "news?"

Wright
Yes

Walter
And you think "sports" when you hear the name ESPN?

Wright
That's right.

Walter
Now let's consider the national chain of Domino's Pizza since we are going to use them throughout this the chapter as an example of

various principles. Most people think "quickly delivered average tasting pizza" when they think about Domino's. Right?

Wright

Yes, and Domino's does a great job of getting the pizza to you, too!

Walter

They sure do. Can you see from these examples that the sizzle or "positioning" is how one's company or product is consistently perceived by its customers? Customers like you?

Wright

Yes, I can. That's interesting.

Walter

Not only is it interesting – but it's so important and powerful for companies.

Wright

Why?

Walter

Positioning helps **increase the odds of success for companies and products in the marketplace**. We all know the sobering statistics about how often new businesses fail or new products flop. While there are myriad reasons contributing to those results, as prudent business people we want to do everything we can to stack the odds in our favor, don't we? If we know that by correctly, creatively, and consistently positioning our company or product we can greatly increase our odds for success why wouldn't we do it?

Wright

But how do we really know that "selling your sizzle" helps increase the odds of business success?

Walter

Thanks to a guy named Doug Hall, who is the author of a great book called *Jump Start Your Business Brain,* we know for sure! What he's done is he's taken this time-honored marketing concept of a positioning or sizzle statement that I'm going to share in this chapter and he's tested and quantified the different portions of it. More importantly, what he has been able to prove conclusively is that the better one is at positioning, the better the chances for success in the marketplace. And who doesn't want that in today's tough market?

Wright

That's great. But can you explain to me how having a market position or sizzle statement helps a company?

Walter

It increases a company's chance of success in two ways, internally – by creating focus – as well as externally – by creating clear and consistent communication to customers and prospects.

Let's use Domino's Pizza here to illustrate the internal benefits of having a clear market position. As we said, Domino's is all about quick delivery. That is a benefit that they determined was important to their customer base. Before the next touchdown, you want that pizza in front of you, don't you, David?

Wright

Absolutely!

Walter

So if their focus is quick delivery and that's what they're building their reputation and brand name on in the marketplace, how likely is it that someone in their purchasing department is going to be spending time trying to source gourmet sauces, for example? Not very likely! Instead, they are much more likely to be looking for ovens that cook faster or new products they can deliver faster. They're going to be looking for ways to improve on delivering on their positioning in the marketplace. No pun intended!

Can you see how having a focused market position helps internally direct companies to spend their money and their time in the most effective way?

Wright

Yes, I see that with Domino's. Can you give me another example?

Walter

Let's look at my company. We talked about how I focus on B2B companies. I spend my time, money, and efforts learning and staying current with best marketing practices for business-to-business companies. I don't spend a minute learning about marketing to consumer markets. That's not my market position. Since every company I know of has limited resources, leveraging them toward a common goal is a more direct path to successful outcomes. If a company tries to be too many things to too many people they will fail because they will not be able to do anything very well.

Wright

You've introduced a lot of new products in your career, is market positioning important for new product development and successful new product introductions?

Walter

It is mission critical. Why spend the time and effort to develop a new product if you don't know what the sizzle or market position will be and whether the intended marketplace finds that to be of value? I once heard the renowned new product development expert Donald Reinerstsen suggest that all new product development start with sketching out the sell sheet or sales brochure for the product. This simple task forces the development team and the company overall to define what they are really expecting in this new product when it is ready for launching and to think about the market positioning of such a product BEFORE they get started. This sell sheet basically becomes a visual set of specifications for marketing, engineers, production and everybody else in the process of developing that product. Like Stephen Covey advises us...start with the end in mind.

Wright

Now that I understand about the internal benefits of having a market position, tell me how it helps with current and potential customers.

Walter

Ah, yes, this is where success is truly defined – in the marketplace – external to the company's environment. Positioning is the foundation of all of the communication with the marketplace. It is the cornerstone of the concept of integrated marketing – speaking with one voice, saying the same thing over and over again to customers and prospects. You know Volvo means safety because you've seen some mention of it in every advertisement that has come out for their cars over the years. Their current slogan? Volvo for life.

Wright

Well, that makes sense to me.

Walter

You see, using a powerful positioning or sizzle statement to build one's integrated marketing communications campaigns makes it easier for the market to more quickly become familiar with the company or product.

Wright

So customers learn from a company's advertising or marketing efforts?

Walter

Absolutely! And it is the responsibility of the company to continually send the same consistent message to the market; otherwise they make it too hard for customers and prospects to understand who they are and what value they provide.

I have seen several times in my career where, after a few months or a couple of years, companies get bored with the look or message they are sending and want to change it simply for the sake of change. This can be a dangerous move. These companies need to remember that the average B2B prospect needs to be exposed to a similar message at least eight times before it even registers in their brain. So if a company keeps changing their message in terms of its positioning, it will NOT make any headway in making prospects aware of them not to mention creating enough interest for the prospect to consider buying the product.

Wright

So it makes sense to pick a good positioning and stick to it for a while?

Walter

Yes. The English novelist George Eliot said it best, "Decide on what you think is right, and stick to it." To quantify the value of consistent messages I've heard numbers that indicate that if a company spends a dollar in an integrated marketing campaign – one with a consistent positioning and look – it is like spending $1.35-$1.50, since that message builds on earlier exposures to that same message. In contrast, if the message changes frequently a one-dollar investment may return only 50 cents' worth of benefit. Adults learn through repetition and consistency. The least we can do for our prospects is to treat them like adults, don't you think, David?

Wright

That is the very least, yes. When I look back on all the projects that I have started and introduced that failed I always come back to a lack of spaced repetition.

Walter

It's a common mistake.

Wright

You know it's just that you have to keep at it and keep at it and keep at it. Advertising actually is an education tool. You're literally teaching people what you do or who you are or what you sell. I never looked at it that way before.

Walter

Exactly, repetition of a consistent and meaningful message is key.

Wright

So how can our readers tap into this powerful sizzle stuff and come up with a powerful positioning cornerstone for their own marketing efforts?

Walter

Like I said before it really is not that difficult to do. There are four major components to a sizzle statement. I'll explain each one separately indicating how much it can increase one's chances for success. I will also provide a few questions or brainteasers to kick off this process for the reader.

Wright

That doesn't sound too hard. Let's get started!

Walter

Sure, but let me remind the reader of something before he gets started on this exercise. It is paramount that he respond to these questions **as if his customers or prospects were answering them**. So to get started on the right foot, I suggest writing down a description of whom these folks are that a company currently sells to and whom it is trying to reach. This group of people is known as one's Target Market and the better one knows them the more meaningful and effective the positioning will be.

Wright

In what terms should the Target Market be described?

Walter

Some of the more common characteristics for B2B markets include: size of the company in dollars or number of employees, Industry Group Codes (SIC or NAICS), the title of the employee being targeted. But don't be afraid to describe them in terms of common problems or goals, too. That really helps to make the exercise even more meaningful.

Wright

Once the reader does this, then he knows who he will be talking to, right?

Walter

Right. He should picture them in his mind and think, "How would those folks respond to these questions?"

The first component that the reader should consider from his target market's perspective is the **BENEFIT** his company or product provides to the end-user or buyer. Think of it simply as the answer to "what's in it for me" or the "WIIFM" from the customer's viewpoint. To break through the everyday clutter of messages and real life one MUST answer this question to the liking of the prospect in order to gain his attention and interest.

The more strongly one can state a **BENEFIT**, the more effective the positioning and sizzle. Doug Hall says the **BENEFIT** needs to be overt, not at all subtle and his numbers prove it. Go to market with a weak benefit statement and the chances for success stand at only 13%. If the benefit statement is strong, much more overt and meaningful, chances nearly triple to 38%! The key here, again, is that one really has to look at this through the end-user's eyes and think about the value that is delivered to that person.

Separating features from **BENEFITS** can be tricky for any company, especially one that is not used to thinking that way. So let's look at Domino's again. Their key **BENEFIT** is that the customer gets to eat sooner rather than later. This is an important payoff for those who are ordering a pizza because they are hungry or because of time-related constraints, like half-time. This **BENEFIT** is the result of a variety of features and processes but those are NOT the **BENEFITS** to the end-user or consumer.

As we've said before, I work with a lot of engineers and they tend to get very excited about new patents or new processes. And while we're always respectful of their achievements and their breakthroughs, the question always comes down to "What does that mean to the person who is buying the product?" If there is little or no meaning, value, or **BENEFIT** to the end-user, then those breakthroughs have less of a positive impact in the marketplace than perhaps the engineer would like. One always must look at the features or technology through the eyes of the prospect.

Wright

Are you sure about those numbers you quoted? From 13% to 38%?

Walter

That's what Doug Hall tells us and I believe him because it makes perfect sense. Are you going to be more interested in buying something if you know what it can do for you or how it does it? I would guess that you don't really care how those Maserati engineers design that car for speed and style. You just want to know it might be helpful to you in attracting some new girlfriends, right?

Wright

You got me there, Rosemary. I do understand what you're saying. But can you give the readers some idea about how they could learn to think this way for their businesses?

Walter

I sure can, but, David, they don't have to go this alone. In fact, one easy way some companies get started with this process is by asking their current customers these same questions they are asking themselves. Here are a couple to ask:

- What is the number one way our customers **BENEFIT** from our company, product, or service?
- How do we make our customers' lives easier?
- What problem do we solve for our customers?
- Our company helps its customers by....?

- What's in it for a customer to buy from us versus someone else?

Wright

Those questions sound like they would generate a lot of discussion from both customers and from insiders at the company.

Walter

That's very true and that is exactly what we want them to do. One wants to generate a lot of **BENEFITS** so that later the list can be honed down to the top two or three – based on the customer's viewpoint.

The second component for a great sizzle or positioning statement is the supporting evidence for these benefits, or what we call, the REASONS WHY. While the two or three main benefits should entice the prospect the REASONS WHY should make a believer out of him. Simply stated the REASONS WHY tell the prospect why he logically and/or emotionally should believe that the company can and will deliver on those benefits.

Doug Hall tells us that the stronger and more believable the **REASONS WHY**, the more improved the chances of success. A low reason to believe nets an 18% success rate while a high reason to believe garners a 42%.

Remember all those features and patents that didn't belong in the **BENEFITS** section? They belong here – loud and clear! Customers are cautious and skeptical, so the marketer has really got to prove to them through features, accreditations, guarantees, testimonials, patents, market research finding, etc. that the benefits promised will be delivered. Again, one must consider this from the perspective of the end-user.

One of the reasons Domino's can deliver quickly is because they stress quick, yet safe driving by its delivery teams. I'm sure they have other processes in place to support their positioning – they simply choose not to share them all with us. And that's okay, too, especially for that kind of business where the price point is low and the frequency of purchase is high.

Here are some questions that the reader can use to generate the **REASONS WHY** for their key benefits.

- What **REASONS WHY** support each of the company's key **BENEFITS**?

- What **REASONS WHY** are most important in supporting those **BENEFITS**?
- How can these **REASONS** be communicated so that they are easily understood and believed?

Wright

So to have a great positioning we need to consider our key **BENEFITS** as well as our supporting evidence or **REASONS WHY** that show that we make good on our promises. That's two components, Rosemary, what are the other two?

Walter

The other two are **UNIQUENESS** and **CREATIVITY**. Let's talk about the first one here.

This component has everything to do with supply and demand in the marketplace – so one really needs to know about the competition and about how customers and prospects view the competition.

The basic idea here is that the more **UNIQUE** the product or service is in meeting the demand for specific **BENEFITS** the stronger one's chances for success. Doug Hall shows this component to be the one that can be leveraged the most. A business or positioning statement with a "low dramatic difference" or low level of **UNIQUENESS** weighs in with a 15% chance of success and one with a "high dramatic difference" or high level of uniqueness shows a 53% chance of success.

Wright

Did you say 53%? That's pretty high odds!

Walter

Yes, it is, but I think it makes a great deal of sense. If a product or company is simply perceived as a 'me too' or commodity player pretty much doing what everybody else does that means there are a lot of choices for customers out there to get the benefits they need. If, on the other hand, the product is – or can be made to look like it is – **UNIQUE**, that it is the only game out there, the chances of business success increase significantly. Think about Microsoft. They are pretty **UNIQUE** in what they do and what they offer. They don't have a lot of competition and the customer doesn't have a lot of choices about where to get those **BENEFITS**.

Now let's talk about carryout pizza and our old friend Domino's. While there are a lot of pizzerias one could call for a variety of reasons, when one wants quick delivery there is only one company that comes to mind – yours truly, Domino's.

Wright

So Domino's made themselves unique not by offering a unique product, but by how they positioned themselves in the market. That is pretty neat.

Walter

Yes, it is and it's made them a lot of money over the years. And while any business can use this kind of "pre-emptive" positioning it is not easy to keep the required internal focus over the years like Domino's has. Hats off to them!

They really did follow Eliot's advice, they found something that was right for them and their market and they stuck to it.

Here are a couple of questions for our readers to answer regarding their **UNIQUENESS**.

- What is our company better at doing or delivering than the competition?
- We are the only company that....?
- What do our customers tell us makes us different, better?

Wright

Thank you for that great information, examples and questions. Should we talk about **CREATIVITY** now?

Walter

Yes, I've saved the best for last, David. When I talk about **CREATIVITY** here, what I am getting at is the way things are communicated to the marketplace, the slogan, the tag line, the jingle. Is there anyone in the US over the age of 30 who doesn't remember the line "Where's the beef?"

Wright

I don't know how they couldn't!

Walter

You can probably still visualize that little old lady reciting that line – and then reciting it yourself the next day at the water cooler. Basically, what she was communicating to us was the fact that Wendy's had larger hamburgers than the competition. They probably had 33% more or whatever the number was, but they didn't just come out and say, "Our burgers are 33% bigger, bye-bye." They translated a key **BENEFIT** and **REASON** into creative language that quickly, concisely, and humorously communicated to its target market. That's the element of **CREATIVITY**.

Domino's has used delivery-related lines over the years to reinforce their key benefit. Do you remember, "Get the door, it's Domino's" or "Domino's delivers"? A correct, consistent and **CREATIVE** message that resonates with the target market is what market positioning is all about.

Wright

How we say things is so important. I remember one time playing devil's advocate in a workshop on **CREATIVITY**. The instructor was talking exactly about this same subject, about how things are said. I stupidly said, "Well, I just want the facts so I can make an informed decision." And he said, "Well, let me give you a "for instance." I said, "Okay." He said, "What if this young lady over here comes up here and says 'when I look into your eyes, time stands still?'" I'm thinking, "Man, that sounds great." He said, "Or she could have said your face would stop the clock." So I shut up and sat down.

Walter

You got it then, right?

Wright

Exactly.

Walter

By the way, can you recall what the tag line was for McDonald's at the time when Wendy's was running the "Where's the beef?" campaign?

Wright

No.

Walter

Neither can I!

Walter

The first three components of the sizzle or positioning statement really set the foundation for **CREATIVITY**, the fourth component. Remember, we want the message to be correct, then to be creatively translated, and finally to be consistently communicated to the target market. This order is important because a lot of business folks like to come up with tag lines or slogans or approaches to ads BEFORE they even know what they want to say or what is most important to their audience. This is a waste of time and is potentially dangerous.

Wright

How could that be dangerous?

Walter

It could be dangerous if a company favors the **CREATIVITY** (the way it is said) over the **WHAT NEEDS TO BE SAID**. For example while, "Where's the beef?" was definitely **CREATIVE**, cute, and memorable it would NOT have been effective – and may have even been considered false advertising – if Wendy's didn't, in fact, have larger burgers than competition. Worse yet, if they had a more important **BENEFIT** they wanted to communicate, like food temperature or taste, that tag line would have been completely inappropriate and they would have missed their opportunity to communicate and leverage their true benefits.

David, this is a mistake I see all too often. One way to avoid making it is to do the "thinking" work first. Write it down. Let it gel for a couple of weeks and review it to make sure it still makes sense. Make sure that it represents the strongest possible statement for the company or product. Then hand it over to an in-house team or outside creative source to brainstorm headlines, approaches, etc. Pick a favorite from those ideas, double check it communicates the sizzle strategy you want for your company and then start communicating it.

Wright

Do you have a sizzle statement or tagline?

Walter

Yes, it is "creating customers for business-to-business companies." That's what I do. While it may not be super creative or clever it succinctly communicates the key **BENEFIT** I deliver and to whom I deliver it. If people want to know more about how I do that, I can get into the **REASONS WHY**. If they want to know why I'm **UNIQUE** in delivering that value I can answer that, too! I've taken all of that "thinking" work from writing a sizzle strategy statement and consolidated it into that tagline. I've said, "I want to be known as is the person who creates customers for business-to-business companies." That's my positioning and I use it consistently in all of my marketing and communication vehicles.

Wright

Sounds like the best way for companies to increase their chances for success is to figure out who they want to be, what value they deliver to their customers, creatively encapsulate that into a memorable message and then put their time and money behind that. Do I have that right?

Walter

You do, David. Pretty simple stuff, huh?

Wright

I think you've made it simple for our readers, for sure. If you had the opportunity to tell our readers in closing something that you think that might benefit them and help them understand this whole process better, what would you say to them?

Walter

I would ask them to simply "get started." Read through each of the component sections above, answer the questions, and you'll see it is not very difficult. They will learn so much about their customers and themselves in the process.

Keep thinking, "I'm doing this because it has been proven to increase the business' chances for success." What more motivation does a business person need?

Wright

Anything else?

Walter

Yes, remember the three "**C's**"—**Correct** message, **creatively** executed, and **consistently** communicated. Stay focused on your positioning over the years and you'll be red hot in the market.

Wright

Oh my! Well, what an interesting conversation. I've really learned a lot.

Walter

Well, thank you!

Wright

And I think that this is going to be a great chapter for people to understand focus and spaced repetition and all these things that are so important that we read about but that we don't always do in business, do we?

Walter

Not every business does them, but the more successful ones do it more often than not.

Wright

That's a great, motivating way to look at it.

Walter

Thank you so much, David, for the interview.

Wright

You're more than welcome. Today we have been talking to Rosemary Walter. She's a marketing consultant who creates clients for business-to-business companies. She works successfully through her company, Mosaic Marketing Management, and she has proven to us today that she really knows what she's talking about. And I really do appreciate it.

Sizzle Statement Strategy Worksheet

Target Audience:	**Who are you trying to convince?** *Define them as best you can.*
Benefits:	**How does your company or product help its customers?** *List two to three ways.*
Reasons Why:	**Why should your target audience believe the benefits will be delivered?** *List at least one for each benefit.*
Uniqueness:	**What makes your company or products better than the competition?** *How are you different?*
Creativity:	**How can you summarize the above in a creative, catchy way?** *Brainstorm and play around with words and images. Consider hiring outside folks to help with this task.*

Additional Book Resources

- **Covey, Stephen R.** *The 7 Habits of Highly Effective People,* **New York: Fireside/Simon and Schuster, Inc. 1989**
- **Hall, Doug.** *Jump Start your Business Brain,* **Ohio: Brew Brain Books, 2001**
- **Reinertsen, Donald G. and Preston G. Smith.** *Developing Products in Half the Time,* **New York: John Wiley and Sons, Inc., 1998**
- **Ries, Al and Jack Trout.** *Positioning: The Battle for Your Mind,* **New York: McGraw Hill Companies, Inc. 1981**

About The Author

Rosemary Walter is a marketing expert, author, speaker and consultant who creates customers for her business-to-business client companies, thereby increasing their sales and profits. She works successfully with marketing and non-marketing folks like engineers, sales, and manufacturing staff. Rosemary holds both a BS and MS in advertising and marketing communications and has nearly 30 years' experience in business and marketing management. She was part of the team that introduced Chicken McNuggets® to the world.

Rosemary Walter

President, Mosaic Marketing Management, Inc.

309 E Rand Road #330

Arlington Heights, Illinois 60004

Phone: 847.483.5018

Fax: 847.483.5019

Email: Rose1Walter@MosaicMM.com

www.MosaicMM.com

Chapter 2

ALLEN STAM

THE INTERVIEW

David Wright (Wright)

It's my pleasure, today, to welcome Allen Stam to *Marketing Magic*. Allen is a marketing consultant who specializes in teaching companies how to make tradeshows really pay off! He has won awards nationally and offers companies proven strategies to motivate exhibitors and generate revenue. His training seminars are customized and are offered at his client's location or at their actual tradeshow booth. Allen offers 50 training modules that cover pre-show activities, how to double the traffic at the booth, how to close sales faster following the show, how to track results and much, much more. He has helped exhibitors at association conferences, tradeshows, local and national conventions, and at special events. Allen, welcome to *Marketing Magic*!

Allen Stam (Stam)

Thank you, David.

Wright

The first question I have for you is fairly easy. Why should a company or organization exhibit at a tradeshow?

Stam

I really believe it's the most cost effective method of getting prospects to buy the products or services that you offer. It should be included in the marketing mix only if a company or organization wants to be more profitable. You can never go on that many sales calls and meet that many people in such a short period of time. It is truly the only marketing venue to display your products or services in front of hundreds of potential buyers in just a few days. Sometimes it's just as important to simply keep your name in front of your current customers. There are usually several reasons why a company markets themselves at tradeshows.

Wright

So how does an exhibitor select the right tradeshow?

Stam

There are three things to keep in mind. First, start with a local or regional tradeshow to get experience before exhibiting at larger national tradeshows. The cost is much less while learning how to work the tradeshow to achieve the maximum benefit. If you are an experienced exhibitor, then consider exhibiting at a larger show with a larger attendance and of course, a larger budget. Second, a company or organization should only exhibit at a tradeshow if the buyers of your products or services are planning to attend. You need to do some research to see who will be attending the tradeshow that you are considering. Talk to the show planner. Get the names of previous exhibitors and talk to several of them. Find out why they exhibited, if they were successful and if they plan on exhibiting again. Third, make sure that the tradeshow is focused to your target market. Talk to the associations that are associated with your target market and read industry and association magazines. Gather information on what are the best available tradeshows in your industry segment.

Wright

So is an exhibitor tradeshow plan necessary?

Stam

It definitely is! You'd be surprised how many companies I've provided training and coaching to that didn't really have an effective and thorough plan. How do you create a budget unless you know what's involved? Most of all you need to define your goals, both quantitative and qualitative. And then you need to execute from your plan. There are so many things to consider and plan for that a company or organization won't be successful unless it is entirely documented for each tradeshow. Some examples include planning pre-show activities such as the booth design, the carpet color in the booth, staffing needs, booth location selection, booth theme and giveaways. You need to plan for activities at the tradeshow such as how to capture and document leads at your booth, who is setting up and breaking down your booth, what other networking events will various staff members be attending, and who's in charge of your booth. And never forget to plan the post show activities. Don't wait until after the tradeshow. This includes creating a post-show e-mail message, planning who will follow up on the leads and how to measure the success of the tradeshow. These are just a few of the hundreds of activities you need to plan for.

Wright

I can see from just a few of the things that you are mentioning that a plan is necessary. I have done a few tradeshows over the years and can see why they were never very successful. I needed a plan!

Stam

That's right, David. There are so many things to consider. Here are three additional ideas for you to think about. First, it is not just about showing up at your booth. Success only comes with the proper planning. Your plan is an agreement between all the departments that are involved in the tradeshow. Second, you need a tradeshow plan for each tradeshow. Each tradeshow could present a different opportunity with different goals. Third, your tradeshow plan needs to be directly relevant to your overall marketing strategy. Remember you need to out-think and not out-spend the competition. Here's the place where you start to out-think them.

Wright

That is definitely true. I think we have made every mistake in the world when it comes to tradeshows. Sometimes, however, you get lucky. We exhibited at a tradeshow one time in New York and fortunately the booth next to us had an incredible amount of traffic because of the promotion they did prior to and during the show. We got a lot of traffic just because of our booth location.

Stam

That is great that you got lucky because of your booth location. I coach companies and organizations on several aspects of selecting an effective booth location for a particular tradeshow. There are several questions you should ask yourself. The first one is who are the exhibitors that are next to your booth? Ask yourself how they relate to your business and do you think they will create a lot of traffic? Call them ahead of time before selecting your booth location. Also, how can I partner with an exhibitor on the opposite side of the tradeshow floor to help drive traffic to each other? Your booth location again will play an important factor. Most exhibitors don't even consider these questions. Most importantly, ask yourself what areas of the tradeshow floor will get the most traffic. Consider where any raffles are held, where food will be served at breaks, where the restrooms are, and if your booth is centrally located. Hopefully the next time you won't have to rely on luck, David!

Wright

I think my luck ran out and I will have to do my due diligence in selecting our booth location next time. I have seen everything on the tradeshow floor. Is there any tradeshow etiquette that exhibitors should follow?

Stam

Yes, there are a lot of things that you should do and shouldn't do in your booth. I mean it starts with really basic concepts like don't eat, don't chew gum, and wear comfortable shoes. Actually I have an article, *To Do or Not To Do, That is the Question – 25 Tips for Booth Success.* A free copy is available to anyone that is interested by simply sending an e-mail to ToDo@TradeshowAcademy.com. The most important thing to remember is just to make attendees feel welcome when they walk by your booth. How do you feel at a retail store when all the employees are talking to each other and not giving you the time of day? Or if they're busy on a personal phone call or eating behind the counter?

Wright

Oh, yeah. I have had that happen plenty of times.

Stam

And then likewise how do you feel at a store when someone looks at your credit card and thanks you by your name? Or when someone takes the time to want to know about what you need and how they can provide you with a solution?

Wright

Exactly.

Stam

There are a lot of factors to exhibiting at a tradeshow. Likewise, there is the right way to do them and the wrong way. Think about how you should treat someone when they come to your booth.

Wright

Right. So do you have any advice on how to get attendees to stop at your booth? This was always our biggest challenge.

Stam

This is a crucial step in your overall tradeshow success. Remember, the more attendees at your booth mean more potential sales and more sales mean more success. My first suggestion is to be unique! This can include such things as your booth design, how everyone is dressed in the booth, what you give out at the booth, how you give out your promotional item or what games or celebrities you have at your booth. People will remember you after the tradeshow if you were different from the other exhibitors. Second, a smile and possibly a little humor go a long way to making someone feel comfortable enough to want to come into your booth. People do business with people they like. If you look like you are having fun and are likeable then why wouldn't they stop if they have any interest at all? Third, ask the right question when they walk by your booth to grab their attention. What are the most popular questions that you have heard at tradeshows, David?

Wright

I have probably heard questions like, "Hi, how are you doing?" "Are you having a good tradeshow?" "Would you like a brochure?"

Stam

Exactly. These are all the wrong questions to ask! The attendee could answer your questions with "Great," "Yes" and "No thanks." You should never ask a closed question that will result in short, quick answers because the tradeshow attendee can simply answer your question and keep on walking right past your booth. What you really want to do is ask an open-ended question that is fun or unique. For example, you can ask them "Let me show you a great idea that should make you lots of money" or "Guess what this is and you will win a prize" or "I have been waiting all day for you to stop by." Ask open-ended questions such as these, and you will definitely get attendees (prospects) to stop at your booth.

Wright

I can think right now about all the people that didn't stop at our booth because of the questions we asked!

Stam

Even just smiling and saying "I have a big idea for you today" to an attendee walking by your booth will almost always get them to smile, stop at your booth and ask "What's the big idea?" There's no better way to start a conversation than having the attendee ask you a question. I can't tell you how many times someone has mentioned to me that they were really glad that I got them to stop. Sometimes your best business will be a result of the effort you put in to asking the right questions to get them to stop at your booth.

Wright

Wow, those are great tips for any exhibitor!

Stam

Thank you. I have studied numerous tradeshows to see how attendees react at different booths. The more successful you are at your booth the more traffic it generates. Just think if you're walking down a tradeshow floor and there are two booths across from each other, and you don't know about either one. You see about 10 or 15 people at one booth and there's no one at the other booth. Which one would you stop at? You're definitely going to stop at the booth with all the people! You want to find out what the buzz is all about. The more people you have at your booth the more successful you appear. People do business with people who are successful.

Wright

OK, so now that an exhibitor asks the right questions they will get a lot more booth traffic. How do they qualify a prospect so they aren't wasting their time?

Stam

Well, I always say that this is as easy as one, two, three. It's a three step approach. It starts immediately after you've stopped someone at your booth. It's simply asking them a series of three questions with the first question being the broadest and then each subsequent question narrowing down the focus to determine what their interest is. Remember also that they need to be open-ended questions like I mentioned before. So let me give you an example. First give the attendee a 5-10 second overview of what you offer and ask them what type of similar services they have purchased. Based on their answer, you might ask what their needs are within the next six to twelve months. You're simply trying to find out what they are looking for that would solve their problem. Ask them a question that is relevant to their company and what type of problems they have encountered. You should be able to find out if they have any interest in what you are offering. You will need to customize your questions to find out if they are an actual buyer of your products or services or if they help make the decisions. If you aren't sure then ask them what products or services they are responsible for purchasing. You will be amazed at the information you will receive. If you have a two year sales cycle, then you want to modify your questions to determine their needs within the next two years. Offer them a free trial or maybe a free sample to see what their reaction is. Remember; don't ask them if they would like a free trial or a free sample. They can simply say no and you won't know the reason. Instead, ask them if it would be useful for them to evaluate and if so, when is a convenient time to sign up for a free trial.

Wright

Those are great ideas as I can remember taking a lot of time with people only to find out they weren't really interested or they weren't the buyers.

Stam

David, most of the time an exhibitor will find that it only takes one or two questions to determine if they are a potential buyer. Ask your open-ended questions and then just listen to what they are saying. Also, make sure you follow the 80/20 rule. Listen to them 80% of the time and talk at most 20% of the time during your conversation.

Wright

That is so true. I think we all make the mistake of trying to tell a potential buyer about all the great things we have to offer instead of listening to what they need and why they need it.

Stam

Exactly. Sometimes just reflecting back what they are saying will lead them to tell you more about what they are looking for. You won't even have to continue to ask questions. Remember, don't spend time with unqualified prospects. I have some techniques that I do at my workshops on how to move these non-buyers out of your booth easily and quickly without any negative reaction. It's important that you only spend time with the qualified prospects, and that's why you really need to qualify them quickly.

Wright

So you mentioned that they should do most of the talking. What do tradeshow attendees really want to hear when you're talking?

Stam

Well, David, let me start first with telling you what they don't want to hear.

Wright

Okay.

Stam

They don't want to hear about the features of your products. They don't want to hear how great your company is. They don't care how many locations and how many employees your company has. They don't care how long you've worked for the company. They don't want to know all about your product warranties. They don't want to know all about how your product works. So what do they want to hear? They want to hear what is new. They came to hear ideas. They want to hear about potential solutions to their problems. They want to know how you are different from everyone else in your industry. Provide them with quick ideas and demonstrate solutions. Keep it brief.

Listen to what they are saying. Your goal is really to listen and not to tell. If you walk by most exhibitors' booths you will see that it's usually the booth staff that's doing most of the talking. Be different and listen and you won't go wrong!

Wright

Should an exhibitor compare their products or services to their competitors?

Stam

Yes, by all means. I think it's important to delineate how your company is different from your competitors. However, it should be done in a positive way. It should point out your unique selling proposition. Specifically illustrate how the products, services, features or benefits that are offered by your company or organization are different from others. Your discussion should again be focused on solutions. Never at any time should you ever put down the competition even if you're asked point blank questions about your competitors.

Wright

I have been fairly unsuccessful at every tradeshow I've ever gone to, and I know this because I just didn't know what I was doing. How do you guarantee success for tradeshow exhibitors?

Stam

Well, it starts with some of the things we have talked about. It starts with a tradeshow plan. An exhibitor needs to do the proper planning and then they need to execute according to their plan. It's crucial you have a plan if you want to be successful. Success means really different things for different exhibitors all of which should be tied directly to the goals that have been set for that specific tradeshow. I think you can guarantee success for an exhibitor if they can double their booth traffic which I guarantee to be able to help exhibitors accomplish. So it really starts with a good plan, followed by getting the traffic into your booth and then following up after the tradeshow. It doesn't matter what you do before or during the tradeshow if you don't follow up. This is a major weakness with most exhibitors and needs to be carefully thought out.

Wright

I remember one tradeshow I exhibited at. There was nothing happening in my booth. And the booth next to me had lots of people coming in and milling around. I finally asked what he did to attract so many people to his booth. He said he got the list of all the attendees and sent them postcards. They showed where his booth was located and gave them an incentive to stop by.

Stam

Great idea.

Wright

You know I didn't believe it. I thought, "Well, why didn't I think of that? That's so simple."

Stam

There's nothing like a personal invitation that will bring people to your booth. The more you can market before a tradeshow the higher success you're going to have at your booth. You can do e-mail marketing as well as direct mail marketing. However, personal phone calls are always the best.

Wright

True.

Stam

It is especially true for invitations to your current customers prior to the tradeshow. You want happy customers in your booth for other potential buyers to listen to and talk with. What better marketing is there at your booth than a testimonial from a happy customer?

Wright

Allen, what's more critical for tradeshow success, the location of the booth or the design?

Stam

Well, both are really essential, not to mention the numerous other factors that all play a part in your exhibiting success. I am sure you've heard a realtor proclaim location, location, location in trying to sell your house. Well, that's really true for your booth as well. If you waited too long to sign up for a booth with a good location then I would consider doing another tradeshow as this is a crucial element. You can have a great location also, but if you don't have an overall great booth appearance then you won't get the results you are looking for. Remember, be unique! This includes the booth as well as the booth staff. Booth location and booth design really go hand in hand. You need a key location on the tradeshow floor, but you also need a booth that is eye catching and inviting.

Wright

Should an exhibitor give out promotional products?

Stam

Absolutely! Promotional products are commonly known as tradeshow "giveaways" in this venue. This really is a misnomer. They should always be used strategically. They're not just a giveaway. They should tie into your overall booth theme. There are three different methods a promotional item can be used at the booth by a tradeshow exhibitor. First, use a promotional item to drive traffic to your booth. Make it unique. You want to create a buzz on the tradeshow floor to drive more prospects to your booth. Don't just hand out a promotional item to anyone that wants one. Make attendees earn it and use the time to qualify them while at your booth. The more traffic the better chance you have of meeting the top prospects. Second, you can use it as a gift to give to someone to thank them for taking their time to see a demo, take a survey, sign up for a trial, or just spend a little time at your booth. It's always good to thank someone and you can use a higher end promotional gift as a way to thank them. And a third method that I would recommend is really creating what I call a one-two marketing punch. Mail the first piece prior to the tradeshow just like we talked about with direct mail. The mailer should then provide an offer to stop by the booth and pick up the second item if they bring the first one with them to the booth. For example, you can mail them sunglasses along with a catchy letter about all the new bright ideas that they can see at your booth. Tell them to wear the sunglasses to your booth and they will receive an auto sunshade. Can you imagine the buzz you will get with 10 attendees at your booth all wearing sunglasses? Remember to be different! This will always get attention and drive more traffic to your booth. There are numerous one-two types of promotional items that aren't too expensive. You need to target your best prospects and potential buyers because this type of promotion will cost more money. It's a great technique that you can use to try and selectively attract more people to your booth.

Wright

How does an exhibitor close the conversation with a potential buyer at their booth?

Stam

It is essential to lock in the next step with the potential buyer while at the tradeshow. Set a specific time for you to call to follow up. Give them options instead of leaving it vague and open-ended. For example, for the hottest prospects you can ask them if next week or the following week would be a good time to call and follow up with them. If they say next week, then ask if Tuesday or Wednesday, for example, would be better. An exhibitor will have better success if they lock in a specific time. Their follow up call will sound something like "I am calling you today at 9 am as we agreed upon at the tradeshow." Impress them with your follow up and show them that you really want their business!

Wright

So what can an exhibitor do to maximize their tradeshow experience?

Stam

Well, there are so many more ways to increase the success at your tradeshow than just simply showing up and exhibiting at your booth. Most companies fall into the trap of just coming to exhibit and don't think beyond their booth. Here are just a few examples of other marketing activities that you can participate in. Advertise before the show in program guides or e-mails that the show manager is sending out. Advertise in the daily show newspapers that are often given out at the show. Advertise on the shuttle buses that run from the major hotels to the convention center. Advertise on the kiosk outside the entrance to the tradeshow floor and include your marketing literature. As you can see there are numerous ways to advertise. An exhibitor can also sponsor the tote bags or lanyards that are often given out when an attendee registers at the convention. You can also sponsor lunches, cocktail parties or golf outings.

Wright

I can see that an exhibitor really needs to know what their budget is before determining what additional marketing activities they can afford.

Stam

That's true. An exhibitor needs to be selective and have specific goals for spending money on other methods of marketing at the tradeshow. However, there are several other opportunities that don't cost anything! These are often overlooked. For example, an exhibitor could schedule a press conference and issue a press release during the convention for a new product or service they are introducing. There is nothing better than free PR!

Wright

I totally agree with that.

Stam

I also recommend that an exhibitor host a break out session or a workshop to provide information of value to other attendees while marketing yourself and your company or organization. Exhibitors should have additional staff members available for other networking opportunities that are offered throughout the convention.

Wright

An exhibitor has lots of contacts from their booth after the tradeshow. So now what do they do?

Stam

Well, it's a race to the finish line. Remember that we talked about location, location, location. Now is the time to follow up, follow up, follow up. It's really essential to the overall success of the tradeshow. You can't wait for prospects to call you. An exhibitor needs to follow up as they promised to do at the tradeshow. The first step in following up after a tradeshow is to prioritize all the leads. I recommend a three tier method of prioritizing your leads. The top ones have been qualified as having needs over the next few months. They might even have immediate needs where they want you to contact them within the first week after the tradeshow. This is where your listening skills will pay off. You can't prioritize a lead unless you have enough information about them during your discussion. Plus, you can't prioritize a lead unless you successfully qualified them at your booth. You need to call these hot prospects within a two to three day period after the tradeshow. The next tier of contacts includes those individuals that have been qualified but do not have an urgent need to be contacted. The bottom tier of leads are those who are not currently qualified but may have needs in the future.

Wright
It seems critical to contact everyone you have met at a tradeshow but sometimes the numbers can just be overwhelming.

Stam
I agree. I recommend sending out a "thank you for stopping by our booth" e-mail message to all contacts. This should be prepared in advance so that it can be sent out immediately following the tradeshow. Customize your message to the top prospects and the ones that you have committed to following up with. The e-mail may also include an invitation to sign up for your monthly e-mail newsletter or to visit your website for some current tips or tradeshow specials.

Wright
That makes a lot of sense.

Stam
If there are just too many contacts then I would recommend that you start by calling the top tier leads first. You've already determined that the bottom tier leads are not key prospects for you or your business in the immediate future. However, we have gotten a significant amount of business from these bottom tier contacts so an exhibitor needs to make sure that they follow up with everyone, even if only by e-mail. You never know when their needs change, their position changes within the company or they change companies.

Wright
At the end of the day, how does an exhibitor determine if their tradeshow was successful?

Stam
Well, the best method that I would recommend is to set quantitative goals prior to the tradeshow that you can measure against following the tradeshow. Make sure all of these quantitative goals are

included in the tradeshow plan. For instance, is one of your goals to obtain qualified leads at a booth? It should be written to include how many leads are desired of each tier. The more you exhibit, the better idea you will have as to the number of leads you can expect. If you get professional tradeshow coaching then you should be able to double the number of leads from your previous tradeshows. Other goals might include a specific number of signed contracts, a specific amount of sales within 6 months, a number of surveys that are filled out at the booth, or the number of website hits you receive on specific links provided on marketing literature available only at that tradeshow. You can easily measure the success of the tradeshow against quantitative goals such as these. Evaluate your goals from tradeshow to tradeshow to see what is realistic.

Wright

I can now see that it's really important to track the results to determine if a tradeshow is a success.

Stam

Yes. The better you can quantify your goals before the tradeshow the better you are able to measure your return on investment. There are also other qualitative goals that you can evaluate over time to determine if your tradeshow was a success. They're not as easy to measure. For example, one goal might be to be to have your company seen by your current customers at a major industry tradeshow. If you aren't exhibiting they may wonder if your company or organization is still in business. Remember, people want to do business with people and businesses that are successful. The tradeshow floor is a great way to see the customers you haven't seen for awhile, especially if they are located outside of your local area.

Wright

Plus, it's a lot less expensive making appointments with your customers while at the tradeshow.

Stam

Yes that is definitely true. Another idea that most exhibitors typically don't think about is finding out more about your competitors while at the tradeshow. Set a goal to learn more about what your competitors are doing. There are also so many other intangible results that are hard to measure such as how much exposure you got at your tradeshow booth, or through a press release, or while hosting a break out session. The key is to track the results and evaluate the ROI for all tradeshows. This will drive your decision making process to select the best tradeshows for your company or organization.

Wright

Well, what a great conversation. I've learned a lot. I'm going to be calling you before our next tradeshow.

Stam

That's great. I truly hope this helps exhibitors make their tradeshows more profitable!

Wright

Today we have been talking to Allen Stam, founder and owner of Tradeshow Academy, Inc. Allen is a tradeshow award winner and exhibitor from coast to coast. And as we have found out today, as a tradeshow expert and professional coach, Allen knows a lot about what he is talking about. So when you are thinking about doing your next tradeshow, I would definitely give Allen a call. Allen, thank you so much for taking the time with me this morning to help me understand a little bit more about tradeshows. I really personally appreciate it.

Stam

Thank you so much David; it's been my pleasure.

About The Author

Allen Stam, founder of Tradeshow Academy, brings over 10 years of experience in tradeshow marketing to corporations and associations. Allen is an award-winning marketing expert and has proven his expertise at tradeshows from coast to coast. With a diverse background in sales, marketing, engineering, software development and program management, Allen knows how to connect with tradeshow staff and exhibitors from all business segments. He has helped numerous corporations, associations, and organizations turn their tradeshow experiences into more and better business! Allen is a member of Trade Show Exhibitors Association (TSEA), Center for Exhibition Industry Research (CEIR), National Speakers Association (NSA) and the Washington, D.C. chapter of NSA.

Allen Stam

Tradeshow Academy, Inc.

626C Admiral Drive #318

Annapolis, Maryland 21401

Phone: 800.758.7880

info@TradeshowAcademy.com

www.TradeshowAcademy.com

Chapter 3

JAY CONRAD LEVINSON

THE INTERVIEW

David E. Wright (Wright)

It is a privilege and pleasure to welcome Mr. Jay Conrad Levinson to our program. Jay is the author of the best selling marketing series in history, *Guerrilla Marketing*, plus 24 other business books. His guerrilla concepts have influenced marketing so much that today his books appear in 37 languages and are required reading in many MBA programs worldwide. Jay writes a monthly column for *Entrepreneur Magazine*, articles for *Inc Magazine*, a syndicated column for newspapers and magazines and online columns published monthly on the Microsoft and GTE websites. Recently, Jay has turned much of his attention to the development of the Guerrilla Marketing Association, a dynamic, interactive forum allowing aspiring marketers to learn the fine points of guerrilla marketing directly from Jay from certified coaches, through telephone training sessions, and online publications. And this is just scratching the surface. Jay, thank you for taking the time to speak with us today.

Jay Conrad Levinson (Levinson)

Well, David, thank you for inviting me. I consider it an honor to be engaged in conversation with you.

Wright

Well, thank you. It's unlikely that any of our readers would not be familiar with your ground breaking book, *Guerrilla Marketing*, or one of the other many companion books that you've written sense, but just in case, would you mind telling us a little bit about your background and how you came to write *Guerrilla Marketing?*

Levinson

I'll be happy to. The reality starts on a February day, like today, in Chicago, and the temperature is 13 below zero. I was waiting for a bus, and I had a big job in a giant, wonderful advertising agency in Chicago. Everything was going well, but 13 below zero and the way my ears felt certainly didn't feel like it was going well. So I asked my advertising agency if they would transfer me to San Francisco. They said they couldn't do it because I was too connected with my clients and they didn't want to let me go. So when I said I'd leave and move to San Francisco anyhow, I had accepted a job offer from another advertising agency, the client said, "Hey, Jay, we don't care where you live as long as you continue to write for us." So those were Quaker Oats and Alberto-Culver of Alberto VO5. So I said, "yes" to them and I decided just to be a consultant to the job that I had accepted. And I found as I started working from my home, which overlooks San Francisco Bay, I'm a hard worker and a fast typist, David. I found that when I was protected from meetings, committees, memos and really nice people coming into my office to shoot the breeze, I could accomplish in three days what used to take me five days. I spent about a year and a half working from my home three days a week, and I thought, "There's nothing really special about me. Everybody ought to try something like this." So I wrote a book about it, *Secret's of Successful Freelancing*, and that book became very successful, but how many freelancers are there? So I expanded the idea in that book and I called it *Earning Money Without a Job*. People said, "Are you the guy who wrote the book Earning *Money without Working*? I said, "Oh no, no! You've got to really work hard, but you don't need a standard nine to five job."

That led to me being invited to teach a course at the University of California in Berkley in their extension division based on *Earning Money Without a Job*. The title of the course was *Alternatives to the 9 to 5 Job.* Then one day my students asked me what sounded like an easy question. It turned out it was not an easy question. They said, "Jay, can you recommend some books for us on marketing a business for people who don't have much money?" And I gave the wrong answer. I said, "Sure." I said, "I'll scout out some books and I'll have them to you the next time we meet." So I went to the library in Berkley, but now we're talking about the early '80s. There were no books on marketing for people with limited budgets. I went to the library at Stanford. I went to the City of San Francisco and Sacramento. I looked in the public libraries. All the books on marketing were written for companies with $300,000 a month to invest. That certainly was not the kids in my classes. So I put together a list of things they might be able to do based on what I had learned working for big companies. At any rate, my list was about 520 ways to market your business that cost very little. Well, that's no title for a book. One day I was reading the newspaper and a man named Blair Newman, who happened to be a boyhood friend of Bill Gates, was quoted as saying that what this economy needs is some kind of guerrilla marketing. And I thought, "Wow! That's a good title for the book." The book I had written for my students was about going after the conventional goals, but using unconventional means. So that became the title of the book for my students.

The book took on a life of its own as my agent found out about it. And gosh! Now it's written in 39 languages, which means I don't understand 38 additions of my own book. But the book was written to satisfy a need. There was a big need of small businesses coming of age in the world. There was a need for inexpensive marketing ideas, and here I was with a book I'd written for most of my students, which fills the world's bill as well.

Wright

Before we get into the nuts and bolts, I would really appreciate hearing your thoughts on the definition of marketing. You know many business people toss around the words "marketing," "sales," "PR," etc., without really understanding the subtle differences between them. In the most practical terms possible, what is your definition of marketing in general, and then what is guerrilla marketing?

Levinson

Well, marketing, David, is any contact that anybody in your business has with anybody else on planet earth. It's not necessarily formalized. It is any contact, how the telephone is answered, the attire worn by your representatives, it's every contact. It's a process. It's not an event. It's not a thing you do a few times a year. It's a continuing, never-ending process. And if you do it right, it's a circle. The circle begins with your ID up for hire to bring income into your life and it becomes a circle when you have the blessed patronage of repeat and referral customers. If you transformed that idea into a circle, you will then understand what marketing is about. So that's what marketing is. It includes a lot of things.

I'll give you the differences between guerrilla marketing and traditional marketing. I used to compare guerrilla marketing with textbook marketing, but I can't do that any more because guerrilla marketing is the textbook in so many university MBA programs. So I have to compare it to traditional marketing. There are 20 differences. These 20 differences, all of them, are just common sense, but these are the real differences. If people can understand these differences and change their business around to do these things, they'll find that their business becomes a whole lot more profitable. In addition, they get a lot more balance in their life because guerrilla marketing is very against the notion of workaholism and being away from your family. It's definitely possible to get work done in standard working hours or less. What marketing preaches strongly is the idea of balance. When I say I've worked a three day week from my home at the edge of a forest overlooking a beautiful blue bay, and I've done it since 1971, I still have to let you know there's nothing really special about me, so thinking anybody ...nobody has to be a workaholic. People who are workaholics choose to do work over everything else in their lives, and I feel sorry because there's lots of other things other than business, other than profits, other than marketing.

Here are the 20 differences between traditional and guerrilla marketing. Number one: Traditional marketing says, "To market you must invest money." Guerrilla marketing says, "Well, if you want to you can, but you don't really have to." Your primary investments should be time, energy, imagination, and knowledge. If you are willing to invest those, you won't have to invest as much if any money.

The second difference: Traditional marketing intimidates a lot of people. As you noticed, David, they're not really sure what it is. It's smoky and it's enshrouded by a mystique. Is sales part of marketing? Is internet presence part of marketing? Well, that mystique disappears with guerrilla marketing because the second difference is that guerrilla marketing completely removes the mystique from marketing. Anybody who's read any guerrilla marketing books or joined the

Guerrilla Marketing Association, there's no mystery to marketing for them anymore. They see clearly what it is and what it isn't.

The third difference: Traditional marketing has always been geared to big business, as I mentioned to you when I wrote this book and I was looking for books, I couldn't find any of that were written for people with small budgets. So traditional marketing is geared to big business. Guerrilla marketing is geared very much to small business. Now, although it's true that Fortune 500 Companies buy up several thousand copies of the *Guerrilla Marketing Book* at a time to distribute to their sales and marketing people, the soul and the spirit of guerrilla marketing is in small business. The essence of guerrilla marketing is small business. Now, it's true, a lot of big businesses can use techniques that I'd recommend for small business that cost nothing. They can do that too. Just because they're big companies doesn't mean they have to be a big spender.

The fourth difference: Traditional marketing bases its measurements on sales. Did our sales go down? Or on responses to their offer. How many responses have we got to our offer? Those are on store traffic. How many people came into the store or visited our website? Guerrilla marketing says those are the wrong numbers to look at. There's only one number that tells you the truth, and that is your profits. That bottom line tells us the truth very clearly. A lot of people can enjoy high sales while losing money all along. They can get a lot of responses to an offer, but they may be in a money losing spiral down. So you've got to look at profits because that's the number that lets you know if you're doing it right or you're not doing it right.

The fifth difference: Traditional marketing is based on judgment and experience. That's a fancy way of saying guesswork, and guerrillas can't afford to make wrong guesses. So guerrilla marketing is based as much as possible upon laws of human behavior. Example: we know that 90% of all purchase decisions are made in the unconscious mind. We also know a slam-dunk manner to access the human unconscious mind and the way we do that is through repetition. Now put those two facts together. Decisions are made in the unconscious mind and you can access that unconscious mind through repetition. Then you begin to have a glimmer of an understanding of how the process of marketing works, and that's just one of many examples of how guerrilla marketers use psychology.

A sixth difference: Traditional business has always said, "Grow your business and then diversify." Guerrilla marketing says, "Oh boy! That gets you in over your head and gets you in a lot of trouble." At least the companies like Coca Cola say, "Our name means beverages," and then buying a winery and losing $87 million, and saying, "Well, maybe our name means soft drinks." Other companies have corporate egos that make them think that they can diversify when in reality they are really misdirected if they diversify because the guerrilla answer is forget diversifying. Think about maintaining your focus. Think who you brought to the party and stay with that person. Stay with that focus. It got you to where you are, and your job now is to keep getting better at what you are doing rather than diversifying.

The seventh difference: Traditional marketing has always said the way to grow your business is linearly, which is by adding new customers one at a time. You know, it's the old way. Well, that's a pretty expensive way to grow. Guerrilla marketers know there are better ways to grow a business. They grow their businesses geometrically. That means they enlarge the size of each transaction. They aim to have more transactions per sales cycle with their customers, and they tap the enormous referral power of each one of those customers. Each one is the center of a network, and they grow linearly in the old fashioned way. Now they are growing in four directions at once: larger transactions, more transactions, referral transactions, and standard linear transactions. It's pretty impossible to lose money, let alone go out of business if you understand just that idea about growing geometrically.

The eighth difference: Traditional marketing believes marketing is over once they have made the sale. Because of that mindset, 68% of business that is lost in the United States is lost not due to poor service and not due to shabby quality. It's lost due to customers being ignored after they've made the purchase. That's why guerrilla marketing preaches fervent follow up so you can get in touch with those customers and let them know you appreciate their business. Life is not just all business. Connect up with them as a human being as well. Follow up and let them know that you really care and that you're grateful, and you're not going to lose 68% of your business like so many other businesses do. It's just the human thing to do.

Wright

We're kind of privileged to visit with you today, Jay, because many of our readers and clients have tremendous products to sell to people. These are people who have invested years of their lives and a great deal of their own money getting the product ready, but then they hit the wall which is marketing, and they are rarely prepared. Have you found this to be true? What would you tell someone who has run into this wall?

Levinson

I'd say it's a really easy wall to surmount because all it takes is a simple plan, not a complex plan. Guerrillas start with a very simple seven step marketing plan. That's all. Once you start with the plan, then you've got to promise yourself that you will commit to that plan because that's what really makes marketing work. That's what really makes marriage work. That's what really makes a business work, or completing a marathon. It's a commitment to your plan. You must be committed and that's how you get over the wall. The plan is your stepladder over it and the commitment to the plan is how you get down the other side and make it to the finish line. But there is no finish line because guerrilla marketers know that the journey is the goal. People do run into a wall in marketing, and you know, David, you can't blame them for seeing that wall because they think marketing is complicated. But as I was showing, we just talked about eight of the ways guerrilla marketing is different from traditional marketing. The point still being that if you break it down into simple components, what guerrilla marketing does starting with a seven steps marketing plan, then that wall isn't as high. It's more easily surmountable. You have a road map. You know where to go. Gosh without a plan, that's like taking a journey without having a road map. It's not going to work out.

Wright

So does guerrilla marketing explain the seven steps?

Levinson

Oh, yes. It tells you just the seven different steps. Seven simple sentences that you've got to complete. All of them are short sentences except for the fourth sentence, and once you've finished those sentences, are you ready for this? It takes five minutes to write a guerrilla marketing plan. I've taught this at Berkley for ten years and I gave these students five to write a seven sentence guerrilla marketing plan. They all did it and many of them used that same seven sentence marketing plan for the next many years in guiding their business because it gave them a map into uncharted terrain. I know you've discovered that doing business is pretty much uncharted terrain. There's lots of surprises out there and they say it's a jungle out there. That's why guerrilla warfare is necessary to proceed faithfully in that jungle towards your goal. I wrote *Guerrilla Marketing* to make it as simple and safe as possible. I'm telling you one of the big things that as you launch a guerrilla marketing attack to do it with slow motion. Don't be in a hurry. My average client takes a year and a half to launch a really successful guerrilla marketing attack, and my newest book, *Guerrilla Marketing for Free*, talks about a hundred ways you can market for zero, zero cost. It's not as complicated as they think. And it's getting easier now than ever before for a small business to really make inroads into a big world and get a small chunk of a very large pie, or if they want a large chunk. But don't forget, I think the most important thing is to necessarily just to build your business and increase your profits, but also to have that balance in your life.

Wright

So, what I hear you saying is that you believe the reason most people don't take it upon themselves to learn how to be successful marketers is they think it's too … it's overly technical or complicated or too time consuming?

Levinson

Yes. Yes, that's exactly right, David.

Wright

I scanned amazon.com before calling you today, and I was amazed at how many guerrilla titles you've produced. Would you mind picking one or two of these titles and telling our readers how you translated the basic guerrilla philosophy into other marketing applications like internet marketing, home based business marketing? In other words, can your strategies really work across the business models?

Levinson

Yes, they really can because of the reason they were written. As I told you, I wrote the first guerrilla marketing book in 1984, but those books have sold 16 million copies so far. I wrote the first one to satisfy me, which happened to be a need in my classroom, just to learn about marketing inexpensively. Later I started giving talks because as an instructor at Berkley you get invitations to give talks at conventions that are passing through the San Francisco Bay area. I would give talks and people would ask me to be more specific about the weapons of guerrilla marketing. They said, "You sure talk about a lot of the weapons. I wonder if you could describe them?" So I wrote another book called, *Guerrilla Marketing Attack,* which describes the weapons of guerrilla marketing, and the myths as you and I are talking about, and some of the psychology that I brought up. Then the feedback I got, people said, "Boy, that's great when you talk about the weapons. Would you consider doing a chapter on each weapon?" I like writing sensationally. So I wrote 100 chapters – there's 100 weapons – but only of maybe two and a half pages each. There's a description of each weapon that a business might need.

And then I noticed that a lot of people were reading the books, taking it seriously, growing their business, and they were ready to just move up to the next level. So I thought, "Wow! A lot of these people know how to do it now, so I'm going to show them how to do it with excellence." So I wrote a book about the golden rules of marketing called, *The Guerrilla Marketing Excellence, the 50 Golden Rules of Guerrilla Marketing.* Then, as you identified, suddenly here comes the internet and nobody has a clue how to really do it right. It's just a sure path to financial oblivion if you do it wrong. So my publisher said, "Can you do a book to help people do it right?" So I knew I could, but I know how long it would take for me to learn it. But I knew a person also who had been teaching, also who had several books on computers. He'd been on the internet since the '80s, and his name was Charlie Ruben. I said, "Charlie, would you help me do a book about guerrilla marketing online?" And he said, "I'd love to." And together we did *Guerrilla Marketing Online* and *Guerrilla Marketing Online, Second Edition* and *Guerrilla Marketing Online Weapons.* And along comes my friend, Seth Godin. Seth Godin said, "Yeah." He said, "There's so many home based businesses and they can use a lot of the techniques you write about. Let's collaborate on a book for home based businesses." So we wrote *Guerrilla Marketing for Home Based Businesses.* And Orville Ray Wilson from Colorado, who's a master salesperson and believes in the guerrilla techniques wants to collaborate with another author, Bill Gallagher, on guerrilla selling because so many people sell, and they need a lot of these guerrilla characteristics in their selling to literally double their sales output with new ideas. And so we wrote *Guerrilla Selling.* That's been a very successful book.

These books are written to fill a void, and in response to what people need. Technology has undergone a revolution in the past 10 years, not because it's become more powerful or pretty or graphical. It's because it's become less complicated. So I wrote a book about that. I didn't come through with any background of technology. I had a totally different kind of background, but I wrote a book for people like me who had no technical background. I called it, *Guerrilla Marketing with Technology,* because I felt that there was a need for such a book. The one I just talked about, *Guerrilla Marketing for Free,* was because I know some people really want to start out with a shoestring and they're wearing loafers, so they have no shoestring. So they can't spend anything except what I said: time, energy, imagination, and knowledge.

Last week a new book that I wrote came out that I co-authored with two people called, *Guerrilla Retailing*, because retail businesses across America are being hit hard and most of them just are in the dark as to how to compete against the Wal-Marts, the big box stores, and they need help. And so we came riding up on our white horse and hopefully provided *Guerrilla Retailing.* So those titles are in response to needs and that's the key to all business, David. If you can find the needs, then go into business just filling them. Don't try to create your product or your business and then look around for people who want them. It's much easier first to find the need, then to create your product or your service.

Wright

Let's talk a little bit about the Guerrilla Marketing Association. When you spoke to the office earlier, you seemed really excited about this resource. How does it come about? What can it mean to an aspiring business person?

Levinson

Well, I love the question because it's the way my life has changed. I've written 31 books. That's about a book a year since I started doing this. I realized that, when I see my book at Barnes & Noble, I see things in the book that maybe three, four, or five things that I wish I hadn't said because those things have changed since then. It takes about a year or a year and a half from the time the book leaves my work word processor to the time it's on the shelves at Borders, Barnes & Noble or Books-a-Million. I also think of about five things that I hadn't put in that book, and the reason I didn't put them in the book is that I didn't know them then.

I feel that I did my best in writing the books, but still I wish I could be more in touch with the readers. The Guerrilla Marketing

Association enables me to do that. It's a way for me to write, but have my writings published monthly, and not only write and publish monthly, but to get questions from people who have read and give them answers immediately. Here's what the Guerrilla Marketing Association is. It's a small service for small business, an interactive service where people join as members. As members here's what they get. Once a month they get a publication online. It's called the *Guerrilla Marketing Insider.* At least 30 cutting edge ideas that are on three things. They're *Cutting Edge New*, they're able to be put to use the next day or that day, and they cost either nothing or very little. They get at least 30 of those, plus they get five videos, which they view online, interviews with experts just to make it more interesting and let them really hear it from the horse's mouth some of the home truths about marketing. In addition to that, there's a coaching forum, which means they can ask questions about their business. They can say, "Hey, here's my website. What do you think of it?" They'll usually get an answer within 24 hours. We have a team of 40 coaches, certified coaches, who answer those questions. These are college professors, or authors, or ex Fortune 500 people who love answering marketing questions, and they answer questions for our members on a regular basis. We also have a Wednesday evening phone call. The members on the call can then ask questions of all of us, and they can ask questions specific to their business.

Here's how good this is. Last month we had a member on who said, "Well, I've just written a book and my goal is to get it to be number one at Barnes & Noble. Does anybody have any suggestions?" Well, we happened to have a couple of people on the call as experts, who were in the field of literature and the field of bookselling. And we have some members who had quite a bit of experience in making books grow, who told this member on the phone their ideas for what he might do to boost the sales of his book, especially Barnes & Noble. Two weeks later, the call comes up. He's on the phone. He says, "I want to thank you guys for the help you gave me." He says, "My book is number one best seller at Barnes & Noble." We were amazed, but that was the reality. This is what we're set up to do. We give information that is immediately actionable. We charge $49.97 a month. You can quit whenever you want and there's no long-term contract or anything. Our website has a new idea called the tip of the day. Every single day you go to the website you're going to learn something you didn't know before.

There's also a whole course on guerrilla marketing free for the asking right on the site. It's part of the membership. Our several hours of videos are of a very expensive ($4,000.00) boot camp that I gave in Las Vegas. The video of that is also on there.

Weekly, people get updated on marketing of an e-mail newsletter, we send a very short one once a week. So those are some of the things people get when they join the association. They get access to me. I really am the father of guerrilla marketing, but I'm interacting with them on the phone and on the coaching forum and on the things I write in *The Insider*. So there is a back and forth and we get to be even more responsive to what the members want to learn about, what they want to do, what they need most. And if I don't know the answers, and we both know... neither one of us knows the answers, that's why they have experts and other certified coaches who can answer the ones that I can't answer.

Wright

Before we let you go this afternoon, will you give our readers one last bit of advice? What else would you say to encourage men and women who are serious about trying new ideas to market their goods and services but haven't been able to get off square one?

Levinson

Well, it's a matter of not realizing that it's a big job, but that it's a step by step job. There's ten steps to take to succeed with a guerrilla marketing attack, and it shouldn't take you a long time to do it. Every part of this is easy, except for the eighth step. If you take these steps, one by one by one by one, you'll find that marketing is easy and that you are able to make it work for you.

The first step is to research your market, your product, research the competition, research your prospect and the website of their competitors, research your own benefits.

Step two is to write a benefits list, which is a list of the benefits people gain by doing business with you. And then put a circle around all those benefits that are also competitive advantages, advantages not offered by your competition.

Now, the third step is to select the weapons that you are going to use. I told you, you can find a list of 100 of them at the guerrillamarketingassociation.com. Select the ones you'll use and then put them in priority order, just put a date next to each one of them so you'll know when you're going to launch it.

The fourth is where you create that seven sentence guerrilla marketing plan. That's pretty darn simple. Seven sentences. First sentence tells the purpose of your marketing. The second tells the benefits or competitive advantages. You'll stress to achieve your purposes. The third sentence tells your target audience. Fourth sentence tells your marketing weapons you'll use. The fifth sentence tells you your niche in the marketplace, what you stand for. The sixth sentence tells you your identity, not your image. That's a phony thing. I said your identity, truth and honesty, who you really are. You have a personality. You've just got to be aware that you have one and you're in charge of what it is. Communicate that in your identity. The seventh sentence tells your marketing budget, and it should be expressed as a percent of your projected gross sales. In 2003, the average American business invested 4% of their gross sales in marketing. 4%. So think of how much you'll invest in 2004. Okay, now you've done a marketing plan which is the fourth step.

The fifth step is make a guerrilla marketing calendar. There's an easy way for you to make one and print it out for yourself at the Guerrilla Marketing Association website that lets you plan out ahead a year for what you're going to be doing. It makes everything easy so you don't have to make a lot of decisions.

The sixth step is finding fusion-marketing partners, people who have the same kind of prospect as you or same kind of standards as you, and go into joint marketing arrangements with them. There's a lot of that going on in America today, especially the area of small business. What is does it lets more people know your work and it reduces the cost because you're sharing it with other people.

The seventh step is now to launch your marketing attack in slow motion. You've got to feel comfortable about it emotionally that you're not doing too much, and you've got to feel comfortable about it financially that you're not spending too much. And you won't if you understand guerrilla marketing.

Here comes the hard part. I warned you the eighth step is the real tough one. It stops most people. Talk about a wall. It's maintain your attack. Most people expect marketing to work instantly, and it doesn't work instantly so they quit what they did even though everything they did was right. It takes a lot, but you've got to be committed to it. You've got to maintain the attack. More money is lost in this area than any other area. This is where it stops. Doing everything that's right and seeing that nothing has happened.

Okay, the ninth step, now this is hard, keep track because you're going to use a whole lot of weapons. You're going to hit the bull's eye with some of them and you're going to miss the target with others. Unless you keep track, you're not going to know which is which. So you must know the bull's eyes for the misses because guerrilla marketing is not a matter of using a lot of marketing weapons. It's a matter of being aware of a lot, trying many, and then getting rid of the ones that didn't hit the center of the bull. And keeping track is the name of the game.

Now you get to the tenth step. The tenth step is now that you've done all of these things I just mentioned, start improving in all areas. Improve your message. Improve the media you are using, which means using fewer. This way you can improve your budget. You can spend less and you improve your results. You get more. Real successful companies don't invest a lot of money in marketing. They went through this process I just told you about, a ten step one by one process. They weren't in a hurry, and then they found out that boy marketing is easier than I thought it was. It's the best investment available in America today if you do it right and you just heard how to do it right.

Wright

Boy, I'll tell you. That's a doctorate in marketing. We've been talking today with Mr. Jay Conrad Levinson. It's been an absolute delight, Jay. I really appreciate it. Thank you so much for sharing your thoughts and insights with us.

Levinson

Well, thank you for giving me the opportunity to talk about my core marketing beliefs, David.

About The Author

Jay Conrad Levinson is the author of the best-selling marketing series in history, "Guerrilla Marketing," plus 24 other business books. His guerrilla concepts have influenced marketing so much that today his books appear in 37 languages and are required reading in many MBA programs worldwide.

Jay taught guerrilla marketing for ten years at the extension division of the University of California in Berkeley. And he was a practitioner of it in the United States – as Senior Vice-President at J. Walter Thompson, and in Europe, as Creative Director at Leo Burnett Advertising.

He writes a monthly column for *Entrepreneur Magazine*, articles for *Inc. Magazine*, a syndicated column for newspapers and magazines and online columns published monthly on the Microsoft and GTE websites.

Jay has served on the Microsoft Small Business Council and the 3Com Small Business Advisory Board. His Guerrilla Marketing is series of books, a videotape, an award-winning CD-ROM, a newsletter, a consulting organization, an Internet website, and a way for you to spend less, get more, and achieve substantial profits.

Here is the man to transform you into a marketing guerrilla – Jay Conrad Levinson.

Jay Conrad Levinson

Guerrilla Marketing International

369-B 3rd Street #301

San Rafael, California 94901

Phone: 415.455.9197

www. guerrillamarketingassociation.com

Chapter 4

FORD SAEKS

THE INTERVIEW

David E. Wright (Wright)

Today we are talking with Ford Saeks. Ford's sales-producing, profiting-generating advice helps people reach success in their new or existing business ventures by making every dollar count. He's founded more than 17 companies, received multiple patents, and speaks to thousands each year from startups to Fortune 500 companies. He's a nationally recognized speaker on improving direct & Internet marketing through innovative campaigns. Ford, welcome to *Marketing Magic.*

Ford Saeks (Saeks)

Well, thank you very much, David. I'm glad to be part of this book.

Wright

So what made you become so passionate about marketing?

Saeks

Well, it started when in Minneapolis Minnesota, in 1976. I was sixteen and was working for minimum wage at two jobs. One was bagging groceries at Milt's Market and the other was working the camping desk at the Army Navy Surplus Store. I was living on my own in the housing projects of North Minneapolis and I needed to make more money.

Wright

You were living on your own at age sixteen?

Saeks

Yes, but we'll save that story for another time... What's important here is that I was trying to figure out how to earn more money. I knew there had to be a better way of making more than $1.25 an hour. I sat down with the Yellow Pages and flipped through it looking for a business I could start. I had limited experience and even less money. I needed something easy to get started, flexible hours, and that I could learn fairly fast. I thought about several businesses and selected to start a painting company. I figured—how hard could that be... Just get some paint, a few brushes and I would be in business.

I was on the "work-program" in high school so I only had to go to class for one hour in the mornings and the rest of the day I could go to work. I went to my friends in shop class and had them print me flyers and business cards with "Saeks Painting & Light Construction." I didn't know what the construction part would be, but I knew it had to be light since I didn't have any experience—or tools.

I started marketing by posting the flyers and cards at grocery store bulletin boards, on car windows, and had stacks available everywhere that other store owners would let me. I went to Radio Shack and purchased an answering machine and it was a huge mechanical contraption with real-to-real tape and manual levers. It did the trick though.

This was basically a grassroots marketing campaign where you just take a message to the marketplace and see what happens. Of course I didn't know the technical marketing terms—I was operating strictly on instinct.

After two weeks of my initial marketing efforts I received a message on the machine asking for a quote for a painting job. I was ecstatic! Then the voice in my head kicked in with, "W*hat the hell are you thinking... you don't know how to run a painting business, you don't have any experience; no money!"* Have you ever been right on the edge of taking a risk and talked yourself out of it? Of course—everybody has at some point. But I wasn't ready to quit that easily. I thought, "I have to use my resources."

After making a list of ideas, I decided the best option was to go to a paint store and talk to the manager about my new business venture. Picture this. I was basically a street-smart mouthy kid, age sixteen with long hair, an army jacket and carried num-chucks in an inside coat pocket—not exactly the image of a new business owner.

I went to the nearest paint store on Lake Street in Uptown Minneapolis. I walked up to the counter and said, "Hi, my name is Ford and I just started a painting company and I would like you to explain a few things about different types of paints, supplies and how to quote a job. You see I need to go present a quote in about 30 minutes and need help." After a long stare—the laughter started—and he told me to get out of his store and not bother him. I think he thought I was joking or going to rob the place or something. Well, after a bit of persuasion I convinced him that I was serious and that if he helped me, I would by all of my supplies from him.

He agreed. Then he picked up a pint of paint, opened it and with a new brush began to splatter the paint on my pants and jacket. I said, "Hey, what are you doing!" He replied, "You don't look like a painter and you need to be convincing if you are going to get the job." I thought he was crazy, but what choice did I have at that point. Then he gave me a painter's cap, mixing stick, clipboard, calculator and instructions for measuring the rooms.

Ten minutes later I was at the prospect's house. I walked up to the front door and just as I was ready to knock—I froze with hesitation. I thought—this is crazy—I should just leave. Again, I pushed through it and knocked anyway... what did I have to lose. The door opened and the man said, "Come in and let me show you the work that I would like to have completed." I walked through the rooms with high ceilings, pealing paint, cracked walls and listened. The man said, "We want to have semi-gloss in the halls, flat in the bedrooms and high gloss in the kitchen. We want these windows glazed too." I thought to myself, "W*hat is glazing a window? And flat, semi-gloss and high-gloss... what's the difference?"*

After a few more notes and measurements, I explained that I had to return to my office to complete the quote and that I would be back in about 45 minutes. I thought, *Yeah right—my office—I didn't even own a paintbrush...* I rushed back to the paint store.

The store manager helped me figure out the quote and supplies list. The quote came to $1,025.00. That was a small fortune to me at the time. I went back to the prospect's house and this time the wife was home too. She was huddled behind her husband looking at me with a penetrating look of skepticism. I handed them the quote and explained that it was $1,025 for the job, payable with 50% down and 50% due upon completion of the job. The wife took a look at me—then at the quote—then back at me and said, "Do you have any experience?" I wasn't prepared for that one and didn't want to start my business out wrong and replied, "Here's how we work—if you aren't 100% satisfied with our work, then you don't have to pay!" Then I just shut up.

She looked at her husband and said, "Honey, write the man a check!" Those were bittersweet words to my ears. I took the check and sat in my 1966 Chevy Chevelle with no insurance—or tags—and stared at that check for $525 and thought—this is so cool! I need to learn how to do this more often.

Then reality hit. I didn't have any supplies, experience or a crew to help me complete the job. I went back to the paint store and stood outside it. Every time someone came up to the front door I would stop and ask them if they wanted more work. It didn't take too long before I found a few experienced painters to do the job for me. I paid them 70% of the job. I used the deposit to buy a few supplies and I was in business. That first year, I earned over $36,000 in revenues. For a 16 year old back in 1976, that was just amazing to me.

I learned several lessons from that experience: 1) The power of using guarantees – The better the guarantee the easier to reverse the risk factor in the mind of the prospect. 2) Perception is reality – It doesn't matter if what you say is true if the prospect doesn't believe it, you won't make the sale. 3) Communication – The most valuable element in marketing. Everything you do in business that represents your business IS MARKETING. 4) Preparation & research – The resources are always there if you are willing to take the time to look.

That was what got me really passionate about marketing, which also made me think there's definitely an easier way to make money if you **add value.**

My motto now is, "How can I add value and make a profit?" What I would challenge the people reading this book is to find out where their passion level is about marketing. To take a look at their businesses, whatever industry or country they may be in and look at how they can reignite that passion so that they can get the energy behind their new ideas and use creativity to look at their businesses in a new light.

Wright

After reading an article on your website, you wrote about having a "marketing mindset." Can you explain what you mean by that and why it's so important?

Saeks

A marketing mindset, a.k.a. entrepreneurial mindset, means that you need to make sure that you aren't standing in your own way. You can learn all of the strategies, tactics and how-to information in the world, but you also need to have a strong belief about the benefits of your products and services, the value you add, and the results that your product or service gives to your customers.

Belief comes first and taking action comes second. In that order. Without the mindset you will only produce mediocre results.

The question I would ask today is, "What do you do on a daily basis to make sure that you're evolving and developing your skill sets?"

What I tell the clients I work with and attendees in my seminars is to take personal inventory of their business skill sets. We look at their job position in marketing, whether it's a head of the marketing department, a CEO, a manager, director or it could be a small businessperson that wears many hats. We have them list the top 10 –15 skill sets they think they need in order to be successful. Then we rate them on a scale of one to ten on how well they think they perform in each skill set. Then we create an Action Plan with steps and resources they can use to improve or leverage each area. It might be taking a class, attending a seminar, reading a book, networking, masterminding, hiring a consultant, or delegating the tasks to someone else more qualified.

It's amazing that just by doing that simple exercise, you can find areas for improvement. It just gives you a way to rethink your business and marketing efforts. It's an easy exercise that you can do right now.

The strategy I use to help develop and maintain my marketing mindset is something I learned many years ago. I think it might have been from Jim Rohn or Brian Tracy or someone else—I forget now, but it's called the ***hour of power***.

Here is how it works: 1) Select a skill set or topic and spend about 20 minutes learning something new about it; 2) Then spend 20 minutes applying what you've learned by taking some immediate action step; and, 3) Finally, take at least 20 minutes taking care of yourself—whether it's exercising or eating right or relaxing, meditating or all of the above throughout the day.

It's not structured process from 8:00 to 9:00, but I might spend 20 minutes in the morning jogging on the treadmill. Later I'll read an article at lunch. And then I call a client and actually practice whatever it was that I was reading about in that topic or skill set. The key is to be flexible, yet consistent in your desire to learn and improve the skill set that you've selected to improve.

For example, you can start with copywriting, prospecting, direct marketing, Internet marketing, improving your follow-up skills, or even more specific topics like how to automate your email communications, set up a direct mail campaign, or create a special promotion. Next, plan daily activities to improve one of them. Once you've mastered one, then select your next topic or skill set. If you don't want to improve that area yourself, make a plan to get help, hire your weakness, or modify your efforts to compensate for that area.

When I wake up in the morning and right before I go to bed I read something positive to help program my subconscious. At the end of the day, I like to celebrate my successes too. The title of this book is *Marketing Magic*. At the end of the day, what magic did you create? And if you didn't, what could you do tomorrow to improve one of your skill sets to work on the mindset? Remember, if you don't have your mindset clear—all the how-to strategies in the world are not going to be much help to you.

Wright

So what's the number one thing that anyone spending money on marketing should keep in mind?

Saeks

The number one thing in my opinion is that the market will tell you what's working and what's not. You can love your campaign, but if it's not creating the results you want in terms of producing inquiries, responses, sales, and profits, then an element needs to be adjusted. There are many factors involved that you will need to look at in the entire picture of your marketing campaign—the frequency of the impressions, the marketing strategy, the marketing message, your copy, the number of impressions, and the delivery of the message. It's basically a synergistic approach that you need to use to test and track.

There are so many times I see clients that love their campaign because they invested a lot of money on it from another advertising agency. But you can't judge it by how much money you spend on it. You have to judge it by the results it produces. Period. Many times in display advertising for instance, a smaller advertisement in black & white with effective copy will out perform a full-color page display advertisement.

You don't want to change more than one element at a time when testing. Pay attention to the TV commercials, radio, and print advertisements, and other sources of media—all forms of marketing. I suggest you create a "hall of shame" and "hall of fame" for advertisements and direct mail. Go through what others call junk mail and think about it as idea mail. Not so you can copy what others have done or plagiarize them, but you can model themes after it. Make notes about what you like or dislike. Did it have an attention-getting headline? What was the response action step? What was it about the piece or advertisement that caught your attention?

Start your files today and remember, if you're not getting the results you expect from your marketing efforts then you need to modify either your marketing message, the target market your sending the message to, or the method that you are using to send that message to the target market. It's really that simple. The magic is in the combinations of those elements—not on any particular element. You can have the best product and marketing message (the copy), but you'll still go bankrupt sending it to the wrong target market.

Wright

In your experience, what are some of the most common direct marketing mistakes and how do you avoid them?

Saeks

This in itself could be a 12 volume series. We've made millions of dollars for our clients and with my own products and services around the world and we've learned just as much or more from the mistakes we've made too.

One of the more common mistakes we see—this may sound almost too simple, but it's often overlooked—is not selling *benefits* and focusing just on the *features*. I can assure you that even seasoned marketers may still slip back into focusing too much on features and not enough on emotional, benefit-driven copy to communicate the value to their prospects.

Here's something that will help you improve your marketing efforts. Gather up all of your marketing materials and review your website evaluating them on whether you are communicating the real benefits of your products or services or just focused on features. Often, we become so close to our own products and services that we take the benefits for granted and just promote the features. Benefits are what catch the attention and stand out above the clutter of the thousands of marketing messages that we are bombarded with each day.

Here's an easy way to tell the difference between features and benefits. A benefit is usually something intangible and emotional; where as a feature describes your product, your company or is about you.

The magic words you can use to tell the difference are, "which means?" If you look at your market materials whether it's the back of this book that you're holding in your hand or an advertisement sitting on your desk—read a sentence or paragraph, ask yourself the question, *which means?* This simple exercise will get you to the final emotional benefit.

To give an example, I was in New York City presenting a seminar on direct marketing, and we were having a group discussion about features and benefits. One man who was in insurance sales didn't agree with my explanation. He said that his benefit was *Fifteen years of experience.* And I said, "No, that's a feature." And he said, "No, that's a benefit." So we went back and forth several times, and everybody was looking at us because it's getting kind of heated now and he was really getting upset. I said, "Sir, let me ask you one question. "*Fifteen years of experience*, what does that mean to the prospect?" And then he said, "It means that they can trust me...dammit." And I said, "You're right. They can trust you and *they can trust you* is the benefit and *fifteen years of experience* is the feature!"

You could see the light bulb go off in this guy's head. He started smiling brightly. He started writing notes profusely. A few minutes later he got up and said, "You know, I've got my money's worth. I'm out of here. I am going back to evaluate and rewrite all of my marketing letters." A few weeks later, I received a letter from him about how I had transformed his business and really improved his sales by focusing on the benefits versus the features. For the record, features are important too, but benefits come first. Lead with benefits and substantiate your claims with features.

Maybe another common mistake would be throwing good money after bad. You know *profit can hide a lot of mistakes.* Typically, I'm asked to come in as a marketing consultant to look at how they can improve profits. I look at their marketing expenditures and help them evaluate their returns. Then we look for new opportunities and how we can add value. Many times they are already running TV campaigns or radio campaigns, and they're selling a fair amount. Now if their product has a good profit margin, they may not know they're losing money on that type of marketing or whether or not it's helping. So we have to tweak certain things and measure the response and test again. But throwing good money after bad can be overlooked when there is enough profit margin to cover the poor returns.

Wright

Right.

Saeks

Another mistake is not making a specific offer, specific action step, and asking for the order. Take a look at a few direct mail pieces or magazine advertisements, even the web—mostly the web. You'll find great headlines, great copy, and then it gets to the end, and it says, "contact us for more information." Well, I don't need more information. I need to know what to do next. The mistake here is assuming that the prospect will take the time to figure out what to do and do it. It's better to tell them what to do next. Avoid the confusion or the chance that they may get distracted and use a specific action step.

Another common mistake would be not taking the time, care and energy to build and protect their customer & prospect database. Many companies will send out survey cards to prospect lists and mailings with reply responses to help build their list. But then they have the reply cards sitting there in the box in the corner of their office that no one ever entered in the computer. Or if they did enter them in the computer, there are five different systems. They're using Excel®. They're using Access®. They're using Act!®, or another Customer Relations Manager (CRM) program. They may be using some other custom database program or accounting program, but they don't have control over their database.

The problem is if they did want to go create a specific offer to a targeted group of prospects from their database, they wouldn't be able to mail it because the list might be outdated. That wastes time and money. Building and taking care of your prospect and customer lists is a critical element and a topic that fills entire shelves in the bookstore. The magic step here is to make sure you are building and securing your database. There are no excuses—several websites even offer free database tools.

Wright

One of the problems with my database is I really believe that Act! is smarter than I am. It can be hard to understand. But I agree that protecting your prospect list is a very important element in any business. So how do you measure direct marketing success?

Saeks

Well, I measure direct marketing success by profit. Of course, the first concern is to add value and then make a profit. Sure there are other forms of measurement, but you don't go broke making a profit. That was proven with the dot.com, or should I say *dot.bomb,* of a few years ago. Many businesses thought they could sell products or services below cost and make it up on volume—whatever they thought—if they didn't make a profit somehow—then they went bankrupt. We look at every campaign we run and track the results. Sometimes there are several elements that all work together and in that case we rate the entire process on a scale of 1 to 10, with a close eye on the profit margins. If you're not making money, then it's not working and you need to take a different approach and try something different—it's that simple.

Wright

I've heard you talk about marketing myths. Can you tell our readers one of the more common marketing myths and how to avoid its pitfalls?"

Saeks

Certainly, one of the myths I heard when I first started out was to "find a need and fill it."

Wright

Yes, I've heard that too.

Saeks

The myth: People don't really buy what they need—they buy what they want.

They're seeking to fill some sort of emotional need and then they justify it with logic. For example, my son and I went shopping for a new vehicle for me. I decided it would be really cool to get a Hummer. The H2s came out last year, and I thought, "*Oh, that would be a great vehicle. I'd love to have one. I'd use it to go to the lake, camping and skiing in Colorado.*" So at the dealership I told my son that he could pick out any color he wanted. They had gloss black, midnight blue, maroon, and the classic bright yellow.

He picked out the yellow one. An hour later it was mine and we drove it off the lot. As I was driving the Hummer home and watching the average gas mileage at 10 miles to the gallon, I started to justify my purchase. Did I really need a H2? Hardly. I wanted an H2—not because of the dual airbags, or 17" all-terrain tires or other features—but because of how cool it was and how I felt when driving it.

When you try to educate your market that they *need* your product or service—you're going to have a tough road and a lot of risk involved. If your market can't clearly see the benefits that you offer, you run the risk of spending way more money than you're ever going to make back trying to educate them that they need it.

As an example, the person reading this book is most likely looking for ideas and strategies that they can use to make better marketing decisions and ultimately more money for their business. And if they aren't, they won't make it past chapter 1.

An action step here is just being careful that you don't start believing your own BS. Make sure you're clear on what your target market *wants* and adjust your marketing message accordingly. Make sure that you listen to what the market is telling you, and don't listen to someone who tells you it can't be done if they haven't done it themselves.

Wright

Great advice. When you're launching a new product or a new marketing campaign, what system do you use to stay on track?

Saeks

The system I use is so simple and extremely powerful. This system has made millions of dollars in sales for my clients and me. It works with any business, product, or service, and here it is . . .

The Marketing Mix System™

It is three simple things—it's your combinations of *messages*, *markets*, and *methods*.

Message would be a benefit message. You have to be clear on the benefits and value that you add. Now we've already covered that topic a bit earlier. Make sure that you write a clear benefit message that's going to get attention.

Your *market* is your target market defined by psychographics (behaviors) and demographics (statistics). Who are you trying to reach with your message? Where do they congregate? What do you know about them?

Your method is what you plan to do to get your message to your market. Methods are divided into two categories. Advertising and publicity. Advertising being a method that you pay to send your market, and publicity being a virtually free method used to send your marketing message to your market.

So the message would be the what, the market would be the who, and the method would be the how.

Now, I know what some of your readers may be thinking at this point... "Hey, Ford, are you on crack? This is too basic for anyone in business..."

I would beg to differ! As simple as this system is, it's extremely powerful and can be applied to any business, product or service with outstanding results. Sure you understand the terms and concepts, but the real magic is in the combinations and how you mix the three main elements together to make real marketing magic.

Now when I tell this to people they say, "Ford, you know you charge a lot of money for your seminars and your consulting. This seems too simple." But here's what I tell them. If I give you a telephone number, you can understand the digits, like (316) 942-5553, but if you don't put those numbers in the right order when dialing, you're going to get a wrong number.

So even though people understand what benefits are, understand who they're trying to reach, and understand how they're trying to get the message to them; if they haven't scientifically taken a look at the mix of the messages they're sending to the market with what methods and rated them and ranked them, then there's no way for them to tweak the system to get better results.

Here's an example that illustrates the system in action. In 1987 I invented a line of bicycle storage systems that went from floor to ceiling to safely store bikes inside in limited space. When I first came up with the idea, my message was: Save space and protect your bike. I thought my market was bicycle racers because I raced bikes and I thought everybody who raced bikes had an expensive bike they wanted to protect and store inside and that my product was the perfect solution. My marketing method was to drive around to bike races and sell them. Take them into bike shops and sporting goods stores and sell them direct to dealers.

After several months of trying to sell them through the back of my van and direct cold calls on bike shop owners I only had a few sympathy sales. I was spending time on marketing but wasn't making the project successful. I thought, "There's got to be a better way." I went back and looked at the three main parts of the system, which at that point wasn't really a system in my head yet. I thought, "*Okay. What if I change my message, change my market, and change my marketing method?*"

I performed research, read the industry trade journals and spoke to the bike shop owners about how they made most of their product selections. I found out where the trade shows were for the bicycle industry. That lead me to exhibiting at my first sporting goods trade show and I came back with $75,000.00 worth of orders in three days.

Same product, but using a different combination of the three main elements of the Marketing Mix System™ dramatically improved my results. I changed the message, I changed the market, and I changed the method. The message became "Here's a product that you can make money on in your store—an instant profit center." The market became bicycle dealers, specialty mail-order catalogues like *Sharper Image*, mass merchants like Wal-Mart and Sam's, opened up a whole new avenue of marketing. And the methods I used were trade shows, direct mail, and trade publication advertising and a ton of free publicity.

Review any of your advertisements or promotions and write down all your messages or highlight them with a pen. Next, ask yourself whom are you sending it to and what method are you using to get that message to that target market.

The power of the system is when you rank and rate your results. Start a tracking system and soon you'll start to see trends and which combinations produce the best results. If you're not getting the results you expect then you know that it's the combinations of those three elements. A common mistake some make is trying to send the same message to more than one target market. The message you send to a consumer will probably be different than the message you send to a wholesaler or distributor. One is interested in the benefits of the product, and the other is interested in the benefits of selling the product.

Wright

Why do you feel so strongly that the Internet should be used in conjunction with any marketing campaign?

Saeks

The Internet should be utilized because it's the ultimate direct marketing communication tool. It allows instant tracking of your efforts, immediate feedback, and allows you to leverage all of your marketing efforts. We started on the Internet back in 1993, and I know this book is focused more about general marketing, but we couldn't discuss the topic of marketing without at least including the Internet. Again, this could be an entire chapter in itself and hundreds of books have been written on the subject. The problem with many of those books is that they are outdated by the time they are published. Worse yet, many are written by people that haven't even made any money from Internet marketing.

What sets us apart is that we don't just talk about the strategies and tactics of Internet marketing—we live them in our day-to-day operations. We manage over a hundred profitable websites of our own and many for our clients. We have a special resources section set up for the readers of this book. They can visit http://www.primeconcepts.com/ecommerce and find some of the best tools and resources we've found that can significantly improve their marketing and sales efforts.

Ask yourself if you are using the Internet to leverage your customer service and sales department. Did you just put up a site built from a web design company that doesn't know anything about marketing? Are you making a profitable return on your Internet investment? If not, you will be able to, as soon as you consider the Internet just like you would a trade show or advertisement, or marketing campaign. The problem we've seen with some clients is that they didn't treat the Internet as a "marketing tool" and because it involved technology and a new medium, they turned control of it over to an employee, department, or vendor that wasn't qualified or experienced in marketing.

Those same individuals know how to market—and they understand their business, products and services better than any vendor could—but just didn't take enough control over the Internet marketing process. It doesn't have to be that difficult.

The key is to consider what areas of their sales and business processes are best utilized by using the automation and technology of the

Internet. By now, every business owner or officer understands that they need to use the Internet and the moment they start focusing on how to use it to automate and include certain content on their site they will start to leverage the power of the Internet.

I worked with a company in Washington that had four very large stores that had hundreds of thousands of SKUs (stock keeping units) in each store. They were a sporting goods outfitter chain on the west coast of the United States. They had spent a half of a million dollars on their Internet investment before they brought me in. I was amazed that they'd invested all that money and they'd not only lost money—but their site was actually losing them customers because it wasn't congruent with the quality of their stores. It was a crime that they spent so much money, yet it was a disaster. The online shopping didn't work properly. It was supposed to be tied to inventory and have a member's section with specials, but it didn't function properly. They'd only sold about $60,000 of sales through their Internet site.

After completely reevaluating their messages, their target markets, and their other marketing methods, I said, "You should not be selling online. What you need to do is turn your website into an information resource." Here's why . . .

They operated stores that sponsored all types of outdoor sports races. They had a store in the mountains and a store near the ocean. Each store catered to different types of sports and didn't all carry the same inventory. Their products were constantly changing with different brands, styles, sizes and they changed with the seasons too.

Because of the rapid product changes and specialized use of their products in different markets it was a nightmare trying to control it on the web. Sure it could be done, but not in the manner that they already were committed. After a bit more research and discussion they decided to give my ideas a try. They focused the content of their sites on event sponsorship and outdoor sports education. They had free articles on how to select the best camping gear, kayaking, mountain climbing, surfing, skiing, bicycling...and other sports. They included a section for Race Registration and results and became one of the leading resources for customers to go to find out the who, what, where, when and how for outdoor sports. Included on the site in the articles and other sections were special promotions that drove the prospects and customers to visit the store. They used the fact that their products and services were specialized and best purchased in person with their expert advisors helping them make the best choices.

A few months after completing the changes they actually tripled their Internet traffic, increased their traffic into their stores and sales significantly increased too. The key is to leverage the Internet by deciding what works best depending upon your company and resources. Once they got that under control and profitable, then they added the online store purchasing options back in with new technology and it was successful.

Now take us for example. We're an information publisher and produce "how-to" products, offer consulting and promote events around the world. We have sites focused on individual products that we refer to as "sales letter sites" and others that are "deep content sites" Because they are designed with marketing in mind—and all interact together with reciprocal links—we attract more prospects and have excellent sales.

Start with these concepts: 1) Review and evaluate your current site for what's working and what's not; 2) Create a plan for improving the content and design. Make sure you have effective navigation, page titles and action steps on every page; and, 3) Create and implement a plan for search engine rankings, cross promotions, and Internet marketing strategies. For a special report on Internet marketing strategies and search engine ranking techniques visit: http://www.primeconcepts.com/ecommerce.

Wright

We briefly discussed tracking and test marketing. What are some other elements that you recommend to evaluate and improve results?

Saeks

The key is to test one thing or concept at a time. The first area you want to look at is your first 50 to 75 words of a promotion, because if you don't hook them in those first 50 to 75 words of the promotion, you're not going to get them. And of course, that includes your attention-getting headline. If your headline sucks then they'll never read the body copy. Remember, benefits come first, and then features support them.

Raving testimonials, now here's a big one! The testimonials can be via audio, video, print, and now with the web are very powerful sales support elements. You definitely should be collecting testimonials from your customers about your products and company. Don't just collect the testimonials—you actually need to use them in your marketing materials too! Sure that sounds obvious, but I bet you have testimonials that you've collected that you've never put to good use.

Some say, "Well, do you have trouble getting permission?" No. You don't have trouble getting permission. You just have to ask for them, and if you are in an industry where you can't quote a particular company, then you just put their initials, or that it's from a leading supplier in the industry. Yes, there could be some skepticism as to whether it's true—but it's proven time and time again to be very powerful. Oh, and you don't have to make up your own testimonials. If you have good products and services your customers will tell you. You just need to listen and take action to collect them.

Yet Another element would be including response deadlines in your offers. Scarcity or fear of loss creates urgency for prospects to respond. If you say, "There's only so many left," or "this offer expires soon" and you test with and without—you should find that adding these elements increases response rates.

Bonuses and up-sale offers are great ways to increase sales too. Ask yourself what you could bundle together to make into a new offer? What could you offer as an up-sale? Could you add value with an add-in bonus, discount coupons, something to get them to take action and to continue the sale?

Color schemes and visual syntax also effect response rates too. Color schemes can be warm/hot or cool/cold. Certain color schemes help to trigger certain emotions. Visual syntax is the path or pattern that most prospects would follow due to your layout of your advertisement, web page, promotion, postcard, TV promotion, etc.

For example, if you have pictures in an advertisement you want the movement of the image in the photo to go toward the text, not away from it. The same thing applies with pictures of people, animals, cars, machines, and even the lighting and shadows in a photo. Photos attract attention, but text is what sells. You want to attract attention with color and graphics, but you want to get them to read the copy.

One of the more common tests is to run split headline offers. This is where you have the same offer, but change just the headline and split your promotion into two groups to see which headline pulls the best response rates. We just did a 10,000-piece mailing. We sent 5,000 with one headline and 5,000 with a different headline. The results are still out, but when we find out, we'll know that one headline is better. Then we'll go back and mail the other 25,000 pieces with the headline that pulled the best.

With that said, I left the most important element to discuss last. This would be headlines and copywriting. Spend some time either learning how to write effective headlines and benefit offers for your products and services or hire someone skilled in creating mouth-watering, crawl over broken glass to get your product copy. Let the market tell you what's working—they are the only ones that matter. I'd love to spend another three of four chapters focusing on copywriting since it's so critical in marketing success. If your readers want to learn more about it, they can visit http://www.primeconcepts.com/copywriting for a Free 21 Tip Copywriting Checklist they can use when creating promotions and advertisements.

Wright

Very interesting. So, what final advice would you give to someone who is responsible for improving marketing results?

Saeks

A main thought that runs through my mind is "you can make results or you can make excuses—but you can't do both."

You need to be in control of your marketing efforts. Be a continual student of marketing. I read marketing books, listen to business CD albums, go to seminars and adapt the ideas and concepts to my business ventures—don't just adopt them at face value. I learned that concept from Nido Qubein. Have marketing mentors that you can model and learn from too. One I work closely with in a mastermind group is world-renowned copywriter, Randy Gage. I have many others too, some that I've met and work with, and others that I know only through their materials, but they seem like close friends too.

In the end, don't let your webmaster, graphic designer, advertising sales representative, or your spouse tell you what is going to work, especially if they are not in your business. You're going to know your business, or should know your business, better than everybody else. If you feel out of touch, start today and talk to your customers and employees and find out what's working and what's not. There are no short cuts or magic bullets, but using the concepts and strategies outlined here are guaranteed to make a significant positive improvement to your bottom line. I wish you the best of success. Send me your thoughts and comments to fordsaeks@primeconcepts.com and I'll send you a Free Desktop coaching software on the *101 Keys to Prosperity.*

Wright

Today we've been talking to **Ford Saeks**. Ford's sales-producing, profit-generating advice helps people reach success in their new or existing business ventures by making every dollar count. And I think we've learned here today, Ford, that you know an awful lot about what you are talking about.

Saeks

Well, I appreciate that, David. I hope the people who read this book don't just read it and stick it back on the shelf, but they write down at least two or three action steps they're going to take from my chapter and every other author that was in this book so that they have a concise marketing plan of action they immediately apply and increase their profits!

About The Author

Ford Saeks is positioned as one of the Nations Direct Marketing Specialists. Ford's sales-producing, profit-generating advice helps people reach success in their new or existing business ventures by making every dollar count. He's founded more than 17 companies, received multiple patents, and speaks to thousands each year from start-ups to the Fortune 500 companies. He's a nationally and internationally recognized speaker on improving marketing & sales performance and e-commerce through innovative marketing campaigns.

Ford Saeks

Prime Concepts Group Inc.

1807 S. Eisenhower St.

Wichita, KS 67209-2810 USA

Toll-free: 800.946.7804 (US & Canada)

Phone: 316.942.1111 (International)

FAX: 316.942.5313

www.PrimeConcepts.com

www.FordSaeks.com

Chapter 5

BETTE DAOUST, PH.D.

THE INTERVIEW

David E. Wright (Wright)

Today we are talking to Bette Daoust, PhD. Bette has been over 25 years in various technical and business leadership roles. She brings to the table a successful executive career combining many years working with non-profit and for-profit organizations, both in government and a broad variety of industries. Her positions have included executive, financial, marketing, sales, service management, and have encompassed strategic and organizational development experience. As a consultant, she has worked with such companies as Peet's Coffee and Tea, Mobile BIS, Cisco, Accenture and Avaya to improve business processes. She excels in helping organizations to understand and implement the technical and human side of knowledge management systems.

She first graduated from University of British Columbia with a B.Ed. in Commerce, then Simon Fraser University, MA, and finally, Northcentral University where she got her Ph.D., in Business Management. She's a member of the Alliance of CEOs, Project Management Institute (PMI), Information Technology Training Association (ITT), and various other executive organizations. She has held several executive positions for her local Chamber of Commerce and has served, more than once, on the Board of Directors for Rotary, in which she is still very actively involved after 14 years.

She's also the author of many technical books and will be publishing three new titles in the area of business under the Blueprint Books label in the fall of 2004. The next title is *Blueprints for Best Networking Practices – 150 Ways to Network Yourself.* Other titles include *Blueprints for Branding Yourself* and *Blueprints for Discovery Selling.* She is also in the planning stages of her fourth Blueprint title in the area of knowledge management, *Blueprints for Unleashing Corporate Potential.* Dr. Daoust also holds several trademarks in the area of knowledge management. Dr. Daoust, welcome to our *Marketing Magic* book! Thank you so much for being with us today.

Daoust

It's a pleasure.

Wright

What does marketing mean to you?

Daoust

Marketing has several aspects to it. Firstly, there are the five core areas of marketing that are behind everything, and everyone would recognize these readily: positioning yourself, packaging, promotions, persuading, and of course, performance. These core items all lead into others, research methods for example, or using e-mail, and advertising; you can even include PR. All of those are employed to do global marketing and service your customer. Marketing even extends into the area of selling, measuring and determining customers' responses. The first step to marketing is defining the business solutions. That's what marketing basically means to me.

Wright

Why would someone developing a marketing plan need to define their business solutions?

Daoust

Well, simply put, if you don't understand what you're trying to sell, either product or service, it's really difficult for customers to determine what they are trying to buy from you. So you need an area of focus, sometimes called core competencies. I prefer simple focus. You want to focus on one core area before you decide what to take out to the market place. And if you concentrate on that core, other things will tend to fall into place a little later.

There's nothing worse than someone going out there and saying, "Well, I sell silverware, but I also carry computer hardware, and I can get excellent mattresses too!" This type of sin is especially prevalent in the service industry. Who hasn't met the consultant that knows it all and does it all? So it's a matter of focus, because people want to know where you are coming from, where your expertise is. The business solution is, knowing what we sell; we can determine our ideal customer. That's what it's all about.

Wright

It seems like if you were selling a product or service, you just kind of open the doors to everybody and try to drop a net. So what is the point of defining your ideal customer?

Daoust

Once you have determined what your core product or service is, then you can deduce that just certain people will want to buy that product or service. And if you can spend the time to figure out who that person is, then you're not going to be wasting a lot of marketing dollars. You're not going to be spending a lot of your time trying to make it a big blanket over everyone.

If you can determine exactly who would buy your product; for example, someone with an income between 30 and 40 thousand dollars a year, a homeowner with two children, so maybe your product fits into that demographic. If you can determine who they are, then you're able to target your marketing so that you are only picking those mailing lists, or going to those trade shows where these types of people show up; now you're going to be a little better off because you're using the rifle approach rather than a shotgun. Now you can tailor your product or service in order to really appeal to the specific group that will buy it. In other words, you will now have a unique offering for your client.

Wright

How do you decide the unique offering you have for your clientele?

Daoust

You have to do a little bit of research. Unfortunately, a lot of people don't like to do research. They'd rather just jump on the bandwagon with "Oh, this is a great product. I like it so everyone should." What you have to do is sort of step back, take a look at what that product is, and actually do a little research. Ask some questions. Do a survey. Get out into the field. Show the product to a few people. Go to various stores to see if something similar is selling.

If you do that kind of research, then you're not going to be out in the marketplace, pounding on doors and nobody really wants what you happen to like. If you do your homework, you can discover the unique value of a particular product or service, perhaps open up a niche market. If you find a group of people that are really interested in buying that particular product, then it's a lot easier to market too. Once again, it's pointing that rifle, but also improving your aim with a little market research.

Wright

What's the best way to discovering your value proposition as it relates to your product or your solutions?

Daoust

Interesting question, because most people don't understand what a value proposition is, and basically a value proposition is what you, your product or service, actually bring to the customer. You may think you know what you offer, but you may find that your customer appreciates something completely different!

Here's a really good example. I've worked with a company whose management thought their value proposition was that they had the best people servicing the industry. But when you asked the sales people, they thought it was because they had the most stores servicing the population. So already you know you've got two different things on the value proposition, but when you actually got out and asked the customers, the customers said, "Well, gee, it's not that you have the best people or the most locations. That's important, but what's most important to us is that you're able to deliver your products on time when I need it, so I in turn can service my customers."

So, a little research redefined this company's value proposition and the way they talk to their customers, based on what the customers had said, and the company was able to increase their sales through their marketing efforts.

Wright

How does the value proposition differ from benefit?

Daoust

Well, benefits for a cell phone can be that you get so many minutes. It can be your car will go further because of the mileage. Those are all benefits of buying the product. But if the product itself brings further value beyond just the benefits, such as this particular car enables me to deliver products on time because it's reliable, then you've got better value.

Wright

I see.

Daoust

But the value proposition will always have an underlying principle of features and benefits as well.

Wright

So value proposition is mainly from business to business?

Daoust

No, it's both; it can be from business to customer as well because there is value to the customer. The customer says, "Well, I buy these particular plants for my home because I know they are not going to die." Here the value is that this particular plant store sells great products and I know that I can beautify my home and not worry about these plants dying because they've treated them well in the growing. So there's a value proposition that can be found in business to customer as well.

Wright

My wife has said for years that anytime a plant comes in the house she kills it. It's almost a personal thing she has. I read an ad in a magazine a few days ago that boasted of plants that absolutely, positively, equivocally will not die!

Daoust

Now that's a great value proposition. I'll have to find that store myself; unfortunately, I don't have the green thumb either!

Wright

How does branding play a part in marketing?

Daoust

Not only are you focusing on your value proposition, but you also have to look at the way you "package" items, or even services. By packaging, I refer to the way you present a product or service. It comes down to the three C's: consistency, confidence, and continuity.

Branding is about being consistent. Every time a customer comes into any location or talks to anyone that works for you, they should be getting the same message. You don't want the customer to get a conflicting value proposition, be it from a salesperson or a different store, or the web. Branding is all about keeping the message the same, but it's also about presenting a continuous image.

You always recognize the companies with these messages. Coca Cola does it very well. If you see a Mercedes Benz symbol, you know right away what it is, even without the company name to tell you. Not that a brand is just a logo, but because you know what it stands for as well: it stands for quality, which stands for a number of other values and benefits that you associate with those symbols.

Branding is important no matter what the size of your company. It stands for what you offer the customer. So if you decide to get Mobile BIS, you should know exactly what you are going to get. Peet's Coffee & Tea does it very well, you can depend on the quality you're going to get… a special coffee ground at level three is going to be the same no matter where you go because when they roast it daily, then they ensure it's shipped to all of their stores on that daily basis.

Wright

Once you have a brand, what are some of the ways you can support it?

Daoust

Supporting a brand can actually be quite simple, it just encompasses everything, what you see on the website, what you see on letterheads, brochures, displays, everywhere. Supporting your brand means paying attention to all the "small" things, like some detail in the signage, or even the colors used. So once again, it all comes back to consistency no matter where you put your brand identity.

Wright

Yes, I'm reminded of the repetition and consistency that I've noticed even in cartoons.

Daoust

That's right.

Wright

Like Dagwood and Blondie.

Daoust

You know exactly what they're all about. That's their brand.

Wright

What types of marketing strategies can be used in order to market a product or service?

Daoust

Well, one great way is to do an interview. Do a chapter in a book. Write a book. Go out and do some public speaking. Put on a seminar. Get yourself in front of people. Go to networking meetings. Become part of the community. Get yourself known through joining community organizations, being on the Board of Directors. Connecting people together is a great way to do it as well. If you come across something that has nothing to do with you, don't say, "I do that too," but rather, "I know someone that might be able to help you." Keep the connections going.

Wright

How does marketing collateral fit into the overall marketing plan?

Daoust

People always say, "What are you talking about when you speak of marketing collateral?" All I'm talking about here are the photos you take that go on brochures or websites; those make a piece of collateral. Another is the brochure itself. Everything you say about the company becomes a piece of content. A photo, a brochure, an audiotape, a videotape, those are all pieces of collateral. These fit together in a package, which is the image that the company projects.

If only you had a way to put them in one location so that everyone had an opportunity to use that information. There is usually a marketing component of a company, and there is a sales component, and quite often they don't use each other's materials. I don't know what it is, but they often develop each their own independent package to represent the company. They just tend not to talk to each other as much as they could.

If there was a method that they could put all of the information that they're giving the customer in one central location, this marketing collateral could be used by sales and it could be used by marketing. If the HR department was looking for new employees, they could use the same identical information to keep people up to speed. When they have a telephone call that comes into the system, people working at reception or in the call center should be able to call up that information and read the same message. So if the collateral itself is kept in one central location, then all of a sudden it can have multi-purposes and multi-uses and allow the company to even further their brand.

Wright

When does your personal package fit into brand identity?

Daoust

Personal package poses an interesting problem. There are very unique cities around the U.S., and everyone has a different dress code as we go through each of these cities. The Bay area around San Francisco is a lot more relaxed than the actual city of San Francisco itself, which would be different from New York, not to mention cities on other continents, other cultures altogether. You must be aware that if the culture of your company is to wear raggedy jeans, then that's the impression you're going to give to potential customers all over the U.S. and abroad. Perhaps you should use an image consultant so that when you're out in the public promoting your services or promoting your product, people have a clear idea of who you are and that they can take you seriously. That's how it really fits in.

Wright

When promoting your business, what activity should you be involved in?

Daoust

Now, this is a subject dear to my heart. I just wrote a book, which will be out this fall called, *Best Networking Practices*. In this book, a million ideas are covered, like going to networking events, for example. I'm not promoting going to any and all events to meet people and perhaps form some business relationships: you have to do a little research ahead of time to make sure the events you chose are perfect for what you want to sell.

If you are selling lipstick, not that you would sell lipstick, but for example, you probably wouldn't want to go to a meeting for male project managers, although they may buy it for their wives. You would probably want to go to an event like a Chamber type mixer, where there would be more of your target audience. It goes right back to finding that ideal customer. If you know where your ideal customer hangs out and what events they go to, that is a place for you to go.

So that's one activity, and you know that while doing one, you will meet individuals that will suggest other events or networking opportunities. So you can catapult yourself into other events that you judge appropriate places to continue spreading the word about who you are. It is all about branding, and it is about recognition, and marketing is about getting people to know who you are. It's not who you know, it's who knows you! That's what you're trying to do.

Wright

You know, so many people are using sell sheets now, one sheets. When putting a one sheet together, what information should it contain?

Daoust

A one sheet is used to sell you, or it's selling your product or service. It's a basic marketing item. So you not only list the benefits, and the features, but also what makes you unique to a customer, the customer advantage. From this one sheet, you want to get them interested, and then you want them to move into action. So you want to add some sort of action statement on there.

Besides listing the products or services you sell, the benefits, features and value, perhaps a list of satisfied clients, and maybe a quote or two from a testimonial. Maybe even a short biography on the company, a blurb on its principles. If it's yourself, then you also want to give all of your personal contact information. The one sheet is something that you hand out and want to immediately move people to action, so that they will say, "Oh, yeah. I want to find out more about this." And then it makes it easy by clearly giving them a way to contact you. It's what I call an expanded business card.

Wright

So after you put all your marketing and contact information together, who do you send it to?

Daoust

Interestingly, I studied a little bit of the phenomenon of multilevel marketing, and they do this extremely well. The first place to send all of this information is to all of your friends and the people that you know. Believe it or not, they may not be in the market for your product, but they are probably the first people that are going to spread the word. It's what I call a backdoor way of getting the word out. You send it to them and ask them, "Here's some of the information on stuff I'm doing right now. Do you know of anybody that might be interested in this? Can you forward this to them? Or can you give me their information?"

So, that's the first place to send to. The second place is to former customers, places perhaps where you've worked and that may want to use your services again, to bring you back as a consultant, or maybe buy some of the products you're offering. And then the final place that it should go to, of course, is any lists that you buy, or membership lists for organizations. These have about three tiers, of which the last is what I call the cold call list of people that are your ideal client and that you should send that information to. And of course, the ideal is to send it seven times. That is when they may show interest. You know that's a little pricier. If you can start with people you know, that's the ideal spot.

Wright

Is PR – public relations – a part of marketing, or is it strictly advertising?

Daoust

Now, that's a two-folded question. First of all, it is part of your marketing plan; the marketing plan should include a PR plan. Part of your PR is to announce things that are of public interest, or of interest to your clients, but you want to announce them in the proper places. You don't want to just send them to *The New York Times*, "I'm announcing that I have a new client." Perhaps that announcement should be in a trade journal of some sort. You should send press releases for some of the great things you accomplish, as well as some of the great things that are coming up. Press releases are absolutely excellent. And PR also includes items such as radio interviews.

Whether you chose to air new things you are doing, or exciting things to make life better for everyone, when you're doing PR, you just have to remember that it must have appeal, you just can't PR anything without appeal. So that's on the marketing side. But it can also be used, of course, as advertising. Everybody has seen an infomercial. That's a great PR piece. Do you see the two sides of it? I use it as a marketing component because I feel that you can get the word out through press releases, through writing articles, through doing columns, through answering editorials, doing a radio interview, whatever it is, the purpose remains to let people know who you are.

Wright

Should marketing include a web presence?

Daoust

You should never do anything without having a website these days. The first thing people want to know is, "Okay, I've got this one sheet, I want to know more. I haven't got time to call, but I have time to go on the Internet and check it out." Now here's where your consistency comes back into play, your branding: anything that you have out on your brochure, a one sheet, your business card, whatever you're sending out, that message should be identical when you hit the website.

The website not only gives more information, but it should also call customers to action. It should be able to make people want to buy the product. Have a place on the website for them to buy your books, buy your products, book you for a speaking engagement, or at least ask a question, or input items of interest: it's just a good marketing venue for an interactive way to get the customers.

Wright

You talked a few minutes ago about being sure your friends and relatives and neighbors and those people who know you get the information about you. But what should you tell those people that you meet and don't already know you?

Daoust

A lot of people refer to this as the elevator pitch: you step into an elevator with someone who asks what you do; you have eight to thirteen seconds to respond. You need to practice this spiel that is short and to the point, letting them know exactly what you do. Some people call this an audio logo; I've seen that written in a couple of books. Again, be consistent. Refer back to the branding.

It could be your vision, it could be your mission, it's your audio logo, and it should also move the customer to get more information. If you simply say, "Oh, I do knowledge management," they're just going to look at you and say, "Oh, that's nice" and move on. But if you tell them it helps them make more money by improving the way the company uses knowledge and skills, you've got their interest. Some people's elevator pitches seem so rehearsed that quite often nobody takes heed. But if you can convince them that you know what you do and you are passionate about it, then your elevator pitch becomes more believable. You have to make it short, sweet and to the point to get their interest, but at the same time you have to be very believable and not seem rehearsed.

Wright

How can you make sure that people will be interested in your product or service?

Daoust

Now, that all comes back to research. You simply have to know that whatever you are offering is needed in the marketplace. If you don't do that research, and you just offer something, you're going to be back in the same position of running from door to door, selling typewriters in the age of computers. You have to make sure a) that you identify that ideal customer, and b) do some research to ensure that whatever you are offering can be accepted in the marketplace. You also have to do some research on the pricing model of it as well. If you're over priced, you're going to fail too. So marketing won't happen until you get those things right. The price has to be right. You can have pricey items, but if there's no demand for it, there's no point. But you can have a pricey item because there is a demand for it; then you can sell it to that ideal customer.

Wright

Listening to you, you often recount stories. Why do stories help in marketing efforts?

Daoust

What I find is that, as you're talking to people, you've done your elevator pitch, or your audio logo, and they want to know more. You can start to tell them stories so they can get a better understanding. Earlier, we went through a story of a plant store that gave a guarantee. You brought up that your wife kills plants and now she's going to perhaps go to this plant store so that her plants won't die next time. I told a story about a customer trying to define the value proposition that gives a better understanding of the product or service, a better understanding of how people will be using it. And once they see how it's being used, they can start to think about the different ways they can use it themselves. So the stories back up a lot of the items that you're talking about.

Wright

If you're a sole practitioner, why do you need to make time to market?

Daoust

If you don't market, you can be in what we call a consulting cycle. This happens to everybody when they first get into sole proprietorship. They run around; they market; they network; do all of the right things to get the customer. The first customer engages them for a period of time—three months, six months. They work solely for that customer. What happens at the end of that? Oops! I've got to get out there and market and sell myself again and get the next customer. So it's that vicious cycle—market, do the work, market, do the work. All of a sudden you've lost that consistency of message. People think you've gone away in that period of time, so they're not phoning you back. So if you can plan in, either weekly or every two weeks, a half day or a day, to make sure your marketing activities are happening on a consistent basis, when that client's engagement ends, you're ready to move on to the next one, because it's probably already in place. You start to book yourself ahead of time. It's a matter of making sure that you do schedule in some marketing time for yourself.

Wright

I heard you mention this catchy phrase, "faster-better, easier-cheaper." Are you able to manage your time to make your services faster, better, easier, and cheaper?

Daoust

Yes, that's one of the keys things. I like to use the analogy of the Olympic Games. The athletes aim to go faster and to be better at the same time. You know they spend a lot of time practicing, so their time is the one commodity that they are short on. They need to really be organized and schedule things in.

In business, being organized so that you are faster and better means that things are easier to handle and less costly, all of which helps you beat the competition. I know one of my challenges, and I'm sure everyone else is in this boat, is e-mail. E-mail arrives; I've got to read it right away. And I don't know how you're handling it at that point, but I know that if I see an e-mail or I hear the telltale sound of it arriving, then oops, guess what I am doing? That's a true interruption of time. So what I try and do is set aside a little bit of time every hour so I will check my e-mail and see if there's something important I have to answer at that point in time. And then just put them aside, try to put them in an order of okay I must answer these today, or these can be left until tomorrow; try and organize it in that way.

There are all kinds of other things. I'm also a book junkie, meaning that if it looks like it's a good book and it has anything to do with what I'm interested in, I'll buy the book. I end up with shelves and shelves and shelves of books of which I read one chapter each. I don't know if you've been in that spot. You get interested in something once and it's all around you. So try to work on one thing at a time. Something comes in; you know you have to deal with it and you just absolutely try to deal with it and get it finished before you move on to the next thing. It definitely saves a lot of time.

I put on a workshop for the Chamber of Commerce locally here, called *Faster-Better, Easier-Cheaper*, and I was actually not that surprised to find that most people can't organize their time well enough to get everything done that they need to do in a day. It's pretty difficult for most people. So when you're doing your marketing component, that's why I'm saying you absolutely must set aside a time to do the marketing, but within that time you should also be organized about what you're going to do, and what's going to happen within that timeframe. Faster-better, easier-cheaper simply means that your company should use it's time more effectively to achieve better results which in turn makes it easier to serve customers at a cheaper (lower) cost.

Wright

Why should you keep track of all of your marketing efforts?

Daoust

This is because I may decide I'm going to do a postcard. Postcards are very popular right now. I'm going to send it out with a little code on it so that I ask people how they heard about me and they can say, "Well, I got your postcard and here is the code from it." This way I can keep track of the success rate. If I send out a thousand postcards, and I get seven responses, then that is my success rate. But I'm likely also conducting an e-mail campaign at the same time and people respond to that too. If I keep track of the number of responses for each one of these, I can further pinpoint what is working for me and what is not. Then I can drop the campaigns that are not cost effective at all and attempt to fine-tune the ones that are.

There are a thousand and one ways to market products, books, and services. If you did all thousand and one and didn't track what was happening, you may end up throwing dollars out the window that you don't need to.

Wright

So tell me about your Four-Way Test.

Daoust

Ah! I am a Rotarian. From the earliest days of the organization, Rotarians were concerned with promoting high ethical standards in their professional lives. One of the world's most widely printed and quoted statements of business ethics is The 4-Way Test adopted by Rotary in 1943. It asks the following four questions:

Of the things we think, say or do: 1) Is it the TRUTH? 2) Is it FAIR to all concerned? 3) Will it build GOODWILL and BETTER FRIENDSHIPS? 4) Will it be BENEFICIAL to all concerned?

So whatever marketing you're doing, you want to make sure there's integrity and fairness behind it. You hope to develop a relationship with the people you deal with and to make sure it's win-win for everyone. I try to adopt those principles in all of the marketing that I do and all of the services I provide, and I suggest that other people try it.

Wright

What an interesting conversation. I've learned a lot here today.

Daoust

That is great. I enjoyed it too.

Wright

Today we've been talking to Bette Daoust, PhD., who has spent over 25 years in various technical and business leadership roles. And as we have found out, she knows an awful lot about marketing. Thank you so much, Bette, for taking this much time with us on *Marketing Magic*.

Daoust

Thank you.

About The Author

Bette Daoust, Ph.D., has spent 25 years in various technical and business leadership roles. Dr. Daoust brings to the table a successful executive career combining many years working with government, non-profit and for profit organizations in a broad variety of industries. Her positions have included executive, financial, marketing, sales, and service management. She has worked with such companies as Peet's Coffee & Tea, Mobile BIS, Cisco, Accenture and Avaya in the field of knowledge management.

Dr. Bette Daoust

BizMechanix

7734 Creekside Drive

Pleasanton, California 94588

Phone: 925.425.9513

Email: info@BizMechanix.com

Chapter 6

Don Benton

THE INTERVIEW

David E. Wright (Wright)

It's our pleasure today to welcome Don Benton to our *Marketing Magic* project. In addition to serving as State Senator in the 17th District of the state of Washington, Don is well known as a strategy expert focusing on business and campaign management, advertising, and marketing. For 18 years he has traveled the country speaking to audiences of all types and sizes. Don worked for one of the largest insurance companies in the world, was CEO of a computer networking firm, has campaigned with the President of The United States and has owned several businesses. Don holds a degree in business management and communication from Concordia University. Don, welcome to *Marketing Magic*!

Don Benton (Benton)

Thank you, David. It's a pleasure to be with you today.

Wright

I haven't had the pleasure of interviewing a State Senator in a long time. Before we dive into your expertise related to marketing, can you give us a brief background related to your business career and politics? For example, how did you end up serving in the Senate for your state?

Benton

Well, it's a lifelong story really. I've been involved in one way or another in politics my whole life. My father was on the local school board for 16 years, so I grew up around public service and elections. I saw him make a difference and it obviously made me believe that one person can make a difference in our lives. Throughout school I was involved in student body elections and when I graduated I ran for the College Board of Trustees in California, where I was elected to serve for two terms. Then, when I moved to Washington, I continued my community involvement. I soon realized that Washington had an onerous tax system for small business, so I complained to the wrong person, my State Senator. She encouraged me to run for the State House of Representatives, so I did, and I won. Two years later I ran for the Senate, and have been serving in the Senate for eight years. My experience in politics really began at an early age. It gave me a lot of lessons in marketing because whether you're marketing for a business or whether you're marketing for a political campaign, the tactics and the strategies are very, very similar.

Wright

Our book is entitled *Marketing Magic*. We chose that title because to thousands of business people across the country, really understanding how to market their businesses or service effectively can feel a bit like a magic act. We want to take the mystery out of marketing promotion and advertising. Would you give us your definition of marketing and explain why good marketing practices are so essential to business?

Benton

The definition of marketing is really quite simple if you think about it. It's reaching the consumer most likely to benefit from your product or service with a compelling and memorable message. That's really all there is to it. By the way, it's the same for my political clients as it as for my business clients. The only difference there is, of course, the product is *you* in politics. Marketing is essential because without it, you're out of business. It's that simple. Over the years there have been some very, very good businesses with excellent products and service that have gone under due to a lack of effective marketing. I can think of several businesses, I'm sure that our readers and our listeners can too, that had inferior products, but they succeeded and continued to succeed because of great marketing plans and strategies. Proper marketing is really the key to business. It helps if you've got a good product and great service, no doubt about it. But marketing is the key to business and political success.

Wright

When you work with a business, what do you look for and consider when evaluating the effectiveness of their marketing plan?

Benton

Well, the first question is: Is the company growing? If the company's not growing, then the marketing effort needs an overhaul because there is no such thing as status quo in business. You're either growing or you're dying. You just can't maintain the status quo. If you are growing, then the question is: How fast? And is the growth rate appropriate for the age of the company? Because as companies age, their growth rate will slow down. It's at that point that you need to ask the question: Am I growing the right customers? Early on in the company, a new product should have a very high growth rate if it's going to continue to succeed. In the aftermath, as the growth rate begins to slow down, then you look at trying to graduate to a higher end customer and so you're not necessarily growing customers, but you're growing sales in terms of sales figures. You're graduating from a $20.00 customer to a $40.00 customer, along those lines. In marketing, this is really a two stage thing. So, the first question to ask when you evaluate whether or not a company's marketing plan is effective is: Is the company growing. And then the next question is: How fast and is the growth rate appropriate for the age of the company?

Wright

I'm sure there are many different approaches to marketing. In your opinion, are there certain principles that apply to all successful marketing campaigns?

Benton

Absolutely. There are three key principles in determining an effective marketing campaign. The very first thing you have to do is identify the target. (This is where a lot of businesses fall down.) You must find out who the target is for your product or your service? The second step is to fill the need. And the third step is to be compelling and memorable. Those are the three key steps to a successful marketing campaign—identify the target, fill the need, be compelling and memorable with the message.

Wright

Would sound bytes fall under compelling and memorable like "where's the beef?"

Benton

Absolutely, and that is one of the examples that I'll talk about.

Wright

Give us some examples if you will, especially from your own experience of successful marketing endeavors.

Benton

Well, you mentioned one earlier. I am sure you know of a couple of more successful campaigns if you think about it. "Where's the beef?" Well, what was the target? The target audience was people who eat hamburgers. What was the need? The need was a hamburger that had meat in it because people that were eating at hamburger joints were finding that the patties were getting smaller and smaller. Be compelling and memorable. By using a good script, a good actor and a good scenario, you are able to identify the target, fill the need, and be compelling and memorable with that message.

Now over 15 years later, you can stand in front of any audience, as I do in most of my talks, and say, "Where's the beef? What was the name of the company?" And the audience yells out, "Wendy's." That's what I mean by being memorable. Fifteen-years later people still remember that tagline. Another great example of successful marketing is what Motel 6 did with "leave the light on for you." When people come in late what does the wife or the husband usually say? "I'll leave the porch light on for you." What is more welcoming than having the light on for us when we come in late at night? The Motel 6 people did an excellent job of identifying the target—people coming in off the road late at night. They filled the need, the need to be welcomed without hassle, and they used Tom Bodett, a memorable voice, to convey the message. So again, identify the target, fill the need, and be compelling and memorable. Motel 6 couldn't build hotels fast enough to hold all the people that campaign brought in. It's one of the most successful marketing campaigns in history. A more recent example is Verizon. Now here is a company, that if five years ago I would have said to one of my audiences, "What is Verizon?" no one would have known. This is a relatively new company that 95% of all Americans today recognize the name. It's wildly successful in terms of branding. What they were able to do is take the need (And what is the need?), a good clear signal, and they came up with a terrific advertising and marketing campaign, which is "Can you hear me now?" Everyone who has owned a cell phone has said this at one time or another to the person on the other end of the line. "Can you hear me now?" They did an excellent job of identifying the target and filling the need, the need being a clear signal on your cell phone, and using a compelling and memorable approach. They now are one of the most widely recognized brands in America, yet no one had ever heard of them five years ago.

Wright

I think it was Sprint that had the pin drop, they don't do the sound anymore, but on all the TV commercials, after all these years, they still have that pin dropping.

Benton

Exactly, that is just another example of a compelling and memorable campaign.

Wright

What kind of unique challenges do the small businesses face when it comes to marketing and promotions?

Benton

Well, probably the biggest challenge for a small business is expertise. You know I've worked with a lot of plumbers who are great plumbers, but they don't have any marketing expertise or background. It's hard to get. They're taking whatever the newspaper guy tells them or the Yellow Page guy tells them or the TV salesman tells them. So it's really difficult. A dentist that's spent all of this time in dental school is a great dentist, but he doesn't have any expertise in marketing or advertising. Most small businesses are that way. They've spent their effort and sweat equity on improving what they do (their specialty), which is plumbing, dentistry or running a restaurant, but in terms of marketing they haven't had the exposure or training to know what's effective. They then become the prey of sales people out there selling a wide array of different marketing and advertising schemes that may or may not work for them. It's tough to find out that a marketing scheme didn't work for you after you've spent 15 or 20 thousand dollars doing it.

Creativity is another challenge. Then of course, a challenge for all businesses, even big businesses, is the budget. Do I have enough money to invest in this program? But I think mostly for small businesses it's the lack of available expertise.

Wright

Since money or lack of money is such an issue with small businesses, what advice would you give small business owners when it comes to marketing and promotions?

Benton

Be sure every dollar you spend is building name awareness. There's never been any truer statement in marketing or advertising than the following: Name awareness has a direct relationship to market share. The more people know, see, or recognize your name, the more likely they are to choose you over the competition. That is a fact of life and if every business owner understood that, they would be so much better off. We, and I'm a small business owner so I include myself, as business owners tend to spend our money in a lot of areas that do nothing to increase our name awareness in the marketplace. The Yellow Pages is a great example. The Yellow Pages can do absolutely nothing to increase your name awareness in the marketplace because it has no readership. People have to actually need your product or service before they'll ever open the book, so you can never hope to create demand and desire for your product or your service with an ad in the phone book, and you certainly can't build name awareness in it. There are only two ways to get name awareness. The consumer must either hear your name or see your name, and they certainly are not sitting down with a cup of coffee in the morning and reading through the Yellow Pages.

Wright

Are there things that a business person can do that don't cost a lot of money?

Benton

Absolutely! I'll give you an example of what one of my clients did. An insurance agency in Charlotte, North Carolina, wanted to do something special for birthdays. Now a lot of insurance agents send out a birthday card, but to be memorable you ought to do something different. What he did was he went down to the local ice cream parlor and he arranged a deal with them. He said, "I want to buy one hundred scoops of ice cream from you, but probably half will never be used. So will you give me a discount? Will you sell me 100 scoops of ice cream for the price of 50?" The ice cream owner said, "Well, let's see. I get paid for 50 right now, and I don't have to dish those out except maybe over the course of the year. A bird in the hand is worth two in the bush. So, you bet!" He was able to take a coupon for a free scoop of ice cream and put it in with every birthday card that he sent out. Now, the recipient was impressed because it was a gift, a birthday gift, instead of just a card from his insurance agent. The ice cream guy was happier than you could imagine because he got cash up front to pay his rent that month, and then could amortize it over the course of a year as the insurance agent sent out 10 or 12 a month. The insurance agent won too because he was able to send out 100 gifts for the price of 50. These type of things are terrific marketing tools. Another marketing technique that I recommend that doesn't cost hardly anything is for the owner to actually spend some of their own time personally marketing the business. We have done this with a postal annex store and with a sandwich shop. They were very tight on marketing money and didn't know exactly how to reach people and let them know they were there. They knew if they could get people in the store, they'd come back; but they needed to get them in for the first time. One of the things a store owner can do is print up some coupons and spend one day a week out marketing in your neighborhood. Go to every other store in the complex. Go up and down all the streets within a mile of your location. Walk in, introduce yourself, and hand them a coupon for a discount. Invite them to your place of business. It costs you next to nothing to do that and that is one of the most effective marketing tools you can imagine.

Another one is to do press releases through what I call free or earned media. This is where you have an event, or you bring in a specialist or someone to sign books and do a press release on it to get some free earned media in a local press. That's a very effective technique that we have employed on a number of occasions for small businesses. So there are many ways to really alert the community to your location and why they should come and visit you, without spending a lot of money to do it. It's just being creative, using some shoe leather and making the commitment to actually go do it.

Wright

If you had ever sent me a free scoop of ice cream, the owner of the ice cream company would really be happy because I have never eaten just one scoop in my life. I would spend more money when I got in there. And I travel with a drove of kids with me as I go, so...

Benton

Absolutely! On that last question let me just add as proof to the success of that. My printer, who does all of my printing today—and we do a ton of printing here, thousands and thousands of dollars worth every year—walked into my business 15 years ago and introduced himself to me. He gave me a coupon for a discount on business cards. This was at a time when we were doing maybe a thousand dollars worth of printing a year, and now we do thousands and thousands. Him coming in, introducing himself, having us try him, and of course, the continued great service that we received from him over the years makes us not even want to think about another printer.

Wright

Right! Don, the internet has become a powerful tool for marketing and promotion. How do you advise your clients relative to internet marketing?

Benton

Well, you have to understand that you can have the best website in the world and it won't generate a penny if no one knows it exists. So again, marketing, just like you market your location for people to come in physically, you have to market your website for people to come in electronically. It's the same concept. You need to promote the website to the most likely user. Show them how it can fill their need and do it in a compelling fashion. I strongly encourage utilizing the search engine route rather than the internet advertising route. Advertising on other websites and so on are not nearly as effective as spending time, effort, and energy, and money on making sure that the search engines list you in the first page or two of references when someone puts in "auto body/Philadelphia." We have the connections and the techniques to put you in touch with the right people that will do that. We do not do that, but we certainly know who does. That's almost a full time job for many of these companies who work to make sure that you're in the top 10 or top 20 of the search engine hits. We think that's one of the most effective ways after the marketing/advertising aspect of it. Every commercial you do, whether it's on radio or television or even in the newspaper, should have your website on it because you've got to drive traffic to your website, regardless of how good your website is. Again, if no one knows it's there, they'll never find it.

Wright

I've known people who grab hold of one marketing idea and then ride it until it becomes ineffective, then they jump on another one and then another one. Is it better to adopt a marketing approach that includes multiple strategies all working together?

Benton

Well, certainly, you want to have a media mix in your marketing. There's no question about that. I said earlier, you can't create name awareness or create demand and desire with an ad in the Yellow Pages, but that doesn't mean that you don't need to be in the Yellow Pages. There are a certain group of consumers out there who will have the need without being led to it by your advertising, who won't have anyone to ask for a referral, and who will only have the Yellow Pages to reference. So you do need to be there for those people. The question is how much is too much and where do you reach a diminishing return on your investment in any one particular approach? So a balanced approach is very, very important. It depends on what you are selling and what your product or your service is as well in terms of targeting the right consumer. But you never want to put all of your eggs in one basket. I tell my political clients that. Direct mail to the voters is very important, but you certainly don't want to neglect the opportunity to reach people on radio and television, even though those messages reach people who aren't even registered voters, but they do reach people who are. The same could be applied to a business. Here is a business to business example. I had a print shop supply guy, not a printer but a fellow that owned a wholesale business that supplied print shops. He said, "Why do I want to advertise on television when my only customer is a guy that owns printing shops? And what if I buy this television ad and it misses all these people." I said, "Oh, hold on a minute. I remember something I had learned from my Dad when he went pheasant hunting. He said, "When I go Pheasant hunting, I don't take a rifle. I take a shotgun. Now a lot of pellets miss the target so we waste a lot of ammunition, but no one ever complains when I come home with a sack full of pheasants." So the moral of this story is people who own print shops watch television too. Yes, your message on television will hit a lot of people that will never be customers of yours, but will it hit the target? That's the key. Don't worry about targets missed or ammunition wasted as long as you are hitting the primary target. If you run the commercial on cartoons, it probably won't hit the primary target. But if you run the commercial on the news, for example, where business owners, like print shop owners, probably are concentrating their viewing time on television, then yes, you will hit the target. It's important to have a media mix, but you have to be smart about how you use different aspects of the marketing plan.

Wright

Well, what an interesting conversation. I really appreciate all this time you've taken with me today, Don, and I've learned a lot. I know our readers will as well. We have discussed all kinds of things about marketing and since you are a politician, as well as a marketing guru, I'd like a comment on one. I've always been interested in politics but never run for public office. I love to listen to the debates, and I did a training session one time on name recognition. I said to the audience, "I knew John F. Kennedy. He was a friend of mine and you're no John Kennedy." Do you know that every person in the room knew who I was talking about, and it happened years ago.

Benton

Senator Lloyd Bentsen from Texas, as I recall.

Wright

That's right! But then I said, "I'll give anybody in the room $100.00 if they can name one other sentence uttered in that one hour debate." And not one person knew one other thing. So that sound byte is really important. How do you suggest that businesses come up with great lines like that—as you call them, memorable?

Benton

Yes, memorable. "I'll leave the light on for you." "Where is the beef?" "Can you hear me now?" "I won't take advantage of my opponent's youth and inexperience in this campaign. " These are all great and key phrases. Of course, the one you talked about, "I knew John Kennedy and he's no friend of mine." You've really got to sit down, and that's one of the areas where small businesses just don't have the expertise. But a small business owner can sit down and just think creatively. First of all, what do people need? What are they looking for? What is their anxiety level? Fill it with something that is comical and different. Some people call it your unique selling proposition. What makes you different? What makes you stand out? It also helps to use something funny. I remember in California, Cal Worthington had a terrific television commercial series. One of the things he said was, "I'll eat a bug to sell you a car." Sometimes it's the outrageous that people remember. People remember that stuff. Sometimes it's a jingle or a little talk. It's been 25 years since cigarette advertising has been allowed on television, and the only place they ever used it was on television. They never used it in print. "Winston tastes good like a cigarette should." A lot of people remember the "Beep, beep, Double A-m-c-o" for Aamco Transmissions. "Call Roto-Rooter and away go troubles down the drain." It's the music, the jingle, something that's catchy. One of the things that we've used in political campaigns in the past that has been very effective for us is we tag the television commercial my two young boys saying, "And don't forget to vote for my Dad!" People remember that. We haven't used that for six years, and people still come up to my boys in the grocery store and say, "Don't worry. I voted for your Dad too." You've got to try a lot of different things until you hit on it. But once you hit on it, once you find something that you think is it, the key then is focused repetition. Great car dealer, Scott Thomason, took over his dad's single Ford dealership in 1983. From 1983 to 2000, in 17 years basically, he took that one Ford dealership to 11 dealerships generating over 380 million dollars a year in revenue, over a million dollars a day, with basically one concept and one tagline on television. And it was, "If you don't come see me today, I can't save you any money." And it sounds silly, doesn't it? But you know what? People remembered it and that's all effective advertising is—that people remember it and remember you and think of *you* before they think of the competition.

Wright

Today we have been talking to Senator Don Benton, who is a State Senator in the State of Washington. He's also a small business ad campaign management expert focusing on management, strategy development, advertising, and marketing. Don, thank you so much for taking so much of your time today to talk with us on *Marketing Magic*.

About The Author

Don Benton is a marketing and advertising wizard with a 28 year track record of successful business ownership and business success stories. At 20 he started his first company that became the largest independent employment agency in Los Angeles and at 24 was the youngest ever elected to the College Board of Trustees.

His marketing savvy took him from student body President to campaigning with the President of the United States. Currently a State Senator from Washington, Don operates The Benton Group, a consulting firm providing expertise in sales, strategy and marketing to such companies as Viacom, The Walt Disney Company, Comcast, CBS, Fox Broadcasting and many national, state, and local candidates for public office.

Don Benton, CSP

The Benton Group

P.O. Box 5076

Vancouver, Washington 98668

Phone: 360.574.7369

Fax: 360.576.6866

Email: don@donbenton.com

www.donbenton.com

Chapter 7

DAVID G. EDSTROM

THE INTERVIEW

David E. Wright (Wright)

Today we are talking to David Edstrom. David is the founder of the Player Coach and Company, LLC, a nationally recognized speaker, and member of the National Speakers Association. David has worked at all levels of sales and sales management for the past 30 years and now travels across the country speaking to Chambers of Commerce, business groups, and associations sharing his powerful new business development secrets referred to as *The Performance Solution*. *The Performance Solution* is the new business development plan for the 21st century because it addresses the three key factors that govern performance, which means clients will work more effectively, more efficiently, and the real benefit is that they will make more money and have more fun. David, welcome to *Marketing Magic*!

David Edstrom (Edstrom)

Well, thank you. I'm glad to be here.

Wright

So how did you get started in this business?

Edstrom

After returning from Vietnam in 1968, I entered the financial services business first as a producer and then later into sales management, as a producing general agent. These two experiences taught me a lot about people, motivation and performance. This ultimately led me to a large mutual life insurance company in New York as a Regional Vice President. There I was responsible for the growth and development of their Northeast Region, the largest in the company. I then became Vice President of Agency Growth and Development and was responsible for national distribution.

One of the things we noticed was that some producers were selling away from the company for various reasons, so we conducted a survey with many of the company's top producers to find out how we could serve them better and bring the business back to the company. We asked, "What can we do to earn their business?" The response that came back over and over again was, "Help us get in front of our target markets." It wasn't give us more money, give us more trips, more computers and more pencils, although they wanted all those things, but what they really wanted was help in getting in front of decision makers in their target markets. This survey reinforced my belief that the number one concern of all sales professionals, whether one day or 30-years in the business, was "PROSPECTING." This survey ultimately led to the formation of The Player Coach and Company, LLC.

Wright

So the name of your company is The Player Coach and Company. What does that mean? It must have some significance.

Edstrom

Yes, it does. As The Player Coach and Company, we "play" and "coach" at the same time becoming an extension of a client's sales and management teams. If you remember the Boston Celtics and Bill Russell, you know that Bill Russell was both a great coach and great player who led the Celtics to many NBA championships. He was a player/coach! So that's the basic concept behind the name. We're the player/coach to sales professionals and business owners, as Bill was to the Boston Celtics.

Wright

So what is the key to success as you define it?

Edstrom

I believe the key to success is to help others become successful. These words embrace our company philosophy. The number one competency shared by all successful people is their ability to manage themselves; and that means doing those things every day that unsuccessful people refuse to do.

Wright

Do you mean doing things that other people are unwilling to do?

Edstrom

Yes, either unwilling or can't do. Usually that boils down to attitude and making the effort. You can have a great plan, all the skills in the world, all the opportunities possible, but if you won't make the effort, then it's not going to happen.

Wright

What do you think is the most important lesson to be learned?

Edstrom

Well, I think one of the most important lessons is that you've got to be in the game every day. Selling is not something that happens by accident or by luck, although sometimes a little bit of both won't hurt, but rather it's the result of a process and a commitment! "You can't win if you don't get in."

Wright

Have you seen a change from year to year, or do the same principles still apply?

Edstrom

The fundamentals never change! However, what has changed and is in constant change is technology. One of the fundamentals that never changes is the need to continually develop new business. The question is, how can we use technology to help us find decision makers and ultimately produce new business?

It sounds like we're talking about prospecting, but actually, with tongue in cheek, we tell our clients to stop prospecting and start building relationships! People like to do business with people that they know, like and trust, so start building relationships. One way to do that is by helping others. One of the best ways you can help other sales professionals is to help them find new business. This is called ***networking,*** which we define as sharing of ideas, information, resources and ***contacts***. I'm sure we'll talk more about that later.

Wright

What is it about people that determines their performance?

Edstrom

Well, really there are three factors that determine performance. The first factor is ability or skills. The second thing is attitude or effort. And the third is environment or opportunities. We've addressed all three factors in a process which is called *The Performance Solution.*

Wright

So what is The Performance Solution?

Edstrom

Well, *The Performance Solution* brings these factors together to help people work more effectively, more efficiently, make more money and have more fun.

Wright

Is this program applicable to everyone?

Edstrom

I think it is, but if you're specifically involved in relationship selling, it's the solution to greater productivity.

Wright

So specifically, who will find your program most beneficial?

Edstrom

The people who find our services most beneficial are professional sales people and small to mid sized business owners.

Wright

With so much in the papers today about corporations that are looking pretty bad in the higher echelons such as Enron and some of the others, does your company have a philosophy?

Edstrom

Yes, we do and the philosophy of the company is actually embodied in that definition, and that is "the key to success is to help others achieve success." It's almost biblical in that "the open handed giving is always full," and the "key to my success is to help you achieve your success" really say the same thing.

Wright

So it's a servant attitude?

Edstrom

Yes, it's an attitude that we are here to serve and help our customers in order to earn their business. For example, if I had a meeting with a prospective client and I knew that he was trying to sell doctors, I'd try to find a couple of doctors who were contacts of mine and go to that meeting prepared to give that person an introduction to both docs. Frankly, I'd probably be the only one who ever did that! So, do you think I would be viewed differently? Do you think I'm likely to find some new business?

Wright

What products and services does your company offer?

Edstrom

Well, we offer three types of services, which we call the "Performance Formula." This was developed by The Self Management Group (SMG) in Toronto, Canada. SMG is a strategic partner of TPC. Their formula identifies three factors in determining performance. 1) environment, 2) skills, and 3) attitude. Our services are collectively referred to as The Performance Solution and address each segment of the formula. Clients can select one or more of these services based upon their specific needs. The three segments together however, form a solid performance development program.

The first segment, Business Development, is perhaps the most important because it incorporates every phase of the Performance Formula including opportunities, skills, and attitude. Our customers are sales professional and small business owners whom we refer to as Executive Players. This relationship is a membership in TPC, which gives each Player access to all of our programs, including a state of the art and one of a kind internet program designed to provide a venue for sales professionals to share ideas, information, resources and contacts, all on line to help each other achieve new levels of productivity. The software can be used as both an individual Player or by members who are part of an organized business network and are committed to helping each other. This is a promoted referred lead system! Our results have been great yielding two sales for every five contacted introductions.

The second segment is Skills Development and includes several core programs including, *Total Relationship Marketing.* This program was originally developed by Mel Kaufmann while he was an Executive Director with the Wilshire Chamber of Commerce in California. It is designed to teach sales people how to go to events, meet strangers and in the process, turn meetings into money. Many business membership organizations do a wonderful job getting people together, but unfortunately many fall short because their members do not know how to effectively network and get real value from their memberships. Hence, we teach *Total Relationship Marketing*, which is presented in either a workshop or seminar venue.

Other programs include *Self Management,* which is designed to teach executives how to be self managers. We talked about this earlier in relation to effort and its' importance in improving performance. Directly related to this program is *Managing Effort*, which is designed to teach the manager how to coach the "self manager." These are just a few of the skills training programs available through TPC.

The third segment is Personal Development which includes three basic coaching services. 1) On-Line, 2) On-Target, and 3) On-Going.

On-Line is a process that allows us to communicate with clients from remote locations either by phone or by WEBEX, and in either individual or group venues. A producer may have all of the skills in the world and a plethera of opportunities, but if he/she will not make the effort, very little happens. So staying on plan with the help from a ***coach*** gets the self-manager to even higher levels of performance.

On-Target is a process through which we help a client understand his/her target market and identify others who look just like their best clients. Staying focused by working with your best opportunities is a critical concept in time management. Too often sales people spin their wheels working with the wrong opportunities.

On-Going is a retainer relationship through which we provide a closer coaching environment and includes the development of a business plan and implementation or coaching process

Wright

So what do you do?

Edstrom

I try to coordinate the whole program and I actually work as the "Player Coach." I get involved in what the client is doing and help them build their target markets and so forth. We are currently launching the company on a national basis, so I have been focused on that effort.

Wright

Are there other opportunities?

Edstrom

Yes, there are lots of opportunities with the company. Our distribution system includes many management and sales opportunities. Our members or Executive Players have the opportunity to become Executive Player Reps and sell the full line of TPC products. Each Rep then has the opportunity to become a Player Coach responsible for distribution within a specific area.

Wright

Do the people that you've dealt with in the immediate past view this as a simple program that that will impact their business, or do they see it as step by step things they have to do every day?

Edstrom

All of the above. It's really quite simple, but each service stands on its own! However, in order to have a positive impact on their business, they have to make the effort, and the effort takes about 15 to 20 minuets a day sharing ideas, information, resources and contacts through the system. We ask our members to meet 5 new people each week and to give 5 introductions to others. It's that simple!

Wright

So he has to be visible in his society.

Edstrom

Yes, he has to be visible. He has to be out in his environment finding opportunities. He has to be out there meeting people, giving introductions in order to help someone else. By the way, we call these introductions Prestige Introductions, which are all made electronically on line, so it takes very little effort and very little time.

Wright

So within the context of the organization, who should become the executive player?

Edstrom

Well, really anyone who's trying to grow their business either vertically, horizontally or both, and who will make the EFFORT! Those are the people who benefit the most from the program and will take their business to the next level.

Wright

So a real estate sales person or a security seller agent could be an Executive Player.

Edstrom

Sure.

Wright

...rather than the boss?

Edstrom

They could both be Executive Players but perhaps operating in different networks! The *sales person* would be in a network of *sales people* and the *boss* would be in a network of *bosses*.

Wright

So what is an Executive Player Rep?

Edstrom

The Executive Player Rep is a professional sales associate who is first a client using the system, and then an associate sharing the system with others who become Executive Players and so on. It's the only system I know of that actually pays sales professionals for prospecting and networking!

Wright

So what do they get out of it?

Edstrom

They get commissions and obviously a lot of satisfaction by helping others. The compensation system is very attractive because it creates an income flow based upon both new sales and renewal business, while it's an opportunity to be in business for yourself, but not by yourself!

Wright

I see. So you start as an Executive Player with an opportunity to rep the company's products, as well as participating in a network of executive players. How does that work?

Edstrom

An executive player network is simply a network of executives who represent non-competing industries, share the same market and want to help each other succeed. Each network will have 4 or 5 thousand contacts in it. Each player can then search the data base for contacts that meet their profile and request an introduction from the Player who entered the contact into the data base. The executive then requests an introduction from that player by pushing a button. When the executive who has the contact receives the request, he/she selects a pre-formatted letter and pushes another button emailing the introduction along with an attached mini-website describing the requesting executive's credentials including his/her picture. The requesting executive then receives a copy of the email, including the contact info, and then makes a call to arrange an appointment.

Wright

So I guess in contrast let me see if I can get this. In contrast rather than in institutional advertising, this is a real personal kind of solution that takes folks really getting in the main stream of things and meeting other people. Well, seems like one of the bottom line benefits would be he sure could make some lifelong friends doing this.

Edstrom

Absolutely. When you meet people five things can happen and four have good end results. The new contact could be a prospect for you, could be a prospect for somebody that you know, could become an executive player, could be a ***friend*** or finally could be of no value at all. I think those are pretty good odds, especially since we know that in 5 years 50% of our new business will come from people we have yet to meet! So it's all about meeting people, helping people and helping others become successful.

Wright

Are these programs reduced to writing so that when you're gone the company can follow them?

Edstrom

Absolutely! We have a solid infrastructure and support system to follow through on every aspect of the business.

Wright

So let me ask you a last question. What do you see in the future? I mean you've been at it now for 30 years. What changes do you see in the way that we go about marketing and selling?

Edstrom

Well, I think the future will bring new opportunities and challenges but what the internet has done for us now is given us a tool to both find and share information. It's given us a way to communicate in light speed and to do so at great distances and at little cost, as if we were in the same room. Knowledge is power, but the real power is in sharing that information, so I think that the key will always be in building relationships by sharing ideas, information, resources and contacts. Having said that, I don't think the future will change the need to build relationships!

Wright

So rather than coming into your store and buying a widget, these people will come in and buy widgets forever and tell their friends about it as well.

Edstrom

Exactly right. That is word of mouth or network marketing! Years ago, I learned that if you have a problem, make it a process and it won't be a problem any more! And, that's exactly what we've done. The number one problem of sales executives today, as well as in the future, is prospecting!

We've taken concepts and systems which have stood the test of time and integrated them into a process supported by our new sophisticated software, which in a class of its' own, and solved the ***prospecting problem***.

Wright

Well, that's interesting, David, and I really appreciate you taking this time to fill me in on what all of these things mean.

Edstrom

Well, it's my pleasure, David. I know it's a lot to take in one sitting.

Wright

Today we've been talking to David Edstrom. David is the founder of the Player Coach and Company, LLC. We found out this morning that it's not magic, but rather a process. He certainly has taken some principles that work and put them together for this performance solution. Sounds interesting to me. Thank you so much, David, for sharing it for us.

Edstrom

Thanks you, David.

About The Author

David Edstrom is the founder of The Player Coach & Company, LLC, a nationally recognized speaker and member of The National Speakers Association. David has worked at all levels of sales and sales management for the past thirty years and now travels across the country speaking to Chambers of Commerce, Business Groups, and Associations sharing his powerful new business development secrets referred to as **The Performance Solution**.

David G. Edstrom
The Player Coach & Company, LLC
113 A West Gordon Street
Savannah, Georgia 31401
Email: dedstrom@theplayercoach.com
www.theplayercoach.com

Chapter 8

ROBERT BLY

THE INTERVIEW

David E. Wright (Wright)

I'd like to welcome Mr. Robert Bly. Bob is the author of more than 50 books, including *The Complete Idiot's Guide to Direct Marketing,* published by Alpha Books and *A Copywriter's Hand Book,* published by Henry Holding Company. His articles have appeared in numerous publications such as *DM News, Writer's Digest, Amtrak Express, Cosmopolitan, Inside Direct Mail*, and one of my favorites, *Bits and Pieces for Sales People.* Bob has presented marketing, sales, and writing seminars for such groups as the United States Army, Independent Laboratory Distributaries Association, American Institute for Chemical Engineers, and the American Marketing Association. He also taught business to business copywriting and technical writing at New York University. Prior to becoming an independent copywriter and consultant, Bob was advertising manager for Koch Engineering, a manufacturer of process equipment. He's also worked as a marketing communications writer for Westinghouse Defense. Bob, welcome to *Marketing Magic*!

Mr. Robert Bly (Bly)

Thanks, and thanks for having me.

Wright

When I first began to look at your career and the scope of your works, I was amazed at how prolific you've been. You wear many hats and seem to be an expert in many fields. How would you describe yourself? Can you give our readers a brief overview of your life's journey?

Bly

I don't think of myself as versatile or a renaissance person. I really only do basically one thing. I may do a couple of others, but I describe myself, when people ask, as a freelance copywriter. Now sometimes people who are not in marketing don't know what that means. So I say to them then, "You know how you get home and you have all that junk mail? I like that direct mail." That's how I answer it. So then they understand it. And my journey is odd. I'll give this short version and you can find the full story in some of my books. I started out young being interested in science. I wanted to become a scientist. I majored in chemistry in college. And then I realized I wasn't particularly good at it and I switched to chemical engineering because I thought that would be a better job. When you're a college senior in engineering, companies come on campus and interview you. And when I talked with one of the interviewers, the person said, "You seem awfully interested in writing. Our company needs technical writers and your background would be ideal." So Westinghouse hired me as a marketing writer for their Aerospace and Defense Division in Baltimore. And that's how I got started in copywriting and marketing.

Wright

I'd like to start with a question about one of your more high profile books, Bob. You authored *The Idiot's Guide to Direct Marketing* for Alpha Books. My guess is that if you ask 10 business owners how they felt about direct marketing or what they thought direct marketing was, you'd probably get 10 different answers. How do you describe direct marketing? And can you give us examples of direct marketing techniques that you've found to be effective?

Bly

The easiest way to describe direct marketing without using jargon or sounding like a college textbook is that direct marketing is a kind of marketing where the reader has to respond in some way. Either they request a free catalog, a sample or a demo, or they order the product. There is a direct response. That compares with what we call general advertising or Madison Avenue advertising which doesn't ask for an immediate response, but rather tends to build and create an image for a product or build what we call brand awareness. The example would be an auto commercial, a commercial let's say for an auto dealer that says to come in Saturday and Sunday, test drive a car, and get a free bottle of champagne. That's direct response. You're asked to take an immediate action versus when you see a Coca Cola commercial. They don't expect you to call a toll free number and order some Coca Cola or run out then, but they're thinking you'll think about Coca Cola next time you go to the supermarket or the next time you go to a diner. And that's really the difference.

Wright

Do companies use both methods at one time?

Bly

There are some companies that are pretty much strictly just direct marketers. There are some companies that are just strictly what we would call image or brand or general advertising. And then there are a lot of companies, probably the majority, that combine both.

Wright

Is there one size or type of business that should use direct marketing campaigns while others should not?

Bly

I don't think there's a size or type of business that should or shouldn't use direct marketing. I tend to think that if you have a small or even a medium sized business, you know you're not a Fortune 500 company, that direct marketing is really almost the only marketing you can afford because you don't have a million dollar budget like Coke or Pepsi. You're never going to build that big brand awareness that they can do by running a commercial eight thousand times. You would go bankrupt. You would go out of business. So if you're a small business, you need to see an immediate positive ROI, return on investment, from your advertising and marketing and really only direct marketing gives you that. General advertising, image advertising does not.

Wright

So what else can you tell us about direct marketing that might help our readers understand its effectiveness?

Bly

To do direct marketing, you have to have what we call in the business, and most of your readers will be familiar with this, you have to have what's called an offer. An offer is basically what the person gets when they respond to your marketing combined with what they have to do to get it. So an offer might be, for example, mail back the enclosed reply card and you'll get a free inventor's kit that tells you how to make money with your invention. That's an offer. And without that offer, direct marketing is going to get minimal response. With that offer, it will get very large response. So you always have to have an offer, and it has to be perceived as having high value. And it either needs to be free or risk free. In other words, you offer can be, "Send me a check and I'll send you a product," but it has to be risk free. You have to say, "You just use it for 30 days and if you don't like it, return it within a month and we'll send your money back."

Wright

You're considered one of the best copywriters in the country. Many of the consultant services you offer business revolve around the written word. Where does this fit into the larger issue of marketing for small and large businesses?

Bly

Businesses...all businesses close their sales with words. Some businesses are marketing driven and some are selling driven. With some products and some businesses, the person who will close the sale is a sales person, and so using these words, he will sit and talk to a prospect or customer one on one to convince him to buy the product. In other businesses that are marketing driven, there either isn't a salesman or the salesman plays just a partial role. So, it's your marketing, whether it's a website, catalog (if you're selling fashions or whatever), the words, whether they're on a computer screen or printed on a piece of paper, close the sale. And for the businesses that are direct marketing driven as opposed to sales driven, the way you construct those messages, the writing, the copywriting is tremendously important. The more business depends on direct marketing to make the sale, the more important words are. Some businesses don't.

Some businesses, a few of them, are built on cronyism, whoever knows this other person gets the job. And in that case copywriting and marketing aren't that important.

Wright

I've done a fair share of copywriting myself over the years, and I've also created marketing campaigns for my companies. I've always thought a great marketing campaign begins with a great idea. Do you find that many elaborate and expensive marketing campaigns seem to have been built on an ineffective concept or idea?

Bly

Yes. In fact, this is the number one marketing mistake. Whether the copy is poorly written or well written, whether the piece is nicely designed or shoddily designed, is very much secondary in importance to the idea, as you call it. There's an old quote from Samuel Johnson, who said, "Advertising is built on a big promise." Or his exact quote was, "Promise large promises, the soul of an advertisement." So it's the idea of what you promise. How does that product meet a need or a want or fill a requirement of the buyer is much more important than any advertising in the way it's executed. There's an old saying, which I think is largely true, that if you have a great idea, offer a product that people will really want, especially a targeted group of people, you'll probably be successful even if your advertising isn't great. It would be better if it was great because you would be more successful, but that can work. However, if you have a lousy idea, something that's you know or no idea, no matter how eloquently you word it or how cleverly or brightly you promote it or package it, it's not going to sell. And I do think that's true.

Wright

What kind of process do you take your clients through to help them reassess their marketing plans? And do you find many businesses are resistant to change?

Bly

Basically, if people are interested in this, and I'll answer the question for here, but if people are interested, I think that's so important a process that actually on my website (www.bly.com) I have a button on the home page. It's a choice of buttons, and one of them says "methodology." I make the process very visible to my potential clients whether they want copywriting or consulting or what have you. And that actually is part of my methodology. I think people want to know how you will work or how you will solve their problems. In many situations it is useful and beneficial to let them know that. My step in doing a marketing consultation is to gather as much information as I can about two subjects—the product, but also the audience, the potential customers. I've got articles on the website that outline that process in detail. One of the other common problems, you said you yourself, you need a big idea or it doesn't work. The other one is that people, marketing consultants, contractors are lazy. They offer quick solutions without gathering the information first. And almost always the solution or the answer comes out of the existing material. You're not creating anything. You're just presenting it in a different way. So you have a lot of front end research to do if you're helping other people. Even if you are doing your own product, you may know a lot about your product, but it's amazing how a lot of people don't really understand their audiences or their markets and what they want, and they don't bother to do that. If you don't do that, you increase the odds of failure tremendously.

Then you need to define what is the specific marketing problem that you want to solve. Do you want to generate more leads? For example, someone will come to me and they'll say, "Well, we need to increase sales. They're lousy." But that's too vague and I question them. And they say to me, "If we get a prospect in front of a sales person, we close 80% of the time." So closing is not their problem. But their problem is getting a sale person in front of a prospect. They couldn't get that meeting. So then the problem became how do we get more inquiries from prospects who are willing to sit down with a sales person and spend time with them so we can quote them. And once you define that, then there's a limited repertoire in the world of tools and techniques that you can use. And based on experience, knowledge, and testing you can find out which will work for that particular situation, implement them, measure the results, and then refine them and fine tune them. And that's what you have to do.

Wright

You're also considered an expert in the business to business marketing. Can you give us an example of this kind of marketing? And tell us what makes the most effective business to business marketing.

Bly

Let me give you one example of what works, and it happens to be a subject I'm actually writing a book on now. Business prospects generally are information seekers in a way many consumers are not. For example, if I see an ad for Burger King, I don't need to know how the hamburgers are made, how Burger King runs its operations. I just want a good tasting hamburger. But if a business buyer is buying a product or service, they want to understand because whether they do their job well or not depends on how effectively they buy products and services and manage their vendors. For example, if you sell a network firewall, your customer wants to know how the firewalls work. How do I know I'm choosing the right one, right?

Wright

Right.

Bly

One kind of marketing that works very well is—there's a term for it, I don't know if I made it up or someone else did—edu-marketing which means educational marketing. You can win the buyers confidence and generate a high degree of interest by offering to educate them about the problem your product solves or the methodology of your product. For example, if you're selling firewalls, you might offer what's known in the software industry as a white paper, which is a free report called, *How to Measure Your ROI (*return on investment) *from Installing a Firewall.* Because if I am an IT manager and I go to management and say I want to spend $40,000.00 on a firewall, the owner of my company doesn't know anything about IT, doesn't care. He says, "Well, what's that, how's that going to pay off. What am I going to get for that $40,000.00?" So this white paper will show me how I can demonstrate that if he spends $40,000.00, we'll make that back in the first month by preventing internet fraud or preserving network band width or whatever the wave a firewall generates all our life. That kind of marketing works especially well in business to business.

Wright

I was perusing your titles on amazon.com, and I came across your book, *Fool Proof Marketing, 15 Winning Methods for Selling Any Product or Service in Any Economy.* This really caught my eye because I love it when experts break down their ideas into manageable bits. Can you touch on one or two of your favorite methods from this book?

Bly

My original title for this, which the publisher changed to *Fool Proof Marketing*, was *Recession Proof Marketing*. So the book, as you could tell from the subtitle, is really about selling products or services in a recession or slow economy. The book does have 15 specific techniques for doing that. I'll give you one of them. One is to offer your products or services in smaller packages. In other words, in a good economy, let's say you're a consulting firm and your normal consultation is $10,000.00. You'll find that when the economy slows down, maybe your potential clients who normally spent that without a problem, may be hesitant to spend that much money, and so therefore they're not coming to you at all. If you decide to offer a more scaled down version and you call it *The Quick Start Consultation* and that's only $2500.00, a lot of the people who now are not buying you service because of the $10,000 price point will start working with you again and buying the $2500.00 service. You'll make money on that, but also once they start with that, they'll want to continue and will eventually spend the whole 10 grand anyway and go on to the full service. That's one strategy. Another one that's more general, but really almost more powerful, is during a recession or slow economy the service provider who's going to win more business is the one who's going to be most flexible and accommodating. You know that a lot of companies, when they have more business than they can handle, they shift into a little bit of a prima donna mode. We've all called architects who happen to be busy and said, "Well, I can't squeeze you in until the year 2012." There's a funny Tom Hanks movie called *The Money Pit* where he wants to hire a plumber and the plumber doesn't even look at the job. He says, "Give me $5,000.00." Tom Hanks gives him the money. He goes, "When will you be back?" He says, "I'll let you know," and he drives off. During a recession, you can't do that because suddenly the work is dried up and now it's a buyer's market. So you have to be much more flexible, accommodating, and willing to do what the buyer wants in order to get his business. That's another strategy.

Wright

Before we wrap up, Bob, I'd like to shift gears to public relations. I've always viewed PR as a vital component of a great marketing plan. How do you feel about the value of public relations for businesses and what advice would you give our readers related to PR as a part of their overall marketing strategy?

Bly

Well, though I do direct mail and direct marketing, and I say it is the most effective method, direct marketing is expensive. PR is great because it can get great results, fantastic large results, and it's relatively inexpensive. It's something, in fact, you can do a lot of it yourself. Now, I actually have co-authored a book on this topic called, *Public Relations for Dummies*. I wrote it with Eric Yaverbaum, who has a PR agency in New York. I'm a big fan of this. In the book we discuss all the PR strategies, but here's what I would say. The easiest way to do this is to identify the publications (and I'm leaving out radio and TV and the internet) that your prospects read, whether it's the local town paper or if you sell mechanical equipment, maybe it's *Chemical Engineering Magazine*, and write, not ghost write, write. Call the editor and offer to write an article related to your product for the magazine. In other words, if you sell mixing gear for chemical plants, write an article for *Chemical Engineering Magazine* on 10 ways to size a mixer. That will be going back to that edu-marketing we talked about. You can write that article and it might end up being two pages in that magazine, you don't pay for those two pages. You're bio with your company's phone number and website URL runs with that article, and if you bought those pages as ads, they'd probably cost you $10,000.00. And they're yours just for the worth of writing. In fact, some magazines will even give you a little honorarium so maybe you'd get 50, 100, 200 bucks out of the deal. That's the way. That's the place to start with public relations. You don't need to read my book to find out how to do that. If you go to www.bly.com and look on the articles page, you'll see an article there on public relations titled, *In Search of Ink* that tells you exactly how to get editors at pub magazines and trade journals to have you write articles for them and run your articles.

Wright

What about direct mail, Bob? Many of my colleagues have totally moved away from direct mail in favor of internet marketing. What do you think about these two methods of marketing?

Bly

There are a couple of basic answers. Let me give one. You can't predict it. That is just the way it is. Some businesses work very well with print(direct mail), and the internet doesn't work so well for them. Others work great on the internet and it's just a waste for them to do direct mail. And there are a lot of others who are very successful at combining the two methods. The thing, of course, that is in favor of internet marketing is the hugely lower cost. But here's the problem. In direct mail, I can go to a list broker, rent a mailing list of people who are strangers. They don't know me. They don't know my company. I can write a letter and send it to them and they will send me money to buy my product or they'll reply at least to ask about buying my product if I'm generating leads instead of sales. This does not work in internet marketing. If you rent a list from a list broker, an internet list or what they call an e-list and you try to sell people who do not know you a product, you're response will usually be 99 times out of 100 abysmal. You'll lose money. So you say, "How are all these people making all this money in internet marketing?" What you'll notice is that all of the people who make good money in internet marketing, big companies, but a lot of small entrepreneurs and operators have large in-house lists. They have built up a list of 5,000 or 10,000, or 20,000, or 50,000 names of people whose e-mail addresses they own and they can mail to them any time. Usually they did this by offering a free online newsletter. Like on my website, I have an online newsletter that goes out once a month. It's called a direct response letter. I have over 70,000 subscribers. So if I send to that list, I can send an offer to that listing.

I have a new report. It's $20.00 and you can download it by going here. You know the response rate will be high because these people are interested in what I do because they hear from me every month. There are three reason it works to e-mail to your house list. Number one, they're interested in you. They know you and they want more of what you do. Number two, they will accept an e-mail from you versus if they get an e-mail with a from line from somebody they don't know. They won't read it. And number three, mailing to that e-list is basically free. You know I can e-mail a message to 70,000 people at almost no cost. So internet marketing works for people who have built up a large house list, usually easing subscribers into it.

Wright

If you had just five minutes to spend with a CEO of a small or mid- sized company, what would you tell him or her about marketing that might help them the most?

Bly

Here is the other common mistake. We talked about not having the big idea, which was your comment. The other is not having an offer.

Wright

Right.

Bly

Here's the other mistake. CEOs of small and mid size companies will call me and ask for advice. If I say direct mail, for example, they'll say, "Oh, direct mail doesn't work." I'll say, "Really? How do you know that?" Then they'll say, "Well, we did a mailing and it didn't work." That's really dumb.

What typically happens is the small company will write or produce a very poorly executed post card, sales letter or sales mailing. They send it out, and of course, it doesn't work because there's no offer. There's no big idea. There's no value. And then they conclude that the entire category of direct mail doesn't work. The big companies don't do this. For example, you've seen commercials for Blue Blocker sun glasses. So Joseph Sugarman runs that company. He's one of the great mail order marketers of all time. I listened to a lecture he gave. He said that when they did magazine ads for Blue Block they would sell; they never did just one ad. They would do three or four versions of the ad minimum, and usually 10 versions. Sometimes they would do 10 versions and nine of them would bomb. But the one of the 10 versions would make so much money that it would pay for all the other nine, and then they knew that they could keep running at a profit. So if he just ran one of those other nine ads, he would conclude that space advertising doesn't work. He would have stopped. What you should do in direct marketing, if you're small, is look at the big direct marketers like Joseph Sugarman and do what they do. The one thing they do all the time that small marketers don't do, but should, they test. They test two or three headlines, three or four mailing lists, two or three offers. And by testing in small manageable quantities, you can start to find out the combination of copy, art, design, format, list, media that make money, that have a positive ROI. As soon as you find that, it's like a money machine that can make you money. If you get a direct mailing that generates 200 sales for every $100.00 of cost in the mailing, that's like having a machine where every time you pull the lever it turns a dollar into two dollars. And that's what you need to do. You need to test on a small basis.

Wright

Goodness. What a great conversation. I wish I had met you years ago and taken all these notes. My business would be a lot further along. Today we have been talking with Bob Bly, respected copywriter, marketing consultant, and author. Bob, thank you so much for taking this time with me this morning and I really, really do appreciate it.

Bly

It's been an absolute pleasure. Thank you.

About The Author

Bob has written copy for over 100 clients including, Network Solutions, ITT Fluid Technology, Medical Economics, Intuit, Business & Legal Reports, and Brooklyn Union Gas. Awards include a Gold Echo from the Direct Marketing Association, an IMMY from the Information Industry Association, two South-star Awards, an American Corporate Identity Award of Excellence, and the Standard of Excellence award from the Web Marketing Association.

Bob is the author of more than 50 books including, The Complete Idiot's Guide To Direct Marketing (Alpha Books) and The Copywriter's Handbook (Henry Holt & Co.). His articles have appeared in numerous publications such as DM News, Writer's Digest, Amtrak Express, Cosmopolitan, Inside Direct Mail, and Bits & Pieces for Salespeople.

Bob has presented marketing, sales, and writing seminars for such groups as the U.S. Army, Independent Laboratory Distributors Association, American Institute of Chemical Engineers, and the American Marketing Association. He also taught business-to-business copywriting and technical writing at New York University.

Bob has appeared as a guest on dozens of TV and radio shows including, MoneyTalk 1350, The Advertising Show, Bernard Meltzer, Bill Bresnan, CNBC, Winning in Business, The Small Business Advocate and CBS Hard Copy. He has been featured in major media ranging from the LA Times and *Nation's Business* to the *New York Post* and the *National Enquirer*.

Robert Bly

Copywriter

22 East Quackenbush Avenue, 3rd Floor

Dumont, New Jersey 07628

Phone: 201.385.1220

Fax: 201.385.1138

Chapter 9

CHARLES CLARKE III

THE INTERVIEW

David E. Wright (Wright)

Today we are talking with Charles Clarke III, creator of "Bulls, Owls, Lambs and Tigers®: Personality Selling and Personality Marketing," which is more commonly referred to by its acronym "BOLT™." Charles developed the concept in 1968 while completing his Master's Degree at the University of Hawaii in Sociology and Psychology. He later perfected BOLT while working toward his PhD at the University of Maryland and the University of Arizona, and while serving as an Instructor at both universities. From 1972 through 1979, Charles was Professor and Department Chairman of Sociology at Mount Mercy College in Cedar Rapids, Iowa. In the late '70s and early '80s Charles began to heavily invest in residential rental property, eventually owning over 103 rentals. He had founded Clarke Property Investments, Inc. and Clarke Property Management, Inc. He later accepted a position serving as first Vice President of Sales Training over Century 21's entire region of Texas and Louisiana. In this position he developed and implemented many of Century 21's sales training programs. This led to a franchise experience with Today's American Builder, during which Charles was Executive Vice President of International Training for Today's American Builder, based in Houston, Texas. Later he was Regional Director and President of its Florida division, based in Tampa. In the middle 1980's, Charles took all of his former experiences and founded Charles Clarke Consulting, Inc., which is now home based in Gainesville, Georgia, in the Atlanta area. He is president of this full service consulting and sales training firm that works with diverse companies throughout the world. He consults with some of the world's largest companies and fills roughly 200 engagements per year as a world-class speaker, sales trainer and convention speaker. Charles works with virtually every industry, but has specialized in the Home Building and Real Estate industries, and is himself a Builder and Developer in Columbus, Ohio. The bottom line on all of Charles Clarke III's material, consulting, and speaking is that, besides being a lot of fun, "Bulls, Owls, Lambs and Tigers®" is totally results oriented. Charles, welcome to *Marketing Magic*!

Charles Clarke III (Clarke)

Thank you, David. It's my pleasure to be in the same publication with our friend Brian Tracy.

Wright

So what is the premise of Bulls, Owls, Lambs and Tigers®?

Clarke

The premise, David, is that we are indeed different than other people. If you look at 100 random people in a room, there are probably going to be about 25 Bulls, 25 Owls, 25 Lambs, and 25 Tigers. That of course is an exaggeration, but the premise is, "Three of every four people have a very different personality than you do." **If you always market and sell the way you would like to be marketed and sold to, you could be losing half to three-quarters of your potential market and sales.** Bulls, Owls, Lambs and Tigers® is based on two variables: how assertive a person is and how much emotion (all emotions except for anger) they display to other people. These two variables predict a lot about how people buy, when they buy, what they buy, and what attracts them in terms of Marketing.

Wright

So this would be "compatible" with maybe Myers Briggs, or DISC?

Clarke

Yes, it is compatible. Actually the oldest form and record of personality analysis that uses a four-cell personality paradigm goes back to approximately 400 B.C., to the time of Hippocrates. Hippocrates used four categories—the Choleric, Sanguine, Melancholic, and Phlegmatic temperaments—to analyze people's personality. An interesting footnote is that it is said that the disciples of Jesus Christ actually drew upon Hippocrates' four temperaments and his idea that you don't sell everybody the same way in their efforts to "sell" the Word of the Lord, which was more of an intangible sale than a tangible sale of a particular product.

Wright

That is interesting.

Clarke

I've been speaking about Bulls, Owls, Lambs and Tigers® for about 30 years, constantly researching and updating the material. Sometimes people ask me if, after all of those years, this topic isn't somewhat old. I would say that they don't know just how old it truly is. People have been talking about personality selling for 2,400 years. Granted, Hippocrates didn't use this exact phrase, but he essentially said, "You don't sell to everybody the same way."

Wright

Well, Myers Briggs, and DISC sound a little dry when you compare them to "Bulls, Owls, Lambs and Tigers®." "Bulls, Owls, Lambs and Tigers®" sounds a lot more fun and user friendly. You must talk to a lot of people that became interested because of that.

Clarke

"Bulls, Owls, Lambs and Tigers®" really does bring the concept of personalities to life, as you mentioned. It's hard to use a letter of the alphabet or a geometric sign to capture a person's personality, but with BOLT™ there is an immediate impression and image of the four animals and the corresponding personality types. BOLT™ is extremely "user-friendly."

Wright

So tell me, what does "personality marketing" mean, and how is it different from traditional or "old school" marketing techniques?

Clarke

Personality marketing's premise is that not everybody is attracted to the same type of marketing. Again, you could divide the population into four fairly equal categories. If you had four people in a room, a good rule of thumb is to assume that three of those people truly think very differently than you—that their brains are wired up differently, if you will. Three people in the room will make decisions differently than you. They will see different things in a marketing piece than other people would see, and they will respond differently. **If we always market the way that we would like to be marketed to, we could be losing at least one half to three quarters of the people that we're trying to attract.**

Wright

Well, I can see the advantage of knowing what someone's personality type would be, so could you describe the personality types and explain a little more about why it is important to be aware of these personalities in marketing?

Clarke

Certainly. A good sports analogy is that marketing is the baseball pitcher and sales is the catcher. Both are interdependent on one another. In selling you get to see the prospect face to face, and all the variables that go along with that. For instance, you get to look at their body language and hear the inflection of their voice. In marketing, though, we don't have these variables to rely on, so we often just market (as I've mentioned already) the way we would like to be marketed to. The basic, bottom-line concept that we need to be aware of is just that people think differently than we do. That should effect all of our marketing decisions.

Wright

Let me see if I can get my arms around this concept. Let's say that I'm a salesperson who wants to sit down and design a presentation for my product or service. What you're saying is that in all probability the presentation I design will be created to essentially sell me.

Clarke

That's correct.

Wright

And you're also saying that if I walk into a room of 100 people, and interact with all 100, that the probability is that I would be "turning off" approximately 75% of them with my own particular sales and marketing approach...if I didn't adjust to them?

Clarke

That's right. Let me give you an example from the selling arena that backs this up. I recently spoke in front of a group of approximately 1,500 Builders, Developers, and Realtors® in Orlando, and I asked the group, **"Do you believe it is rare for someone to buy a home the first day?"** About 50% of the hands went up. I asked the group that raised their hands if they themselves would buy a home the first day, and almost every person among them said that they would not. As for the 50% of the audience that did not raise their hands when I asked if they thought it was rare that people would buy the first day, they said they would buy the first day and have bought the first day, and they do not think it is rare for people to buy the first day (because they do).

Why don't I go ahead and identify each of the BOLT™ animal personalities by referring you to the two easy to read BOLT™ charts I brought with me. I developed these charts, which illustrate the defining characteristics of each animal personality. The first chart (Exhibit A) is my BOLT™ grid, showing how each animal personality is based on two variables—how assertive a person is and how much emotion they display. Exhibit B is a summary of some important preferences and characteristics of each animal.

Exhibit A

Bulls, Owls, Lambs and Tigers®

LOW ASSERTIVENESS "Ask Oriented" → HIGH ASSERTIVENESS "Tell Oriented"

ASSERTIVENESS

EMOTION: LOW EMOTION (does not show emotions) ↓ HIGH EMOTION (shows emotions)

	Least Assertive 1	Mildly Assertive 2	Very Assertive 3	Extremely Assertive 4
Seldom Emotional A	OWL OWL	OWL With BULL	BULL With OWL	BULL BULL
Mildly Emotional B	OWL With LAMB	OWL With TIGER	BULL With LAMB	BULL With TIGER
Very Emotional C	LAMB With OWL	LAMB With BULL	TIGER With OWL	TIGER With BULL
Extremely Emotional D	LAMB LAMB	LAMB With TIGER	TIGER With LAMB	TIGER TIGER

Exhibit B

	Definitions	Questions They Ask	When They Buy
The Bull	1) Bottom line, get to the point, business first 2) Somewhat abrasive personality 3) **Control** oriented 4) "Hurry up" 5) **Highly assertive, low emotion (except the emotion of anger)** 6) Bull "turn-offs": a) Answering a question with a question (Bulls *hate* that) b) Imagination, testimonial, and trial closes c) Salespeople who are too emotional, and too "nice"	1) How much? 2) What's your **best** price? *3) What does it come with? (Interested in knowing what "extras" they can get.)* 4) How soon can I have it? 	1) When they want to 2) When *you* get out of their way 3) When they are assured they have the best price, and that you won't lower the price **4) Bulls say their preference is to buy the first day, even for extremely expensive items (homes, automobiles, and private airplanes)** **5) Sell the "steak" not the "sizzle" with Bulls** 6) **Fast decisions makers, high risk takers**
The Owl	1) Extremely analytical, detail oriented, business first 2) Person who corrects almost everything you do 3) Loves **order** and systems 4) **Low assertiveness, low emotion** 5) Owl "turn-offs": a) Too much excitement, and too much emotion b) Salespeople who do not stay on track c) Urgency closes	1) Tell me about the manufacturing process 2) What materials are used? 3) What kind of warranty does it include? 4) Questions about value 5) Questions about everything 	1) When all of their questions have been answered 2) Answering all of an Owl's questions could take several visits or appointments 3) Owls buy with logic and justify with logic, not emotion 4) **Slow decision makers, low risk takers**
The Lamb	1) Wants to **please** everyone, social before business 2) Takes a long time to make up their mind 3) Dislikes confrontation and arguments 4) **Low assertiveness, highly emotional** 5) Lamb "Turn Offs" a) Pushy sales people b) Urgency and take-away loses	1) Which do **YOU** like best? 2) What is your best seller? 3) Lambs ask friendly, non-threatening questions 4) "Mr. Rodgers" or "Neighborly" questions 	1) When the purchase has been validated by someone else 2) Validation could take several visits or appointments 3) **Slowest decision makers, low risk takers** 4) **Highest level of buyer's remorse**
The Tiger	1) Dominated by wanting **fun and excitement**, social before business 2) Extremely talkative 3) Distracted by "shiny objects" 4) **Highly assertive, highly emotional** 5) Tiger "Turn Offs" a) Too much detail b) Ben Franklin closes c) Not enough emotion	1) Tigers ask completely unrelated questions, due in part to their distraction by shiny objects and/or "shiny thoughts." 2) Tiger questions often have "nothing to do with anything" 	1) When they are excited 2) Tigers buy on their first visit (or not at all) even for expensive items. If they don't, they rarely return for a second visit. 3) Sell the "sizzle" and not the "steak" with a Tiger 4) **Fastest decision makers, highest risk takers** 5) **Impulsive, compulsive buyers**

Wright

I did look over your charts. Very interesting. So what aspects of each of these four animal personalities that you just identified are most easily misread, misinterpreted, or misidentified, especially in terms of marketing?

Clarke

The most misread personality is the one that is opposite of yourself, opposite of your own personality. That disconnect has a staggering impact on marketing efforts. Let's say someone is a Tiger (a highly assertive and emotional personality). If this Tiger were to put together a display ad, their ad might often miss Owls who want lots of detail in ads. Tigers don't like or respond to a lot of detail in marketing pieces, so they usually don't create detailed marketing pieces themselves. It could work in the other way, too. You've seen in the last few years, David, some of the marketing pieces and strategies where companies send a 14-page letter describing their product or service in deep detail. It attracts Owls only. When something like that reaches Bulls, they just put it in the "round file"—the trashcan. Tigers wouldn't pay it any attention either. So basically the answer to your question of, "Who do we miss," is that we usually miss the people that are opposite ourselves in terms of BOLT™ personalities. That is the personality we are most likely to misunderstand, and the hardest one to reach with our marketing.

Wright

That makes sense. Back to the previous example of buying something the first day, from what you're saying and what I see in the chart, Owls and Lambs would be more likely to say "Let me sleep on it" and <u>not</u> buy the same day. Yet Bulls and Tigers <u>would</u> have a higher probability of buying the first day they saw the product no matter what the price point, even automobiles and expensive homes.

Clarke

Yes.

Wright

Let's now relate this back to marketing and marketing examples. What drives the buying decisions of the animal personalities? What kind of marketing motivates each personality type?

Clarke

As I mentioned, Bulls want to reach their decision right away, so they need to immediately have enough information to be able to quickly decide. What Bulls immediately look for in a marketing piece is the price. They want to know what they have to do in order to buy. If Bulls have to shuffle through different papers, or if they have to look elsewhere to find out how to do this, then they just go to an easier route—which usually means they just go elsewhere. Where Bulls are driven by control, Owls are driven by order, systems, and analytical analysis. Owls want all the details.

Lambs are driven by pleasing other people, by warmth and security, and Tigers are driven by fun and excitement. All four of those elements have to be in a marketing piece, television ad, a radio ad, or a direct mail piece. No matter what kind of marketing it is, those elements must be in there, unless there is a conscious decision to go after just one or two of the personality segments. Usually it's the person putting together the marketing and designing the marketing that eliminates two of those. Every single person has one dominant animal personality and one secondary animal type. Of course, everybody has bits of all four-personality types that come out at different times, but there is still one that is most dominant and one that is second. So if someone's primary and secondary personality types are Bull and Owl, the marketing piece they design will often reflect their personality and include only Bull and Owl elements, and not include Lamb and Tiger elements.

Wright

You know down through the years, I have used television, radio, the telephone, the fax machine, direct mail, and all kinds of methods of marketing. So of those kinds of methods, what type of marketing does each personality respond to?

Clarke

Actually each media can attract all four personalities. It is the message and the way the message is portrayed in each media that makes the difference. Take the media of newspaper and compare the personality of the "The Wall Street Journal" to "USA Today." "The Wall Street Journal" is more of a publication for Bulls and Owls. "USA Today" is more of a publication for Tigers and Lambs (the emotional animals). "USA Today" has more fun sections and is done in color with pictures that fall under the category of "shiny objects"—

and Tigers love shiny objects. If a company were advertising for selling second homes and vacation properties they might have more success if they got out of the "Wall Street Journal" and put together a "fun" ad in "USA Today."

Wright

Very interesting.

Clarke

Owls really respond most to the written word. Owls read everything—the entire newspaper, and all of the copy in your ad. Bulls just like to look at the headliner. That's why the marketing pieces that put so much emphasis on the headliner (those that have an immediate call to action) are the marketing pieces that Bulls usually read. Much of what is effective in marketing goes back to the psychological concepts of how people sort data. I'm referring to the idea that people best receive information in different ways, depending on their BOLT™ personality. Some people are more visual. Some people are more kinesthetic. Some people are more auditory. **Bulls are more "Auditory."** They're the people that say things like, "Hey, just tell me about it. It sounds good to me." **Owls are more "Visual."** They'll say "I need to read it. I need to see it in writing." **The Lamb is more "Kinesthetic"** and makes decisions based on feelings. Lambs would say, "Well, this just feels right." **Tigers are "Imagination"** oriented. They might say, "I see," when there is nothing tangible to see. Tigers are visual in being able to "imagine" things. They need pictures and images and colors. Again, to effectively reach the maximum amount of people you've got to have all four of those ingredients in any given marketing campaign, unless, again, you are going after only a particular personality marketing segment. I won't just say marketing piece because it has to be an entire campaign that takes into consideration all these ways that people sort data. I actually have another chart to illustrate the distinct ways each personality sorts data.

Exhibit C

The Ways Each Animal Sorts Data			
Bulls	*Owls*	*Lambs*	*Tigers*
• More Auditory • They say things like 1. Just tell me about it 2. Sounds good to me 3. I hear what you are saying	• More Visual • They say things like 1. I see what you are saying... 2. Would you put that in writing?	• More Kinesthetic • They say things like 1. It just feels right. 2. I have a goof feeling about it.	• More Imaginative • They say things like 1. I can imagine myself owning that. 2. I can picture myself... 3. I can see myself doing that...

Wright

I see that you have some display ad examples of a Bull ad and a Lamb ad that a company ran. Tell me briefly about the company and the story behind the ads. What were the results?

Clarke

These are two ads that were run in the Wall Street Journal by a company called Epmark, based in Columbus Ohio. They nationally franchise their market-proven Home Building Community Development System conceived and refined for over nearly two decades by The Epcon Group, Inc. Epcon and Epmark are America's leading developer and builder of ranch style condominium communities, designed for "active adults." I am their National Accounts Training and Marketing Consultant. They are very proficient in "Bulls, Owls, Lambs and Tigers®" in their marketing and sales. BOLT™ is deeply ingrained into all aspects of their company. I spoke with Dan Noreen, Manager of Business Development at Epmark, about the impact of the marketing decisions and the two ads, and he had an interesting story to tell:

"At Epmark, we can usually tell within a day or two when an ad runs in a national publication because of the increased volume of inquiries and phone calls requesting more information.

"The 'Let's Share' ad ran a number of times in the Wall Street Journal. There was no perceptible increase in leads, calls, or inquiries as a result of this ad. In retrospect, this was a soft-sell, Lamb-type ad running in a Bull-Owl publication. The ad made no connection with the Bull readership by offering to 'share' with them.

"We switched ads and copy to a dignified businessman professing his previous success and stating his desire for a new business opportunity, "something challenging, something solid." Very much a bull approach. When we ran this ad in the Wall Street Journal it immediately generated a strong response and the leads and inquiries came pouring in. We used an ad designed for Bulls and connected."

As you can see in the example, in the Lamb ad the word "share" was very prominent. Epmark had unconsciously created a warm Lamb ad that wasn't going after Owls, or Tigers, or Bulls. The response was extremely low, so they consciously changed it to a Bull ad that had a picture of a gray haired man with Bull language. Through the new image and the new text, the tone of the ad had changed to one of, "We can help you make more money," a message that always reaches Bulls. Their phones were soon ringing off the hook and emails were soon pouring in, all from just changing the personality of the ad and creating a Bull marketing piece.

Exhibit D

I have hundreds of examples like this where just tweaking a little bit makes all the difference in the world. Like I mentioned before, display ads can work for every personality type as long as the message and the tone and the components of the ads match the target animal personality. I have condensed the elements that appeal to each animal into a chart that outlines what a successful Bull, Owl, Lamb or Tiger display ad would include.

Exhibit E

Display Ads			
Bulls	*Owls*	*Lambs*	*Tigers*
Include the price and picture of the product. Bulls need to see if it is **striking, impressive, and statement-making**.	Using the example of a home selling ad, Owls would want to see a detailed picture of the floor plan with dimensions of the home, as well as specifications. They want to know that the product is **practical, efficient, and functional** with all the details.	Lambs and Tigers (the two more emotional animals) want lifestyle ads, with people in the ads. Lambs say they are attracted by family shots and that they like ads that are **warm, cozy, and friendly.**	Tigers also like lifestyle ads, but lifestyle ads that are **fun, exciting and different.** Ads that are unusual and eye-catching, without detailed information.

Wright

Very interesting. This is truly a new twist on marketing that I had not thought of. Do you have a couple more examples?

Clarke

Yes! Saturn automobiles are an example of marketing towards Owls and Lambs in their "non-negotiating" method of buying. Our research shows that Owls and Lambs like the non-negotiating methodology. But that same method of non-negotiating is a complete turn-off to Bulls and Tigers who like to negotiate. Besides that, the Saturn is an Owl / Lamb automobile and is bought more by Owls and Lambs. CarMax is another example of non-negotiating which again turns-off Bulls and Tigers.

Wright

That is truly fascinating. More examples!

Clarke

A good example of how to target different animal personalities comes from the hotel industry and Marriott. The J.W. Marriott is very Bull (striking, impressive, statement making) with an emphasis on prestige. Marriotts are very Tigers (fun, exciting, and different) and have all the fun amenities. Fairfield by Marriott has all the kitchen and laundry amenities for you to do those practical things yourself at a lower price, which attracts the Owls to the high value. Finally, it's Courtyard by Marriott that is warm and cozy and friendly and has a nice "feel" about it (but with very few amenities), making it very Lamb.

Wright

Again, that is fascinating. In marketing we hear so much about **packaging and colors**. Does this work with your BOLT™ typology?

Clarke

Yes, it certainly does. Colors can make a huge difference. Sometimes the people that call themselves the color masters will say the color of the year is such and such, and they spend large dollar amounts on this. I'm not talking about just paint companies. I'm talking about packaging in general. Do you remember how, maybe 15 years ago, mauve was the color of choice? Well, even though it was the color of the year, a Bull was not going to buy anything packaged in mauve no matter what. They didn't care if it was the color of the year, they still were not be attracted to that color. The animals' favorite colors are kind of interesting. What would you say that the Bull's favorite color is?

Wright

Probably red?

Clarke

People often say red, sometimes because of the connection with bull fighting. But the **favorite colors of the Bull personality type are black, dark brown, dark blue, and dark green**—power colors. Sometimes people will avoid black packaging. I know one particular small company owned by Bulls that has letterhead on black stationary with white text. What has happened with that extreme letterhead is that, though Bulls like black, 75% of the population wouldn't like that at all and are turned off by it.

Owls are into neutral colors like beige and light gray. They say that they really don't like white because it gets too many smudge marks. They would rather have off-white, which doesn't show as many smudge marks and dirt.

Lambs are attracted by pastel colors: light blue, light yellow and soft colors, and Tigers are attracted by primary colors and jewel tones such as red, sapphire, ruby and emerald colors. If a Tiger is in charge of marketing, they often make statements like, "Everyone loves lots of bright colors!" Not true!

Exhibit F

Favorite Colors			
Bulls	*Owls*	*Lambs*	*Tigers*
• Black, dark brown, dark blue • High-assertive, low-emotion colors	• Off-white (not white), beige, light gray and neutral colors • Low-assertive, low-emotion colors	• Pastels, light blue, light yellow, pink (although pink really has masculine and feminine overtones) • Low-assertive, high-emotion colors	• Jewel tones, primary colors, reds, sapphires, ruby, emerald. • Lots of very assertive, very emotional color

Clarke

David, I don't believe I mentioned that Bulls, Owls, Lambs and Tigers® is not gender based. Approximately half of the Bulls are women and about half of the Lambs are men. Likewise with the Lambs and Tigers. What marketers need to keep in mind is that, before creating packaging with various colors, the question should be what one or two personalities are we really going after with this particular packaging. Even different types of checks in a checkbook have different personalities. Bulls and Owls usually select the "standard" types of checks, yellow or gray without pictures on them. Tigers and Lambs choose more expressive and emotional types of checks with pictures of designs on them.

Wright

I'm getting a very clear idea of how this applies to marketing and how it can greatly effect the bottom-line! So what would you say is the single most common and deadly mistake that people in marketing commit as it relates to personality marketing?

Clarke

It's not bringing into focus the other three personalities, the three personalities that we aren't. I'd say the single most deadly mistake would be not considering other people's personality. If I'm a Bull, I tend to think that everybody wants to be marketed to like I do. We continue to just go to the same well, all the time. When we get there, we don't dig deeper into the well each time and so we don't reach as many people as possible. The message itself is obviously very important. The words in a radio, television, or newspaper ad—are very important. Because each animal personality is so different, not every word, adjective, or description will work with everyone. There are certain words and tones that strike a chord with each animal. As I have alluded to, some effective Bull words are "striking," "impressive," and "make a statement." Owl words are "practical," "efficient," and "functional." Lamb words are "warm," "cozy," and "friendly." Tiger words are "fun," "exciting," and "different." If you use Bull words when you try to market to a Lamb, you can imagine that it won't work out well. The same goes for Tiger and Owl words. Words like "wonderful," "marvelous," and "nice" (clear Lamb words) just don't do anything for an Owl because an Owl can't operationally measure those words. Sometimes in print marketing ad you'll see the word "unbelievable." When they read that, Owls think, "Hey, even *they* are telling me not to believe them." Tigers, on the other hand, are attracted by the word "unbelievable."

Wright

I hear the word "awesome" a lot, also.

Clarke

Right. "Awesome" bothers Owls. Sometimes you hear people in their 50's and 60's using words like "cool" or "awesome" because they've heard their children use them. But some of the Owls personalities are very resentful of that. Remember "Seinfeld" and the expression, "Yada, yada, yada"? That was very Tiger. Owls say they resent that as much as "Blah, blah, blah."

Wright

Well, this has been an interesting and fascinating conversation. I know I've learned a lot here today that is going to effect the marketing decisions I make in the future.

Clarke

You know, David, it is an interesting concept, but it also translates to bottom-line dollars and cents for any company that utilizes these concepts. Companies that don't consider all of this, that don't think about and incorporate what each personality will respond to in terms of marketing—whether it's in their brochures, business cards, or television, print, or radio advertising—are really missing the boat. **"Because if I always market the way that I would like to be marketed to, I could be losing at least half to three quarters of the potential people I'm marketing to."**

Wright

I realize we have just "scratched the surface" of BOLT™. How can the readers learn more?

Clarke

To learn more go to our web site at www.personalityselling.com and look for the entire text of "Bulls, Owls, Lambs and Tigers®: Personality Selling and Personality Marketing."

Wright

Today we have been talking with Charles Clarke III. He is the creator of "Bulls, Owls, Lambs and Tigers®: Personality Selling and Personality Marketing." And as we have found out today, and as anyone who has read his work or heard him speak has found out, he really knows what he's talking about, and he is truly on the cutting-edge of Marketing Magic. Charles, thank you so much for taking time with us this morning on *Marketing Magic*.

Clarke

Thank you, David.

About The Author

Charles J. Clarke III, creator of "Bulls, Owls, Lambs and Tigers®: Personality Selling and Personality Marketing," (BOLT) developed the concept in 1968 while completing his Masters Degree at the University of Hawaii in Sociology and Psychology. He later perfected BOLT while working toward his PhD at the University of Arizona and also while serving as an instructor at the University of Arizona and later at the University of Maryland. From 1972 through 1979 Charles was professor and Department Chairman of Sociology at Mount Mercy College in Cedar Rapids, Iowa.

In the late 1970's and early 1980's Charles began to heavily invest in rental properties, eventually owning over 103, mainly in residential housing. He then founded Clarke Property Investments, Inc. and Clarke Property Management. He later accepted a position serving as Vice President of Sales Training over Century 21's entire Region of Texas and Louisiana. In this position he developed and implemented many of the company's sales training programs. This led to a franchise experience with Today's American Builders (a franchise designed exclusively for the new Home Building Industry). Charles was Executive Vice President of International Training for Today's American Builders, and later Regional Director of its Florida division.

Charles took all of his former experiences and founded Charles Clarke Consulting, Inc. in the mid 1980's. He is President of this full service consulting and sales training firm for diverse companies throughout the world. He is a premiere sales trainer and convention speaker. He fills roughly 200 speaking engagements a year, and is a frequent featured speaker at national and regional conventions and sales and marketing conferences.

Charles Clarke III

Charles Clarke Consulting, Inc.

P.O. Box 2817

Gainesville, GA 30503

Phone: 770-287-7808

Fax: 770-287-8994

Email: bolt@personalityselling.com

www.personalityselling.com

Chapter 10

RICK COOPER

THE INTERVIEW

David E. Wright (Wright)

Today we are talking to Rick Cooper. Rick is The PDA Pro. He is your PDA Coach for productivity anytime, anywhere. He specializes in helping business professionals achieve higher levels of productivity and effectiveness by using a personal digital assistant (PDA). He also consults with companies to help leaders evaluate mobile technologies to increase workforce mobility. With over 15 years of marketing, sales, and technology experience, Rick is skilled at helping companies succeed. Rick is also principal consultant for StratAchieve, a consulting firm that specializes in helping companies use technology to support their sales and marketing efforts. Rick, welcome to *Marketing Magic*!

Rick Cooper (Cooper)

Thank you, David. It's my pleasure.

Wright

Since you're The PDA Pro, what tips do you have for using a PDA to increase productivity?

Cooper

Well, first of all there are many different types of PDAs including Palm, Pocket PC and Blackberry. I recommend in particular the Treo from palmOne which can be used not only as an organizer but also for making phone calls, accessing e-mail and browsing the web. Here are a few hints from my book, *101 Tips from The PDA Pro*. First of all, I recommend turning off the system sound. Otherwise, your PDA will make various sounds such as clicks and beeps as you're entering information. This can be annoying during meetings. It really serves no purpose. Secondly, to speed up your productivity, stash the stylus. Instead, use your thumbs to operate the keyboard that many of the PDAs now include. To select options on the screen, just reach up and use your thumbnail. It's much faster than pulling out the stylus. When you're setting up a calendar event, enter a brief description like call, appointment, or meeting at the beginning of the entry. For example, enter "Appt-Sue Jones." When reviewing your schedule, you can quickly identify what's happening that day, whether you're going to have conference calls, meetings, or appointments. Another great suggestion is entering birthdays and anniversaries on your calendar as recurring events. It makes great sense from a sales perspective to remind you to call people or send them a birthday card in advance. A PDA is a great tool to help you stay on top of events and keep in touch with your clients and prospects.

Wright

So what you're saying is if I enter my birthday, March the 11th, it will show up every year?

Cooper

Absolutely. You enter it once as a recurring event and then it's scheduled for decades.

Wright

Oh, great!

Cooper

And you can enter in as many birthdays or anniversaries as you want. It's simple and it saves a lot of time.

Wright

I always assumed that people used that stylus because it has a tiny end and the numbers or letters were tiny on the PDA. So you're saying your fingernail will actually work?

Cooper

Absolutely. You can write with your index finger or your thumbnail. It takes some practice, but the PDA's handwriting recognition software will recognize either the stylus or your fingernail. If you prefer a stylus, you can also get a multifunction pen that includes a stylus. It's easier to hold and write.

Wright

So how can business professionals use a PDA to help generate sales?

Cooper

A PDA is a personal digital assistant, but it really stands for Productivity, Discipline, and Action. You'll be more productive if you have the discipline to take action. It gives you information at your fingertips. You enter information that you can retrieve later. To generate sales, make good use of the contact application. You can use the application that comes with the PDA or a contact management application like ACT or Goldmine. That's an effective combination for most sales professionals. Essentially your PDA should give you instant access to anyone you know. Of course, that requires that you update your PDA anytime you meet someone. Also, enter as much information as you can about the people that you meet, including their birth date, interests, and children's names. For example, if you find out that someone has an interest in sailing or golf, enter that in your PDA. That information can be very useful later. The critical thing is to always carry your PDA wherever you go. Don't leave home without it because it doesn't do you any good if it's sitting on your desk while you're visiting a client.

Wright

So could I put in things like an Internet message? For example, my e-mail address is dwtalks@aol.com. Can I enter that? Do I enter that into the PDA along with other contact information, or is it separate?

Cooper

If you wanted to add my e-mail address, rick@thepdapro.com, you could enter it along with my other contact information. You create a new contact record for each person you meet. Enter the e-mail address along with phone and address information. A PDA can synchronize with the software that comes from the manufacturer or with an application like Outlook. An e-mail address entered in the PDA will then be accessible through Outlook so you can send e-mail messages. Some PDAs, like the Treo, allow you to send and receive e-mail messages directly. You can send text messages to others by using Short Message Service (SMS). Or, you can use Internet messaging software such as AOL Instant Messenger (AIM) to send instant messages from your computer or PDA. When you leave your computer, you can log in to AIM on your PDA and can establish a chat session with someone and send messages back and forth.

Wright

So at the office I use a software program called ACT, I think you mentioned this a few minutes ago.

Cooper

Right. ACT is a contact management application popular with sales professionals.

Wright

So I could download ACT on a PDA?

Cooper

Yes. You have two options with ACT. One, you can synchronize ACT with the existing contact application on your PDA which will transfer basic contact information from ACT. You can also install a special version of ACT on your PDA that will synchronize with ACT on your computer. And that can be very effective because if you spend more than half of your time away from the office, it can really boost your productivity. It tells you what you need to do, who to call, and what follow-up is necessary.

Wright

Yeah, I find myself in my car a lot wanting a telephone number, but not wanting to kill myself looking for it, and then making the decision to either call my office so they can find the phone number or not call it.

Cooper

Exactly. Just imagine having that information at your fingertips. Let your PDA be your partner.

Wright

So a PDA would solve that problem?

Cooper

Absolutely. You have a complete list of contacts on the go. I have over 1700 contacts in my PDA. Anytime I meet a new person or get a business card from a business mixer or trade show, I enter it into my PDA. You can also use a device called CardScan, which allows you to scan in a business card and then transfer the information to your PDA. So, if you come back from a trade show with 50 business cards, rather than taking three or four hours for data entry, it becomes a one-hour process. It does require some editing to verify the data entered. It's very quick and extremely effective.

Wright

I wrote this name down. You said Treo.

Cooper

Yes. That's the best PDA Smartphone available today, in my opinion.

Wright

And, where can you find that? Is it available through a phone company or somewhere like Best Buy?

Cooper

You can purchase the Treo directly from the manufacturer, Palm One, which makes the Palm operating system. You can also find it at most computer or electronics stores such as CompUSA and Best Buy. You can also buy it directly through cellular carriers including AT&T, Cingular, Sprint, T-Mobile and Verizon. Because the Treo is also a phone, be careful about managing the transition from your existing cell phone. Most cellular plans come with at least a one-year contract, subject to penalty for early termination. Do your research first. I would suggest you determine whether you're satisfied with your current cellular carrier. If so, contact them first because they may be able transfer your account from your existing cell phone to the Treo with no penalty.

Wright

Since I use US Cellular, I should call them first. If they don't have it, then I should go to another company.

Cooper

Exactly. Your PDA is your communicator.

Wright

So how do you communicate your message about mobile technologies?

Cooper

I have outlined my message in my book, *101 Tips from The PDA Pro*. I offer information through my monthly e-mail newsletter, Tips from The PDA Pro. I also share tips and strategies through audio presentations available on tape and CD. I speak to professional and trade associations about how they can leverage their time by using a PDA to increase their productivity. This message resonates in particular with small business owners and sales professionals. Both groups usually spend more than half their time away from their office. They need to stay in touch through phone, e-mail, and messaging.

Many business professionals think of the PDA primarily as an organizer because those are the features that were initially marketed to consumers. However, the PDA is really a fully functioning portable computer. PDAs are portable. There are many applications available for PDAs that extend their capabilities. Beyond e-mail and web browsing, global positioning satellite (GPS) applications are available that can integrate with map applications. Some companies are giving employees access to their computer network through their PDAs, creating a competitive advantage. This offers a wide range of possibilities from accessing customer information to submitting product orders remotely. Companies can increase their cash flow and lower costs by using PDAs to process work orders. It's time to pitch the paper and power on a PDA. The benefits are tremendous.

Wright

So everything changes and seemingly gets better. How will mobile technologies change in the future?

Cooper

Well, it's funny. With mobile technologies, everything will continue to get smaller, faster, and easier to use. But there's an ongoing battle between keeping the size of PDAs small enough to easily hold in your hand but large enough to have a screen that you can read. The devices are very small now, but faster video will increase the demand for bigger and better screens. So the pendulum will continue to swing back and forth. But what'll happen is that a lot of different functions will continue to be integrated into PDAs and other mobile devices. PDAs can also double as an MP3 player so you can play music. Some allow you to play video files, making it possible to demo your product or service on your PDA. You can get an expansion card to store audio and video files. Internet access will get better for PDAs. Right now there aren't that many websites that cater specifically to PDAs, so most websites are slow to download, but that's beginning to change. Some PDAs have Wi-Fi capability which offers much faster Internet access. More businesses need to customize their websites to offer content developed for PDAs, reducing graphics and increasing text content.

Wright

So tell me a little bit about your marketing strategy. How did you develop it?

Cooper

Well, it starts with developing a marketing plan. You've got to identify your products and services, determine your target market, and set your marketing objectives. You can establish specific marketing tactics to reach your target market. Those tactics may include sales promotion, advertising, and publicity. All the components work together. Marketing is ultimately about selling products and services. You have to understand the wants and needs of your target market and offer products and services that provide them a meaningful benefit.

For me, it was important to establish myself as an expert. You can achieve recognition as an expert through writing and speaking. Write articles and books about your topic of expertise, and speak to organizations and associations that represent your target market. This will get you visibility and put you in direct contact with people who are interested in what you have to offer. I decided to specialize in mobile technologies, but I found that the category was too broad. So I chose PDAs specifically because of my past experience in teaching people how to use a PDA to manage their time more effectively. To announce my expertise, I chose a moniker, The PDA Pro, to describe myself. I selected my category as PDA Coach because that's unique. No one else has claimed the title of PDA Coach. I'm the first. I also chose my slogan, "Your PDA Coach for productivity anytime, anywhere." This also serves as my promise, informing people that I can help them improve their productivity. You can't be everything to everybody. Sacrifice is the essence of strategy, according to marketing expert Steve Topper.

Wright

So whom do you consult for marketing advice?

Cooper

As a member of the Institute of Management Consultants (IMC), I have developed strong relationships with many talented experts. As a trusted advisor for my clients, I can easily refer them to an expert who can help solve their problems and add value. I have consulted Gary Henson, CEO of BusinessCoach.com, for strategies to create extraordinary results. For publicity, I consult Jill Lublin from Promising Promotion. She's been instrumental in coaching me on how to gain publicity. She says that public relations are human relations. You have to know your market and your audience. I participated in her *Insider's Circle Program,* which helped me develop my public relations skills. I found her program to be extraordinarily helpful in learning how to work with the media. It's critical to have access to an expert when you need advice.

Wright

By the way, I've known Jill for many years.

Cooper

Oh, really?

Wright

Oh, yeah. She's a great, great gal, I tell you, and knows what she talks about. She is also featured in this book. So how do you generate interest in your products and services?

Cooper

You have to provide valuable information and share your secrets. The information that you offer people has to benefit them, and you've got to create some excitement. Be unique and stand out from the crowd. Another thing to focus on is your message. You've got to keep your message simple. For example, I say your PDA is your CYA. That quickly communicates that your PDA can help you to create an audit trail. Whenever I need to confirm something from a conversation, I refer to my journal application where I enter information during meetings. If you can say, "During our meeting on July 8th at 2:00 p.m. you said...," that's very powerful. Most people can't dispute that because they don't take notes to that degree. It also ensures you follow through on your commitments.

Wright

Right. Tell me how important you think publicity is and how do you get attention?

Cooper

As I mentioned earlier, I suggest that people become an expert in their field. Generate press releases with informational value. Speak to professional and trade associations or service groups like Rotary. Publicity is simply a form of communication. It's usually through traditional media but it could also be through some form of electronic media. You can communicate your message through an e-mail marketing newsletter or have an article posted on a website. It's about getting your message across to people. Having a publicity strategy simply means you're actively influencing media coverage of you. I decided to focus publicity on me personally which I find to be far more effective than generating publicity for a company. Americans love people who are larger than life. What do Richard Branson, Donald Trump, and Oprah Winfrey all have in common? They're masters of publicity. They know how to get attention, and they have something meaningful to say.

Wright

How important is your message to your public relations efforts?

Cooper

Well, your message is critical. For one, if your message is confused, then people won't know what you're trying to communicate and they'll just get confused. People will listen if you provide useful information. You've got to share your secrets. Learn your message backwards and forwards. My message is that you can use a PDA to gain productivity anytime, anywhere. I coach people on how to use their PDA to increase their productivity. You've probably heard the phrase "stay on message." Politicians live by it.

Wright

Right.

Cooper

Develop a central message and then get the word out. Stay focused on communicating your message. You should change your message every three months. According to Jill, during that period you're goal is to communicate your message to a variety of media outlets because it takes several impressions before your message sinks in. The whole goal is to offer useful information and in turn be recognized as an expert.

Wright

So which media do you target to deliver your message?

Cooper

Since I have a technical topic, print media is a better fit in my efforts to communicate my message. My target market is small business owners and sales professionals. There's a high value proposition for anyone who spends a lot of time away from the office and wants to increase their productivity. Time is money and more time to call on clients or prospects translates into higher sales. I focus on local print media but also target national newspapers and magazines. Industry trade publications are a bonus. They are always looking for content and can reach a very specific audience. So it's critical to understand your market and provide content that's relevant to them. You have to take your message and tailor it specifically to them. Having a clear message is critical. To keep it simple, I use sound bites.

For example, "Think it and sync it" or, "Don't lug a laptop, palm a PDA." A simple message is more powerful and memorable.

Wright

So the PDA does a lot of things the laptop will do?

Cooper

Oh, absolutely. Nearly any kind of application available on a laptop can be found for a PDA. I don't necessarily suggest that people ditch their laptops as some experts have suggested. Think of your desktop computer, your laptop computer, and your PDA as being your technology triple threat. All three work together to make you more productive. Sometimes a PDA is just not practical if you're doing a lot of typing. But even then you can actually attach an external keyboard to make data entry for your PDA easier and more comfortable.

Wright

You're kidding. You can put a keyboard with it?

Cooper

Oh, definitely. There are several different manufacturers that make keyboards that connect to a PDA. These portable keyboards fold up for easy storage. Some connect physically to the PDA while others connect wirelessly through infrared. You connect your PDA and then type directly on the keyboard. It's simple.

Wright

What about printing? Is that in the future?

Cooper

It's in the present. There are currently utility applications that allow you to print. Not all printers will currently accept a wireless signal beamed from a PDA. If everything is set up correctly, you can print a memo or spreadsheet just by walking up to a printer and beaming the information to it.

Wright

So what advice do you have for our readers who want to become an expert?

Cooper

Well, expertise requires that you find an area of specialization that you're passionate about and where you can be the most knowledgeable person on the topic. Then make sure you can earn money from it. Determine who will pay for your services. Research your area of specialty and narrow your focus as much as possible. Make sure that your knowledge is relevant. There are three required elements: knowledge, passion, and interest. It's not just what you're interested in, it's what other people are interested in. If you're passionate about soybeans but no one else cares, then you know being a soybean expert isn't really going to benefit you. Knowledge requires that you know the information better than anyone else. Passion requires that you have a deep down desire to learn as much as you possibly can. And interest requires that someone else care.

Wright

I guess what you're saying is being an expert on a four-wheel buggy is probably not the wisest vocation.

Cooper

Probably not. It's a journey of discovery that takes some fine-tuning over time. It took over a year for me to fine-tune my interest in mobile technologies to focus on being an expert in PDAs. Of course, I'm building on over five years of experience using a PDA and a life-long passion for technology. I chose my target market of small business owners and sales professionals because using a PDA can enable them to be far more effective and it really adds bottom line dollars to their pockets.

Wright

So what suggestions do you have for businesses that want to increase sales?

Cooper

Well, businesses are often unaware that their sales consultants are not following a consistent sales process. All of your marketing efforts will fail if your employees who are responsible for sales are not effective. I follow a sales process developed by Power Marketing. In his book, *If You Were Arrested for Selling, Would There Be Enough Evidence to Convict You,* Power Marketing founder Ian Selbie says, "Many sales people rest on their laurels of their previous wins giving prospecting a low to no priority. Prospecting needs to be given priority and requires discipline." Once again, PDA stands for Productivity, Discipline, and Action. PDAs are for producers. It gives you that discipline necessary to stay in contact and keep following up with people to build relationships.

In her book, *Blueprints 4 Business Relationships*, Dr. Bette Daoust says that when you're nurturing relationships, you must follow up with questions and requests in a timely manner. As a sales expert, she says, the sooner you respond the more likely they will do business with you. You can ensure that you follow through by using a PDA to track your tasks and commitments. Also from a sales perspective, I don't cold call prospects. I prefer warm calls coming from referrals or based on existing relationships and it begins with people one on one. Get out. Talk to people. Go to mixers and Chamber of Commerce events. Find out what their interests and desires are. Be sincere and find a way to help support them. It's the difference between what we call inner ring and outer ring activities. Inner ring activities are more sales oriented, talking about your products and services. Outer ring activities focus on creating strategic value for others. According to Ian, "Solving customers' business problems and helping make them achieve their business objectives through using your products and services is called strategic selling. Helping to solve them without getting paid is consultative selling." The equity that you're building can be considered an investment on your part. So, really, you can use your PDA to build and maintain more relationships. It helps you to learn more about people, find out what interests them, and follow up by sending information that would be useful whether it's an article, a book or even a note encouraging them to achieve their goals and dreams. If you build strong relationships with people, sales will come.

Wright

Well, what an interesting conversation. I've learned a lot.

Cooper

Oh, great. I'm glad to share my secrets for success.

Wright

I really appreciate you taking all this time with us to discuss mobile technology. I think I'm beginning to learn enough about it to go buy one.

Cooper

Excellent! I would encourage that and when you get your PDA, give me a call and I can coach you on how to leverage your time to increase your productivity.

Wright

Well, you can count on that. Today we have been talking to Rick Cooper. He is The PDA Pro as we have learned in this half hour. He is your PDA Coach for productivity anytime, anywhere. And I don't know about you, but just listening to Rick I believe the man really knows what he's talking about. Thanks a lot, Rick, for being with us on *Marketing Magic*.

Cooper

You're welcome, David. Thank you.

About The Author

Rick Cooper, The PDA Pro, offers PDA coaching programs to business professionals nationwide that want to leverage their time to increase their productivity. With over 15 years of experience in marketing, sales and technology, Rick offers business leaders keen insights in how to use mobile technology to enhance their sales and marketing efforts. Rick is author of 101 Tips from The PDA Pro and a national speaker on business productivity and sales.

Rick Cooper, The PDA Pro
3323 Watt Avenue #280
Sacramento, California 95821
Phone: 800.677.6708
Fax: 800.677.8384
Email: rick@thepdapro.com
www.thepdapro.com

Chapter 11

EDWARD A. BOND, JR., CCM, FSMPS

THE INTERVIEW

David E. Wright (Wright)

Edward A. Bond, Jr., is the fourth generation leader of Bond Brothers Inc., a full service professional construction management firm. Edward is also a speaker, author, and management consultant specializing in leadership and marketing strategies for the Built Environment Professional Service Industry. He is a professional manager who has grown his family's fourth generation construction management business to over 300 employees and is one of the top firms in the area for construction management in building, civil, and utility construction. He is a certified construction manager, and a certified professional service marketer, and Fellow. Edward, welcome to *Marketing Magic*!

Edward Bond (Bond)

Thank you, David.

Wright

So how did your background prepare you for marketing?

Bond

David, growing up in a family business environment, where entrepreneurship was encouraged, I learned very young the importance of building and maintaining relationships. One of my first paying jobs was at 9 years of age and it was through a friend of mine whose family worked on an apple orchard near my home in New Hampshire. They taught me the art of picking apples. Part of the process was in the handling of the fruit so that you didn't bruise it. Apples that were bruised were worthless to the apple farms and were used for cider. While apples that were handled carefully were sold as fruit and you were paid more for them.

As you can see, I was taught at a very young age about incentive systems and how they figured into the care and handling of your product as well as the needs of the end user. Of course, it also helped that my family had been operating their own business in the Boston area for more than a half-century at that time.

Yet the real lesson was about how our input comes to be part of the larger output that we provide to our clients and knowing what their expectations are from the start so that we're not putting the same energy into picking apples off the ground as one would in picking apples off the tree. As we know, the lower hanging fruit might be the most bruised fruit and easy is not always the best sustainable model.

Over time I learned to use those lessons, along with other lessons, to ask myself very simple questions that related not only to what I wanted to do, but more importantly, would any one really need or care if it was done. So in today's market it comes out as knowing whether the services and products we provide are truly desired by our clients versus something we want to do but there is no market. Over time I've come to the conclusion that while not all services can be easily differentiated, it certainly is clear on how the handling of the client can be a differentiator. Just as the apple off the tree is handled by hand and can be checked for damage, if we look hard enough we can see how well we handle our clients and our people.

As a professional service firm, the first thing a client values is the level of performance of the individuals who make that promise. Because while a service is intangible in the purchasing phase, and a lot of assumptions are made by the client during their decision making process, what can be measured is the level of consistency and handling in the procurement stages. We find that clients depend heavily on referrals and references from credible sources in those procurement stages. In our business, a client is buying a pledge from us to deliver in accordance to the scope, time, price, and method. It is entrusting that the integrity of the firm will deliver on its promise as we say we will. For us it's important to know what our clients' expectations are up front. We work to get conceptual agreement to their needs and wants, and a careful understanding of who is responsible for performance measures along the way, and then delivering on those performance measures as a tangible measure.

Along the way we've managed to expand and diversify our services and to increase the value that we deliver to clients. We've enhanced not only our business framework and the process of how we do our work, but we've actually modified equipment and developed specialized equipment and have patented technologies that have increased efficiency, reduced costs, and provided safer methods of operating. This has been accomplished over the years with the hard work of our people and their desire to better understand the needs of the client.

Wright

So what made you so passionate about marketing?

Bond

The passion really started even when I was young and worked in the service industry, as well as being around an atmosphere of family business values. Over the course of my career, I've worked in the hospitality industry, I've purchased professional services, I've been a long time provider of professional services and I've served in non-profit organizations over the years, so there's always been a focus on what it is we're trying to accomplish, and how we take our technical expertise and deliver that in a manner that meets the specific needs of the end users. To me it has always come back to the people, promises, and performance. I worked in the restaurant and hotel industry during the early days of my career. Right after I graduated from college I had the opportunity to step into a start-up professional firm that was providing construction services to the energy market. While I was allowed the ability to put those entrepreneurial skills into the process of running the business, I quickly gravitated to what I knew, and that happened to be making connections with people. So as a superintendent and then a project manager, I understood the importance of keeping the firm's resources employed and matching our resources to those of our clients. This, of course, meant building rapport and understanding with my client. At that time, I was wearing numerous hats while operating the business, and it was natural to pursue more work with the client that I had, and to take on more of their workload as they offered it. So we'd go from one job to the next job. I really liked the clients and the people that they had working with our firm, so we continued to add more resources and grow the business.

I also learned that I needed some diversification because as I grew the business, I suddenly found myself in a position of having 90% of my work with one client. What I realized at that time was the need to diversify my services to other clients in the same industry, and to get the assistance of my existing client to work with me in making some introductions and referrals. I showed my client how the diversity of my services and ability to expand my business would also benefit them in the future as their business needs grew. They became one of my strongest advocates and marketing arms, helping me to actually build my business in the very beginning and making introductions to others in the industry. And I think it's from the relationship base of the marketing that I really come from more than anything, which is trying to build a solid relationship with good clients out there and having good people on board. I don't believe that you can have one without the other.

Wright

So that's how relationships factor into your marketing?

Bond

Absolutely. Our family business has been around since 1907. We're actually one of the few firms nationally that has been owned and managed by the same family in our industry for four generations. I hope that a fifth generation will follow. As a matter of fact, I just read some recent research, which stated that out of the firms starting back in the early 1900s in the construction industry, only 14 that are left are family owned and still operating today. We're one of those 14.

Wright

Goodness.

Bond

And 90% of our work comes from repeat clients year in and year out, so we have clients that go back four generations. We also have been lucky in that we've developed many relationships with clients over the years. And by keeping in touch we have been able to build our business by working with many of them as their careers have developed. Of course in our business, every project stands on its ability to meet the expectations, but as many of us know, it's the level of communication and responsiveness that one gives to good clients that makes all the difference. Over the years when people invest in a professional service firm, they are really investing first in the people and then the firm. That's one of the reasons we have people within our firm that have been with us for decades, and even some for over half-a-century.

We have a lot of history and heritage, and yet we're a very proactive firm in many of the things we do and the way we do it. We're one of the few firms to do research and development and work closely with our clients in helping to develop new and improved methods of operations that will enhance their process. We do things that you normally wouldn't find within the scope of a professional service firm in the built environment. We're also one of the most diversified construction firms in the region. We still have a lot of self-performing skills and abilities that our people provide to our clients every day of the week, and we employee a few hundred skilled tradespeople on these projects.

In many cases, it's through our hands-on experience and knowledge that we're able to find solutions to clients problems. When you have professionals with demonstrated knowledge, hands-on experience, and determination all working together, you find yourself in a much better framework to solve problems that occur on projects, and people who are not afraid of a challenge or taking on difficult projects. Of course, it also helps us to really understand not only what our client's need, but to try and enhance the position of our clients operations by approaching their projects with that can do attitude. We seek ways of approaching their work that saves time, money, and resources, so that it brings total efficiency and prosperity to everyone. Being committed to our client's means watching out for their best interests and helping them to be as successful as possible; we know that being invested in our clients is our best investment.

Wright

So what makes your process different from others in your marketplace?

Bond

Well, to be blunt, I think the difference is that we've got a different framework, and that is one of realizing the real value in supporting our clients needs is in our abilities to prevent and solve problems on our clients projects before they occur, being proactive. And while there is no crystal ball to forecast where the problems will be, it's the ability to ask questions and uncover issues that resolves those problems from occurring in the beginning. It's in part our ability to take our hands on experiences and relate them to future projects in a manner that prevents clients from traveling down that path of risk. Over the course of our heritage, we've put in place billions of construction work and have been involved with major projects around the area. And it's the ability to work with other professionals in a supportive manner, being part of the team for the owners benefit. Many clients in our industry realize that it's the combination of brainpower and backpower that are critical in uncovering issues and resolving them in a timely manner. Having solid systems setup to communicate and resolve issues are critical in our business. Every time you put a shovel into the ground, you can't be absolutely certain on what you'll uncover, but after time, you can be well assured of what might be there and it's the proactive approach to being prepared for those conditions that makes for a total team effort and a positive difference.

So when competitors in our industry were getting out of the business of supplying labor and equipment to their projects, and handling more of the riskier parts of the hands-on work, we made a conscious decision to continue to provide our clients with these services and skills that could minimize their risk exposure. We have many utility and civil clients who needed our services because their work needs to physically be done and we also realized that work had to be done by those who were getting out of the labor business. So we not only provide our services to our clients, but we also work with others that no longer have the ability or desire to get involved with the actual hands-on performance.

From a marketing stand point, we also realized that having the brainpower with the backpower power would be a differentiator for us, it would make us a valuable source and separate us from other firms. We realized that clients needed opportunities to work with firms that could offer concrete consulting services and advice, and would be willing to back up those recommendations with performance measures. Clients want a firm that can demonstrate great consulting services that analyze the risk and opportunities, along with an ability to take that project from the planning stages all the way through build out and commissioning to the occupancy stages. Having the resources and ability to provide those services up front and then bring that conceptual project all the way to the actual build out, is a delivery process that most firms wouldn't be able to offer. It's providing the client with the level of comfort and satisfaction in knowing that there would not be silos or finger pointing as to the level of responsibility and accountability. Clients expect professional service firms to have a full understanding of the risks that go with their projects and to be capable of providing value informed solutions. Of course the integrity of a firm is on the line as they make these recommendations, and it's imperative that promises aren't broken along the way that can disrupt this level of trust and professionalism. For many it's too easy to over-promise and under-perform, which leaves the client in a no-win position. For us, we work to provide a total solution and a process that allows us to better understand what can be done and what can't be done so that promises aren't broken when the activity actually starts up. We work for some of the finest institutions in the country, here in New England, and they have a keen interest in knowing how their capital dollars are being invested for the long term. Clients are much more aware and financially astute about their investments and having accountability for results is paramount.

It's also important to understand the client's decision-making process. They have to look at the professional service firm from the perspective of: what's the capability, what's the compatibility, and how well are these people handling and communicating to us all the risks that are associated with these projects. As a professional service firm we know that a lot of times it's a promise that's made up front and that promise has to be delivered, or else. It's our ability to understand the total process of the project, not only of the construction, but also our ability to get a full understanding of their project desires and then fill the void between what they want and what they need that we offer a much better investment and value proposition. I believe it comes down to having a solid focus, good people and good clients.

Wright

So how can people within a professional service firm be part of the process?

Bond

Remember that even like the apple pickers, every point of interaction or handling of the client is measured in some form or fashion. When a firm gets a good client or good people, they should be clear about what their process is to keep and nurture those assets. Just as certain apples are worth more, certain client's are worth more to a service firm. I think if firms are to be part of the process, what they have to understand is that they're output is only part of the input, or only a part of the total process for the client. To often we look at our output, being that of completing a construction project in my case, and assume that the client should be relishing our efforts, when the reality is that the client hired us for our technical competencies and it's in the handling and extra effort that we put into their project success that makes the difference. I use the analogy of when we build a hotel, that when we're done with the construction, it is now that the hotel owner really has their major job coming onboard to get the hotel into a revenue stream, which is marketing the facility, booking rooms, bringing in conventions, and getting the place full. Certainly if we can look at ways and methods of accelerating the schedule, phasing the sequence of work, or just asking some really direct questions about how their business works, and what it is they're hoping to accomplish, then often we can help them to create a faster schedule or allow them to bring in revenues ahead of time. Case in point, is where working with some energy firms around the country right now to develop robotic technology that will help them seal underground utility gas pipes under live gas conditions. We've been collaborating with the gas industry over the past few years and have produced a method of sealing leaking gas mains that offer non-intrusive and environmental benefits.

This technology development came about by better understanding our clients concerns and problems, and working with them through solutions that went outside the thinking of day-to-day operations. It also comes back to the networking that we do in our business as professionals as well as builders. In today's market, we need to go beyond just looking at our process and input. We look to see where we can help our clients with their needs and output. We strive to see more about our clients industry, their businesses, and their individual needs. We've helped clients in far greater ways than just in building their facilities and keeping their assets in top condition. We work to help them maximize their land potential, we provide facility assessments, permitting, energy reviews, financial and legal guidance, and provide solid references to other professionals that can maximize their businesses.

We find that it's difficult to go in with only one area of specialty and hope that you can capture the market. I think what you need to do is broaden your expertise base out, get into your client's world, find out what's really taking place within their world, see what the similarities are within the industry, and then try to develop that into a core strength in a niche market if you can play that out by providing value.

Wright

So how do you measure the effectiveness of your marketing efforts?

Bond

The measurement of our marketing efforts comes back to what's the sustainability of our business with those clients. Are our opportunities with these clients growing, are we meeting our expectations as a firm, are we offering more opportunities to our professionals? From our standpoint, to be able to measure it, we do benchmarking and internal reviews that offer us a view of where our good clients are and how well we're meeting their needs. We realize that good client relationships are an investment by both parties and we try to match up our abilities and services to those best suited for our firm.

So the framework that we first began with is to look at the clients that have a need and a constant need for the services that we provide, and then we look to find out what the value is that we can bring to that, and can we bring enough value that would warrant them to want to bring us on board as well. I think the real marketing value comes back to you when you hold on to your good clients and they refer you to others in their firm and industry.

In our business, there are two critical forms of capital, the financial capital and the human capital; I don't think one works without the other. So we try to develop again those relationships on a solid basis of skills and chemistry. In many cases it's the project managers that are very much involved, not only with the technical side of the business, but they are also involved with the human side. We want the emotional connection to take place and the building of trusting relationships that makes for long-term partnerships that offer both parties a valuable connection.

Wright

So how do you try to understand the total value proposition?

Bond

By getting in and trying to understand our client's world. Over the years, I have had the benefit of being involved in many of my clients industries, as have others in our business. By sitting on boards of companies, educational institutions, mutual funds, development firms, non-profits, and being a Malcolm Baldrige Examiner I've had the benefit of reviewing the best in the industries. Of course, it also takes a willingness to get involved, be willing to listen and learn, and to help resolve problems and concerns that occur. So when I look for clients, I seek those that look for quality in their professional service provider and that have shown a desire of relationship building. I believe that once people know that you are interested in their best interests, that you're willing to put aside your interests for their benefit, that you're invested in seeing them successful, they will show a respect and professional regard to do work with you. Of course, it's a two way street. We always need to do our own work at top-notch levels and make sure that we're meeting the value proposition of our clients and their expectations. So for example, when we work with our clients we might take a look at their existing budget and search out where the value is within their budget for things that they want and need, and then work with them to make value informed decisions about options that can provide value and save in costs from an operational standpoint.

As a construction manager we buy tangible things out there—concrete, steel, along with the means and methods—and we work with the designers, engineers and the energy companies to be able to bring the whole thing into a frame where either the building has a longer life period or it has less operating costs or it has more flexibility—customizing the needs of each client is a primary focus. For example, it may be in the materials that are used, plastic versus steel, or the method of actual construction, such as directional drilling versus open cut excavation, and things of that nature that in our business, the value is shown directly in correlation to the costs that they get in the life cycle of the product as well. We look for quality clients that understand the value that a professional firm can bring to them in investing large capital dollars. We show a track record of successful clients.

Wright

It seems like they're getting an awful lot more than just a typical company. So what are some of the ways that you have developed into a trusted advisor of your clients?

Bond

The way that we have developed into a trusted advisor is by really focusing in on the client, their business and their industry. And when I say that, I don't mean that haphazardly. We seek to be involved with clients that have large capital expenditures and that need professionals who can assist and service them. Many of our clients will bring us in the early stages of their project concept. We'll work with them to better understand their overall project goals and how these fit into their business goals. We work with them to develop the project so that it meets their overall goals and it flows with the culture of their firm.

Many of the professionals within our firm sit on boards of universities, associations, and businesses. We attend a lot of our client's organizations and events and participate in committees. Yet we don't find a lot of the people in our industry doing the same thing; and if they are, they're not at what I would call the executive decision making ability. They may be at an ability to find work, but they're not at the ability to sign contracts or truly appreciate how the clients business operates and functions. We find that what clients really want is the technical competency along with the decision making ability that goes with it so that they don't have to feel like they're being shuffled back and forth. As professional service providers, most of the people that work within our firm have a very strong technical ability. We were one of the first firms in the country to have certified construction managers, and the first in New England. So we take skill development and education very seriously, it goes into preparing our people and building their foundations. But we also take it very serious in making sure that our people enjoy the people that they're working with, and they enjoy the industry that they're working within. We have people that specialize in health and educational institutional work, pharmaceutical work, commercial work, energy work, and then we try to break those down into smaller markets, depending on the size of the market. This way they can really develop core skills and access to people that are out there that will help our clients when they have decisions that they have to make.

Wright

As the CEO, it's surprising to me to see how active you are in the marketing profession. Why is that?

Bond

Having studied business and marketing in college and graduate school, I found that I truly enjoyed the aspect of providing a service but also providing knowledge and insight into my clients business. Of course at that time, service marketing was not a core subject that was being studied, so I needed to find a group that was involved in service marketing. Professional service marketing really came about when my career started, so I also realized the value of being involved in the beginning. When I transitioned over to my family business, I realized the phone was not going to continue to ring forever from past clients. Marketing was on the horizon and we needed to adapt our methods to stay in front of the client.

So I got involved in the marketing profession very early on and helped shape some of the industry in many ways as well. I became the national president for the Society for Marketing Professional Services (SMPS) after having served as the Boston chapter president. I was helpful in getting our professional certification rolled out and in helping to build the body of knowledge that is used in the professional service environment.

And I think it's a mindset. As I mentioned earlier, I started out very early in my life in the hospitality and restaurant business, which is very much service oriented, and I've always just continued with that framework. Being fourth generation family manager and owner of the business, it's always been part of our trademark to provide service 24/7 before the term was coined. We were one of the few, and still remain one of the few, that provides 24/7 services to all of our clients on a regular basis. That's again why we have the management and we have the manpower and equipment that so many in our industry have fallen away from.

Wright

In your business, where do clients focus their decision-making?

Bond

Clients are focused on their output and how it can be accomplished in the best manner and sequence, they're looking for best overall investment value. When I say investment, it's more than just the dollars. It's their time, their resources, their level of risk tolerance, and their relationships that they've developed, along with a trust factor or referral from a reliable source.

Too often in our industry we hear about commodities and that service firms compete only on price. For me, I see smart firms that know it is not the price, but the total cost that concern's them in how they procure their services. I've found that smart clients aren't always looking at the lowest price, because they realize the overall total cost is the key in working with professional service firms and that smart investments offer better returns. They also will focus on the total value that a firm can provide along with the level of relationship trust that they have for a particular firm. In many cases, this relationship might not have been a direct relationship as much as it is a referenced relationship from others in their firm or industry that they trust. It's a given that you have to be qualified before they will consider you.

From my perspective, we like to develop relationships with clients at three levels of their firm, and we hope that it is with three different people from our firm. We do this because in many situations there are different levels of decision making that take place and it helps us to build a better understanding and rapport throughout the clients firm. We also like to do this because it provides us with solid feedback on where the client is focused and how they measure performance.

We'll start out at the field level where, depending on the client, they may be authorized to make decisions and empowered. More often it tends to be more at the middle management level—project management level—where they're authorized. But overall, it becomes the executive level that tends to have a handle on what's being decided throughout the corporation as a whole. And what we try to do is make sure that we have relationships at three levels, different people at those levels from our firm, so that we can listen to the client's voice to find out what's important, what isn't. We don't want to get misguided in our strategy either in setting up our resources in preparation for something if it's not going to happen. So the pipeline is this three level pipeline, and the decision-making really rests depending on the size of the capital expenditure within that client's base at any one of those three levels. More often than not, it's middle to upper level that's making very large capital expenditures. That's because in our business we have projects that run as small as a few hundred thousand dollars to a few hundred million dollars. We may be involved in the client's environment working with them three or five years before a client ever puts a shovel in the ground. It's a totally different model than when I came into the business over 25 years ago, which was more of what we would call a plan and spec type of environment where they would plan it, spec it out, and then put it out to bid or as often referred to as Design – Bid – Build. Nowadays clients bring us in as professional construction managers and we advise them in the design, construction, costs, schedule, and resource allocations. Our goal is to maximize their investments with the least amount of risk.

Wright

How do you get in a position of understanding your client's expectations?

Bond

Since we are focused in specific industries, we target clients that overlap in their needs for services and we ask them what's important and why it's important. With a broad view of not only their business, but their industry and other industries that correlate to their needs, we able to offer a view and perspective that opens up opportunities. And we've found that once we've demonstrated this view, we are more often invited to participate in helping them.

We also have the benefit of having clients for years and the time that we get to know their business and them personally makes a big difference in being able to get up to speed and help them create the measurements and expectations. Today many firms are outsourcing more of their projects and have fewer people on board that can help facilitate the total process and they're looking for firms that will help out.

So while we have worked with many of these clients for 50 or better years, we understand sometimes their systems better than they do, and sometimes we'll have people on board that have been part of their industry and have the experience that they need.

We'll bring people in there that really understand their system, that know how to make a difference, and than we'll go in there and work with the client to unearth their expectations and what it is they need. If we don't, then they can't measure it and we can't measure it either. So our real goal is to be able to have deliverables and measurable milestones, just like a critical path.

Part of the process is understanding the milestones along the way that we need to meet and knowing that the client is committed to the process. There are certain steps that we need to take to meet those milestones, and if we don't meet those milestones, then we're actually going to be pushing other things out onto a critical that weren't critical before. We take these things very serious, and that comes back to good communication and understanding of what their expectations are, how they perceive issues, and where they see risks in the equation, and how we plan to handle that and administer that from a construction viewpoint.

Wright

After having the luxury of four generations in your business, what do you expect of marketing's role in the future?

Bond

I see marketing's role as growing stronger in the future. Too often we see very talented and knowledgeable professionals who do not have the ability to really connect with people. And the foundation of any professional service firm is first and foremost in their people. All of the partners that I have in our businesses are very strong on the technical and skill side, as well as the relationship building side. I think that professionals that have strong marketing skills, matched with strong financial and management skills will go a long way.

Marketing's role is not just that of business development, it digs deeper into roots of why the firm is in business and what the main objectives and strategic focus of the firm is for everyone involved. It's the ability to take that long-term focus and transmit it into actionable items that makes for a successful firm in my view.

Clients want to deal with professionals that are knowledgeable, likeable, and empowered to make decisions. Marketing takes place every day by every person who works in a service firms. It comes out in the way we interact, follow-up, make promises, deliver on those promises, and perform over and above what the client expects.

In our business it's important to recognize that it's our client's money, its large investments, and we need to work with them to keep them in business.

And from the marketing side we have two audiences that we need to keep educated and informed about our profession and business, and that's the external client, our customer, and the internal client, our people. Truly a well-orchestrated firm today balances the two of these into their organization, because just like a bruised fruit is not worth the same, a disappointing client or professional provider can be like a worm in your apple—nasty!

Wright

Well, what an interesting conversation. I've certainly learned a lot today. Edward, I really appreciate the time that you have taken with me to explain your business and your marketing principles. This has been fascinating.

Bond

Well thank you David, I appreciate that and it's been a pleasure speaking with you.

Wright

Today we have been talking with Edward Bond. He is a management consultant. He's a professional manager who has grown his family's fourth generation construction management business to over 300 employees, gotten all the certifications that you can imagine, and as we have found out today knows an awfully lot about his industry and takes the time to learn his clients' industry which is surprising in this day and time. Edward, thank you so much for being with us today on *Marketing Magic*.

Bond

Thank you, David. It's been a pleasure.

About The Author

Edward Bond, CCM, FSMPS, CEO of Bond Brothers, Inc. provides construction management services to the built environment. The firm was started in 1907 and he is the fourth generation of the Bond family managing the firm. Know for his ability to distill complex issues into common terms, he is a popular national speaker and sits on the boards of private, public, and non-profit boards around the country.

Edward A. Bond, Jr., CCM, FSMPS
Bond Brothers, Inc.
145 Spring Street
Everett, Massachusetts 02149
Email: ebondjr@bondbros.com
www.BONDBROTHERS.com

Chapter 12

MERRIE SPAETH

THE INTERVIEW

David E. Wright (Wright)

Today we are talking to Merrie Spaeth. Merrie is acknowledged as a pioneer in the communications field. Her mission is to make communication a strategic business tool. Her influence model and training programs are used by some of the world's most admired and successful companies. As an advisor to the late Ronald Reagan, she was credited by the *Washington Times* for taking the White House into the next century. She is regularly interviewed by major business publications and is a regular commentator for *NPR* and does a weekly column, *Words Matter*, for *UPI*. The author of *Market Place Communication*, she teaches at the Cox School of Business at Southern Methodist University where she has been awarded numerous distinguished instructor awards. Today we're talking to her about what she calls corporate America's greatest unused marketing asset—their own employees—and what she calls corporate family members. Merrie, welcome to *Marketing Magic*!

Merrie Spaeth (Spaeth)

Thank you!

Wright

All companies and organizations say their employees are the most important asset or something like that. Why do you call them the most underutilized marketing asset and what's a corporate family?

Spaeth

David, thank you. The reason that I say that most companies are underutilizing or not utilizing their most important marketing asset—their employees—is because when you look at how companies or organizations communicate with key constituencies (and I would put customers or potential customers at the top of the list of important audiences), companies communicate with advertising, marketing materials, signage, statement stuffers or anything like that. There's a long list of communication vehicles that we call "controlled material." Companies actually discourage most of their employees from talking about the company, its mission, its products, and its services. They have a number of ways they do that without meaning to. If you can get your employees talking enthusiastically about your mission, your products, and your services, you have added credibility to your marketing material and created a competitive edge that is hard to erode. A corporate family is all the people who are involved. For example, let's take a large hospital. Think first of the people who work for the hospital: the administrative staff; the physicians, who may or may not be paid by the hospital; the nurses; and the rest of the health care staff. But you also have the patients and their families. Even donors! All those people are part of the corporate family because they all talk to potential customers. Most companies don't include this comprehensive view when planning their marketing.

Wright

Is it true that the customers that are treated badly talk more than the ones that are treated well?

Spaeth

That's true. People will look for someone to tell about a horrible experience. For example, I have been feuding with a telecommunications company about an insurance policy over a lost telephone. They've lost the paperwork, and the insurance company won't honor it without the paperwork. I've been over to this company seven times, and you can bet I have told at least 77 people about that. On the other hand though, my car was vandalized and Sewell Cadillac, here in Dallas, really lived up to their advertising promises. In fact, they surpassed my expectations, and I've told people about that. There are ways that companies can enlist their customers and their customers' families to pass on good news or good experiences. Very few companies actually try to do it or know how.

Wright

You say that most companies have an obsolete definition of communication. What's yours and how did you develop it?

Spaeth

Most companies think about what they want to say, or what they think a particular audience needs to know. Our definition of communication is asking who is my audience, and what do I want them to hear, believe, and remember, and to influence that. The insight came to me on our first day in business in 1987. I was talking to the head of Southwestern Bell Telephone, and he was describing their quality initiative. He said, "Merrie, we have a team of people and they talk to customers, both small individual customers and large commercial customers, after the customer has had some interaction with the company. And what we've learned is that the customer does not remember what we thought we told them." When you ask how much does the individual remember from what you say, a lot or a little, everyone knows the listener only remembers a small amount. We set out to understand that process, to understand how to influence it, and then to understand how to integrate it into marketing, sales and customer service. We want to understand, anticipate, harness and align that process. It requires a radically different way of thinking.

Wright

So how does that fit with the influence model?

Spaeth

The influence model maps out the three major routes of information. The model first identifies all the audiences, both internal and external, that the company or organization wants to influence. The first route we call the controlled or formal network of communication, because the company controls the messages and sends them directly to the audience in the form of advertising, marketing material, statement stuffers, newsletters, signs, annual reports etc. The second route is through the media and the third is verbal communication, which we define as everything from making a presentation to a Chamber of Commerce or a citizens group all the way to person-to-person communication. To influence the target audience, a company has to use all three of those networks and use them proactively. Most important is what we call message alignment. Let me explain. A company prepares marketing and sales material to reach its potential customers. We look at the message and the actual words that are contained in that marketing material. Then we go to the third network, verbal communication, and we look to see if we hear employees of the company actually using those words, and if they are using them, are they only using them in a pitch situation? And are only sales personnel using them? Generally you find a huge drop off between the words and messages in controlled materials and what employees are doing and saying. Finally, we examine if employees or members of the corporate family articulate these words and messages when they're off the job.

Wright

So the alignment then would be to...if I was an employee of yours, I would try to match my words with what you had in your written marketing material?

Spaeth

Yes. If the target audience hears the words in ads but doesn't hear employees repeating them, the implication is that employees don't believe them. And we need to hear them with enthusiasm and passion, not spoken the way telemarketers use them: "Thank you for doing business with Bank Wimble," or "We value your service." Again to use Sewell Cadillac as a good example. Their ads tout customer service, and in my recent experience, people delivered on what the ads promised. The words I heard were the same words in the ads. You see, we think the employees make marketing material real.

Wright

Is there a quick checklist or self-assessment that our readers can do?

Spaeth

Yes. The acid test is, "Are employees proud of their organization and do they want to verbalize its messages?" And we mean this internally as well as externally.

Wright

Well, the more they say it the truer it will get.

Spaeth

They have to be true. When I ask companies if they show their own ads and marketing material to their employees, the answer frequently is, "No." There are three reasons. First, they've never done it before and I hear "Oh, gee, it'd be such a hassle. "Next, is expense—"You know it would cost money, and how would we do it." But the third reason is the one that slays me. Companies say, "Well, our employees would know that it's not true."

Wright

Goodness!

Spaeth

If you apply our Influence Model™, companies are asking employees to be the personal carriers of messages that they don't believe in. If you go back to our philosophy of influence—to affect what people hear, believe, and remember—the audience immediately figures out that the speaker, customer service rep, or employee doesn't believe what he's saying.

Wright

So if you're not aligned then you could recruit someone as a telemarketer and say, "Well, your job description is basically to mislead our prospects."

Spaeth

That's what a lot of companies are asking their employees to do.

Wright

So back to my question, is there a checklist?

Spaeth

Yes. First, identify all your internal and external audiences. Next, gather all of the controlled material together—your ads, your employee newsletters, annual reports, web page material, posters, marketing material... everything that you prepare and control. Third, compile a list of what we call "good words." That is, the words you want your various internal and external audiences saying about your company, its products, services, people, track record and so on. Fourth is a "listening walk." Listen to what your own people are saying both internally and externally, and listen for these words. That's the initial assessment. The second phase examines whether the company equips its employees and, by extension, the members of its corporate family, to talk about the company and its services. Finally, are people enlisted and encouraged to gather information and carry the company's message forward? Or are they penalized if they do something that's "wrong?" If a company follows this self-analysis, they will get a very good idea of whether they're actually involving employees and regarding employees as components of overall marketing.

Wright

So are there any key obstacles to involving every employee as an ambassador?

Spaeth

The first one, David, is that companies have to think differently. Look at how the direct marketing companies like Mary Kay and Amway think. They have an active plan to involve and include everybody; most companies don't. There's a very different attitude about who carries the company's message and communicating to your employees that they are ambassadors on and off the job. The next obstacle is undoubtedly to provide what I would call an appropriate level of training so that employees understand some basic techniques and are motivated to want to communicate the message. The training budget is always the first thing that gets cut in the down economy. Every company professes to think that communication is terribly important, but when you look at what kind of training they provide, it's usually very task-oriented. This kind of training is perceived as an additional cost rather than a crucial way to get your employees involved and turn them into ambassadors for the company.

Wright

So how is this different from a focus on customer service?

Spaeth

It goes significantly beyond customer service. Good customer service to me is interpreted by satisfying the customer during a single transaction or encounter as part of the job. We look at who employees talk to and equip them with messages to use on and off the job and beyond their job related area of responsibility.

Wright

So it's almost like a super referral. You're just talking about your company all the time.

Spaeth

No. It's recognizing that there are many opportunities to carry the company's message, to make the marketing real and personal, and to motivate them to understand that this is part of the job. To their friends, relatives and neighbors, they are the face of the company.

Wright

Let me get off the subject for a second and ask you a question that I was really interested in asking when I read your biographical notes here. You were an advisor to the late Ronald Reagan.

Spaeth

I was the media director at the White House, yes.

Wright

I've heard so many commentators talk about this subject. But what do you think made him such a great communicator?

Spaeth

Where to start? I miss him so much. First of all, he learned the value of telling stories as opposed to lecturing and relying just on facts. He understood that stories—what we call anecdotes—really bring facts alive. Second, he practiced, practiced, practiced. He spent years refining his delivery techniques, and I refer to him as the first television president. He understood people have been watching television for decades and that has changed what the listener expects of the speaker's communication skills. He understood, and we believe this is true, that watching television changes how people process information.

Wright

Well, whoever was helping him, he sure was a great communicator.

Spaeth

Yes, he was. I learned a great deal from him.

Wright

How does this actually work at the employee level?

Spaeth

We worked with a regional grocery store chain's pharmacists who viewed themselves as highly trained professionals. They didn't see themselves as part of the overall marketing effort. They thought that was somebody else's job. When we videotaped what they were saying, especially to dissatisfied customers, and we compared it to store's marketing and advertising, we could see how badly out of alignment it was. The advertisements promised service, accessibility and convenience, but when somebody came in with a problem, the first response was, "Well, you know it's been very busy today." That may be true, but it undercuts the advertising and marketing message. When the pharmacists realized that they are the living extension of the marketing material and we walked them through our methodologies, we transformed their behavior. When somebody came in with a problem, the pharmacist said, "I am so sorry because our commitment is to get it right for you. Our commitment is to get it perfect, and I'm going to fix it right now." That's a dramatic difference.

We filmed the pharmacists in off-the-job situations. Their friends and neighbors are always complaining about drug prices. A typical, defensive response was, "Well, nobody has low prices all the time. Sometimes we have lower prices, and sometimes the store down the street has lower prices." Again, totally out of alignment with how we're spending our marketing dollars. Most important, we take people through a thought process. You can't tell employees to do this. You have to facilitate a willingness to do it. The second time we filmed this encounter, the same pharmacist said, "You know, if you will come into my store, I will show you around personally, and I'll show you the relationship between price and service and what service is really all about. Are you willing to do that?" And of course, the person said yes. A very different outcome.

Wright

So what role does training play in your program?

Spaeth

It's crucial. This is a methodology that we have developed because you can't tell people "just go use these words." They'll look at you and say, "Yeah, right, buddy, sure. You know I'm not going to go hype myself like that." You must give people training that enhances their everyday skills as well as makes them feel comfortable experimenting. We've copyrighted these techniques so participants feel they gain immediately useful skills and they are empowered and motivated to use person-to-person verbal communication on behalf of the company. They must feel they can be successful, that what they say is true and reflects well on them as well as on the company. Plus, there is an undeniable element of team building.

Wright

You use a lot of real examples on video as part of your methodology. Is there a reason?

Spaeth

Yes. Video today is the most important training tool because people look at it and they will mimic it or imitate it. You can tell people, for example, "Please have a smile when you greet the customer." But when you show people what they look like when they greet the customer, they are horrified. As you know most of our training examples are very funny, but they are also very effective. We see people can transform themselves. And we use it in very sophisticated ways far beyond just facial expressions. We illustrate how to structure what you say and how to influence what your listener remembers and passes on.

Wright

What do you mean structured information?

Spaeth

We divide information in very specific categories: acknowledgements of listening, headlines, and then various forms of proof and validations. Another reason for our video examples is that most of our examples are screamingly funny. We believe that people learn best when they are having a good time.

Wright

So are you talking about body language?

Spaeth

That is important, but structure comes first. If you have a clear headline, illustrated with compelling information and stories, you can be mediocre in the traditional elements of style and still be very effective from our perspective. Facial expression does influence how people listen, and eye contact influences whether your listener thinks you believe what you're saying. Vocal quality convinces the listener you're excited about what you're saying. These are a direct result of how much television we've been watching. But we start first with the structure of information: what's a headline, what's a proof, what's an anecdote, what's a quote, and how to put them together so that you influence your listener.

Wright

Do you do any training as far as personality profiling is concerned?

Spaeth

Occasionally it's part of an overall executive assessment. When we're coaching very senior executives, and they have a variety of management challenges, then obviously understanding the person is important. But with Ambassador efforts, we're talking about things even very large companies can do to enlist every single employee.

Wright

I was in a workshop recently and this workshop leader gave us a sentence. He said, "I knew John F. Kennedy, and you're no John F. Kennedy," and asked the audience who said it. Of course, everyone knew it was the Quayle debate. And then he said, "I think that thing lasted for an hour or more, could you give me one other sentence that was uttered in that?" And no one knew. So do you give any sound bytes out as marketing tips when you train?

Spaeth

Well, to understand the audience and influence what they "hear, believe and remember," of course, is our mantra. We are known for Bimbo Awards, and everybody remembers why thy never want to be a bimbo. They are named for the young woman who announced, "I am not a bimbo." You see, when you use a negative word and deny it, the listener frequently eliminates the denial and actually hears the opposite of what the speaker is trying to say. Every month we have a Bimbo memo with the top two or three bimbo comments of the month.

We e-mail it and people love it. Despite being funny, it is a serious teaching tool because it reminds people of the importance of learning these lessons. So "no bimbos" is the short sweet backdoor entry into our communication training.

Wright

That sounds like such a natural idea. Why isn't every company or organization instituting an employees' ambassador's program?

Spaeth

I think the first thing it requires is that you think very differently. Most people tend to think that marketing isn't their job. It's the marketing department's job. Or recruiting isn't their job. It's the HR department's job. It's a radically different process for most companies to understand that they can build these concepts into a marketing program. Now, of course, the direct marketing companies have thought like that for decades, and when I first started talking about it, people would laugh at me and say, "Well, what can we learn from the ladies in the pink Cadillac's?" It turns out that there's a lot you can learn from them. So thinking differently is the first and biggest step. From that flow many implications: how you prepare people, what different training is provided, how employees are equipped and how information is updated. Most companies do things the way they did them last year, including marketing or advertising. When companies start to think differently, they gain a remarkable competitive edge.

Wright

Well, I've been booking speakers for about 15 years now, and it just never ceases to amaze me that the first thing to go, you've already said it, but the first thing to go is the training budget. And it should be the last thing to go.

Spaeth

True. An ambassadors program can be cost-effective. When you look at your employees as a marketing asset, you grow the program over years. The successful hospitals that we work with build this into their planning models and then each year it grows, whether it's using nurses as recruiters or getting patients and their families to talk to their friends and neighbors. What you can't do is stop, start, stop, start, stop, start. Those kinds of mixed messages only convince the employees that they shouldn't be talking about the company.

Wright

In our area we have three really top rated hospitals. I've heard my neighbors comment that all three of these hospitals do a tremendous amount of television advertising. From the media, we hear about the rising cost of hospitalization and the insurance premiums, and my friends wonder if the advertising pushes up the cost of health care and why the hospitals need to advertise at all if there's such a crisis. Should they be thinking of their employees as ambassadors?

Spaeth

Absolutely. Hospitals in particular can utilize the program successfully because although they may pull from a national constituency, they also have a geographic base. All hospitals should have a very active speakers bureau deploying their doctors and their nurses and other specialists like nutritionists. They should be talking about the area where they're experts, but also using the opportunity to promote the hospital and educate the public that there are, in fact, a number of crises in health care that our elected officials are not moving to address. To do that successfully, the hospital should ask for volunteers, and provide training and assistance turning information into truly motivational quality material. And they should be enlisting all their employees as ambassadors because those routes of communication are so powerful.

Wright

Do you know of any hospitals that do that?

Spaeth

Yes. Crestwood, a Triad hospital in Huntsville, Alabama, and the Baylor Health Care System in Dallas. But any company can launch an employees as ambassadors program.

Wright

This has been a fascinating conversation. I could go on all day.

Spaeth

Well, I hope these comments are useful to your readers.

Wright

Well, it certainly will be useful. Today we have been talking to Merrie Spaeth. She is a pioneer in the field of communications, and she has been talking today about her influence model and the training programs that are used by some of the world's most admired and successful companies. And we have found out also that she knows what she is talking about. Thank you so much, Merrie, for being with us and taking so much time to enlighten us on training and your influence model.

Spaeth

Thank you.

About The Author

Merrie Spaeth has served U.S. Presidents and corporate CEOs providing communications strategic counsel, crisis management and executive training. A popular public speaker and teacher, Merrie's pioneering approach to communications gives organizations a proven methodology for influencing an audience. Her firm provides communications services to a range of clients from not-for-profit to global Fortune 500 companies. A prolific published writer, she is the author of "Marketplace Communication," numerous articles and a regular column for UPI.

Merrie Spaeth
Spaeth Communications, Inc.
3405 Oak Grove Avenue
Dallas, Texas 75204
Phone: 214.871.8888
Fax: 214.871.9015
E-mail: mspaeth@spaethcom.com
www.spaethcom.com

Chapter 13

KELLY MCDONALD
HISPANIC MARKETING EXPERT

THE INTERVIEW

David E. Wright (Wright)

Today we are talking to Kelly McDonald. Kelly is a marketing and advertising expert with more than 20 years of ad agency experience in both the General Market and Hispanic market. Prior to starting her own Hispanic marketing company, Kelly was Director of Client Services at one of the nation's top Hispanic ad agencies. With clients such as Toyota, BlueCross BlueShield, Subaru, Nissan, Budweiser, Bank One, and Kimberly Clark, Kelly has helped clients grow their business by strategically targeting U.S. Latinos. As a speaker, Kelly educates organizations about cultivating Latino customers with cultural relevance. As a volunteer, Kelly has taught English as a second language to Latinos for years. Her marketing firm employs Latinos from the United States, Mexico, Central America, and South America. Thank you so much for being with us today, Kelly.

Kelly McDonald (McDonald)

Thank you.

Wright

So why is the Hispanic population such a hot topic right now for companies and brands?

McDonald

The Hispanic population delivers what I call the "three L's": It's large. It's lucrative. And it's a loyal audience. And from a marketing perspective, that's what every company wants, whether you offer a product, a brand, or a service. Every company wants a large enough group of people or a large enough target audience to sell their products and services to. They want those customers to be able to afford their products and services. And they want to be able to retain those customers, or have them buy more frequently. So from a large, lucrative, and loyal standpoint, the Hispanic market, more than any other specific target segment, delivers those "three L's." No other segment actually delivers all three in the same way. For example, the baby boomers are a large and lucrative consumer segment. They are the largest and most affluent population in this country's history. But they are absolutely not loyal. They're very fickle, and it's very difficult for marketers to retain boomers because they're always looking for the next best thing.

Wright

Right.

McDonald

If you're trying to hit those "three L's"—large, lucrative, and loyal—there is no better, high-potential prospect to target than the Hispanic consumer.

Wright

So how big is the Hispanic population now?

McDonald

As of 2004, it's 43.5 million.

Wright

Wow!

McDonald

And that's a conservative number. We know that many people did not fill out the 2000 Census because of fear of their immigration status. And forecasts for Hispanic population growth are also impressive: the Hispanic population is projected to be 56 million by 2010, and 80 million by 2020. That translates to *one in five.* By the year 2020, one in five U.S. residents will be Hispanic. I think that's another reason why brand and marketing companies are so interested in this consumer—looking to the future, no one can afford to overlook one-fifth of the country's population.

Wright

Yes, they all have to have toothpaste and tooth brushes, cars and TVs, don't they?

McDonald

Absolutely.

Wright

To develop effective marketing messages, do you recommend using Spanish? If so, why? And what about bilingual Hispanics?

McDonald

Spanish is absolutely a cornerstone for effective Hispanic marketing and messaging, but it's not the only one. It starts with Spanish, because research shows that 74% of the Hispanic households in this country choose to speak Spanish at home. So even among those who are bilingual, the language of preference is Spanish. Spanish is the language that they are most relaxed in, most comfortable with; that's the language in which they'll be most receptive to a marketing message. For most Hispanics, Spanish is the language of their heart, their soul, and ultimately, the language of their wallet. It may be the language that my mother speaks, or it may be the language that allows me to express myself best. Spanish is different than English. There are words in Spanish that we don't have in English, words that just don't translate. For example, "*ganas*" is passionate, but "*apasionado*" is passionate, too. *"Ganas"* is more intense, more emotional, and we don't really have a word that comes close to that in English. So for many Hispanics, even those who are bilingual, Spanish is the language that allows them to express themselves more perfectly, more accurately. By recognizing that the majority of Hispanic consumers prefer Spanish, companies have a solid foundation on which to build. Further, we know exactly how many people speak Spanish at home, because that was one of the questions that the Census asked in both 1990 and 2000. In any market, any zip code, we can identify exactly how many people are receptive to Spanish messaging.

Wright

I have kind of been keeping up with these trends by reading articles, and it seems that if we're marketing to Hispanics, we should use the litmus test of "what language they think in."

McDonald

Correct. That's one of the things that researchers are trying to get at. Often when surveys are done, researchers feel that they are not necessarily getting the most pure answers to these types of questions. They feel that respondents may be providing the answer they think the researcher wants, not necessarily the true answer.

Wright

Right.

McDonald

So one of the more recent questions I've seen in market research is: "What is the language that you pray in"? If the respondent states that the language they pray in is Spanish, you know then that Spanish is truly the language of their heart.

Wright

Is it a good idea to translate marketing materials into Spanish?

McDonald

I believe that marketing materials should be in Spanish, but in terms of translating them straight from English to Spanish, I recommend against that. There are too many mistakes that can be made. There are too many possibilities for error; and when the errors are made, they're grave. It is much better to actually create something "organically," from scratch, in Spanish. It is also going to reach the consumer with more relevance. Let me give you a recent example. We were working with a bank client, and this bank has brochures for their key products like savings accounts and checking accounts. They asked us to translate their brochures into Spanish. In their brochure for personal loans, which is in English, the copy suggested that the reason that someone might want to take out a personal loan would be to fund the things that they've always wanted, such as a motorcycle, an RV, or a boat. When we looked at that, we said, "If we just translate this, it's not going to reach our Hispanic target consumer in a meaningful way, because Hispanics index very low in the purchase of motorcycles and RV's." If the bank had sent that off to a translation service, they would probably have an acceptable translation from a grammar standpoint, but from a messaging and marketing standpoint, it wouldn't be relevant. A better example might be that a personal loan is a great way to buy a computer that the family can use, or take a family vacation.

We find more relevant reasons with what this consumer cares about and consumes. That's where it's really about marketing. If it were just about translating from English to Spanish, our jobs would be very easy! You really have to think about what your consumer wants. Just as men are different from women, and the old are different from the young, there is a cultural difference and a family dynamic difference between the Hispanic and the general market culture. The world is chock full of horrible, horrible, horrible translation mistakes. A recent example of one is the "Got milk?" campaign. "Got milk?" when translated into Spanish is *¿Tiene leche?,* which means, "Are you lactating?" I don't think that's exactly what the milk producers of America want to say! Fortunately, they were aware that this translation wouldn't work, so what they created in Spanish was "Más leche" – "more milk." There are countless examples of translations gone wrong. The best strategy is to develop a message organically to reach your high potential target, building a message in a meaningful way around the features and benefits you want to convey.

Wright

Right. So help me out with some terminology here. What is acculturation? Is that the same as assimilation?

McDonald

No, some people use the terms interchangeably, but it's actually incorrect to do so. Assimilation is when one forfeits one's culture and adopts another. Acculturation is the process by which a person adopts or borrows traits from another culture while keeping core values of their first culture. It's the acquisition of a second culture. Until the 1980's, most immigrant groups in the United States were forced to assimilate rather than acculturate. For example, my great-grandmother emigrated from Germany in the early 1900s and she literally came over on a boat. When she arrived, there was no way that she was able to go back to Germany and visit her family. Travel, and especially international travel by boat, was only for the wealthy. There were no planes. There was no e-mail. There were no phones. There was no way you could stay in touch with your loved ones. And so immigrants had to learn English and basically forfeit everything that they knew, everything that was their culture, and fully assimilate into the U.S. culture because there was no other choice. What's changed in our lifetime is technology. I can fly from Dallas to Mexico City faster and cheaper than I can get to Chicago. So if I have family and loved ones in Mexico, they're accessible. I can visit them. I can go home in a matter of hours. I can drive it. I can fly it. I can also e-mail. I can also make a phone call, and all of this is very inexpensive, and it's widely available. So there really is no reason any more to just leave one culture behind and adopt another. It is entirely possible to retain the aspects of a culture that we want and admire while acquiring traits and habits from a new culture that we also want and admire. And that is what acculturation is.

Wright

So how does one factor acculturation into one's marketing message?

McDonald

It starts by identifying the level of acculturation that your high-potential target has achieved. We have an acculturation model with four key Latino mindsets. You'll note that I'm not using the word "demographics." That's because it's really not about age or gender or income or education. There are four key *mindsets* that really illustrate the four levels of acculturation. We call the least acculturated Latino a "Cultural Loyalist." This Latino is foreign born and a recent arrival. They've been in the country less than five years, and are Spanish dependent. That means they're going to tend to live among Spanish-speaking people, work among Spanish-speaking people, and they tend to have very traditional values based in the culture of their origin. This is the least acculturated target profile. The next mindset is the "Cultural Embracer." The Cultural Embracer is also foreign born, but has adopted the U.S. as their permanent home. They do not desire to return to their country of origin to live - this is their new home, and consequently, they are eagerly embracing new foods, new music, making new friends, and learning new things. This target profile may be bilingual or they may not. But even if they are bilingual, they are "Spanish-preferred." How could they not be? They're foreign born—Spanish is their mother tongue.

Wright

So cultural orientation changes with length of residency, but also with expectation of ongoing residency?

McDonald

Right. The longer the immigrant lives in the U.S., the more English they're going to learn. However, most will always prefer Spanish. But there are also important differences in attitude. Cultural Embracers are very aspirational, very progressive, working hard to get ahead. This continues into the next level of acculturation, what we call the "Cross Culturer." The Cross Culturer is U.S. born, but first generation. So mom and dad are from somewhere else. This individual is a very powerful emerging consumer in our country, very influential within the family because they're often the family translator. This individual is bilingual, but more importantly, bicultural, meaning equally comfortable in the Hispanic and the Anglo cultures. This individual is very fashion-forward, very educated, very professional, but also very much in touch with their Latin roots. How could they not be? It's really sort of a unique blend of best of both worlds. Finally, the last level of the acculturation is the Cultural Integrator. The Cultural Integrator is U.S. born, but second, third, fourth, fifth generation, and so on. They're "English-preferred" or "English only" and yet very proud of their cultural roots. The way that marketers should look at this is to ask, "Who is my high-potential prospect?" Let me give you an example. If you are a bank or a money wiring service, then your high-potential prospect is not the U.S. born. It's the foreign-born. Because the foreign-born are the greatest users of money-wiring services to send money home to loved ones. So if I was the marketing director at a bank and I was promoting money wiring services or check cashing services, my prospect isn't the entire "Hispanic market." My prospect is a segment of the Hispanic market, specifically foreign-born, recent arrivals. If I were the marketing director of a mortgage company, I would be targeting the Cultural Embracer and Cross Culturer. Do you see how the acculturation model works?

Wright

Yes, it's fascinating. Can you give an example or two of a company or brand that's doing really a great job with their Hispanic marketing?

McDonald

Sure. Toyota is a great example of a company that's doing everything right. Toyota recognized the value of the Hispanic consumer early on, and has been marketing to the Hispanic market for about a decade in Spanish. One of the things that they're doing right and that I so admire about them is that they are not just making culturally relevant ads in Spanish. In Texas, Toyota has focused on operational readiness for Latino customers at dealerships. They want to make sure that when a Latino consumer sees a message about Toyota and visits a dealership, that the dealership is ready to assist this consumer in Spanish. Buying a new or used vehicle is an important transaction, and Toyota wants all of their customers to be as comfortable as possible and to have the best possible customer experience. So Toyota has been investing heavily in making sure that their dealer body provides not only what we call "Latino ready," but "Latino friendly" environments. The goal is that the Spanish-preferred or Spanish-dominant customer is comfortable and at ease, and usually this means being able to do their entire transaction, from the sales presentation and financing, to service, parts and accessories, in Spanish. This is a much more holistic, integrated marketing approach than simply making an ad.

Wright

What are the key industries that are most right for Hispanic marketing efforts?

McDonald

Well, any industry that offers a consumer product or service is appropriate for the Hispanic market, but there are definitely some key industries that are under-penetrated and certainly under-marketed. Those industries include the automotive industry, the insurance industry, banking and financial services and investments, real estate, retail, telecommunications, healthcare, food and grocery, beverage, and apparel. These are key industries, and all are under-penetrated and under-marketed from a Hispanic marketing standpoint, and yet the Hispanic consumption is large. And the growth of the category is huge.

McDonald

Do you have any other tips or dos and don'ts for our readers?

McDonald

Yes, I think the key tip that I would give anybody embarking upon developing a Hispanic marketing initiative would be three-fold: Number one is *learn your market and learn your customer.* A Cinco de Mayo promotion is not necessarily going to work well in Miami because Miami's Hispanic market composition is mostly Cuban. And Cinco de Mayo is a Mexican holiday. You're going to want to make sure that you understand who your target consumer is and what's important to them and don't misfire. So do your homework and research and learn. Number two, *prepare your operational infrastructure,* whether that means training your staff, hiring more bilingual people, setting systems and procedures in place to handle Spanish-speaking customers and training staff who are not bilingual to be Latino-ready and Latino-friendly. And number three, *pay attention to this now.* Build your business plans to include the Hispanic market as a target segment. This is the biggest thing to happen to marketing since the Internet. And like the Internet, this is not a fad, it's here to stay and it's going to be an increasingly important part of your business growth. Nobody would dream of creating a comprehensive, integrated marketing plan these days without a comprehensive online component. I predict that no one will be developing a comprehensive, integrated marketing plan in the next five to ten years that doesn't have a Hispanic component. So don't look at this as an afterthought. You're going to need to learn about this market segment now or you're going to need to learn about it later, but you will need to learn about it because this is a permanent paradigm shift. Businesses and organizations that truly want to serve their customers and their communities need to understand who their customers are and how their communities are changing, how the shifting demographics around them are changing their market composition.

Wright

Well, I have to say, Kelly, you're not what most people would expect when they think of an expert in Hispanic marketing. You're a blonde haired, blue-eyed Irish gal.

McDonald

Yes, it's true!

Wright

So how did you become an expert in this field?

McDonald

Well, I grew up in Milwaukee, Wisconsin, and was never exposed to Hispanic culture at all. Then I moved to Albuquerque in my early 20's. It was like that scene in *The Wizard of Oz* when Dorothy opens the door and the whole movie goes from black and white to color. Suddenly, my world was filled with color. I started to learn about the Hispanic culture, started collecting Latin American art. I started studying the language more intensely, and I just immersed myself in everything I could that was Latin. I'm just drawn to it. I can't really explain it. It's like, why is someone drawn to jazz? Because it just touches something in you. Then several years ago, after more than a decade in the general market ad agency business working with top global ad agencies, I had the opportunity to become Director of Client Services at one of the top Hispanic ad agencies in the country. It was there that I really was able to wrap my professional life around my personal passion. And you know ...I just fell in love with the culture and the business.

Wright

By 2020, one in five U.S. residents will be Hispanic. Wouldn't it be a smart move for people to learn Spanish?

McDonald

Oh, I encourage everybody to learn languages. I'll quote from Mattel, the makers of Barbie, who have a Barbie doll called "Spanish Teacher Barbie." And on the side of the box, it says, "I like speaking Spanish, because speaking Spanish allows me to make twice as many friends." I think there isn't anybody among us who wouldn't think that being bilingual or poly-lingual is a good thing. In Europe, most people speak multiple languages and that's just part of the culture there. So I think that we would all agree that having language skills is a positive thing. It opens the mind to new cultures and attitudes. And there is no question that the second primary language in the U.S. is already Spanish and will continue to be so. So if you choose to learn Spanish, you will have an opportunity to practice it every day.

Wright

That's great. What an interesting conversation.

McDonald

Well, thank you.

Wright

It sounds like your business and your passion are in alignment.

McDonald

Yes, they are. I'm very fortunate because I get to do what I love.

Wright

I really appreciate you spending this much time with me today, and I wish you the very best in your business.

McDonald

Thank you.

Wright

Today we've been talking to Kelly McDonald. She is a marketing and advertising expert with 20 years of ad agency experience. And as we have found out today, she knows a lot about marketing. Thank you so much, Kelly.

McDonald

Thank you, David.

About The Author

Kelly McDonald is a marketing and advertising expert with 20 years of ad agency experience, on both the General Market and Latino sides of the business. She worked in top positions for several global ad agencies, including Young & Rubicam, TBWA Chiat/Day and Temerlin McClain before making the move to Latino advertising and marketing.

Working with clients such as Toyota, Nissan, Subaru, BlueCross BlueShield, Kimberly-Clark, Bank One, Alltel and Budweiser, Kelly has helped clients grow business by targeting U.S. Latinos strategically and creatively.

Kelly was drawn to the Hispanic culture twenty years ago when she left her home town of Milwaukee and moved to Albuquerque, New Mexico. She began studying the culture and collecting Latin American artwork.

But it wasn't until Kelly worked for one of the country's top Latino ad agencies, that she immersed herself in the Latino culture. Her love for the Latino culture extends beyond business: Kelly has taught English as a Second Language to Latinos for years as a volunteer. Additionally, Kelly and her husband travel extensively throughout Mexico, and her mom has lived in Mexico for fifteen years.

Kelly's dream is to educate American businesses and organizations about the potential of cultivating Latino consumers and share marketing insights to reach Latinos emotionally, rationally and with cultural relevance.

Kelly McDonald

McDonald Marketing

2700 Thomas Avenue

Dallas, Texas 75204

Phone: 214-880-1717

Fax: 214-880-7596

Email: kmcdonald@mcdonaldmarketing.com

Website: www.mcdonaldmarketing.com

Chapter 14

BRIAN TRACY

THE INTERVIEW

David E. Wright (Wright)

Today we are talking to Brian Tracy. Brian is one of America's leading authorities on the development of human potential and personal effectiveness. He is a dynamic and entertaining speaker with a wonderful ability to inform and inspire audiences towards peak performance in higher levels of achievement. He addresses more than four hundred thousand men and women each on the subject of personal and professional development including the Executives and staff of IBM, Arthur Anderson, McDonnell Douglas, and The Million Dollar Round Table. His exciting talks in seminars on leadership, sales management, and personal effectiveness bring about immediate changes and long-term results. Brian has a bachelors in communication with a master's degree, and is a chairman of Brian Tracy International, a human resource company based in San Diego, California, with affiliates throughout America and in 31 countries worldwide. Brian Tracy, thank you for being with us today on *Conversations on Customer Service and Sales.*

Brian Tracy (Tracy)

It's a pleasure, David. Thank you.

Wright

Brian, trainers have changed sales format several times down through the years. It seems that recently relationship selling is recommended as the most successful format. Do these changes represent advances in techniques?

Tracy

Well, selling has really never changed. They've done fifty-five thousand interviews with customers to find out the process that they go through to buy, and there's a specific process that the customer goes through that the salesperson must dovetail their presentation and their interaction with. First of all, the customer has to like the person and trust the person they are talking to. So on that basis, relationships are very important. If I don't like you, I won't buy what you're selling, no matter how good the price is. So therefore, you have to have some kind of a relationship because the most important word in selling, I believe, is the word "credibility," which means that your claim is believable. And since human beings are primarily emotional, if I like you, I believe you more. If I dislike you or I'm neutral toward you, I'm far more skeptical or suspicious of what you say. So relationships are essential. Just the same as dating or going out with another person, the person has to like you a little bit in order to go out with you on a date. With regard to selling, the process is always the same.

First of all, the customer decides that you're a likeable and trustworthy person. Then the customer is open to talking to you. The customers only enters the sale when they realize that they have a need, and up until the time that you ask them the right questions and uncover the problems, and suggest perhaps that they could be better off in a cost effective way, customers are usually not interested, or at least detached, distanced, skeptical, unsure, uncertain, and so on. It's only when you touch on a need that the customer has, and the customer realizes, "Aah, I have that need. I didn't realize it before." Only then do they become interested because needs are what trigger interest. In nature it would actually trigger emotions, and only then do they become interested in finding out how that need can be satisfied in a cost effect way. It's something that really never changes. It starts off with the relationship. It goes to the identification of the correct need. It goes to the presentation of your product or service as a solution to that need, and then answers the question and closes the sale.

Wright

Yeah, that sounds a lot like when I first started several years ago, the sales process was divided into three parts, or at least the training that I had. The formation gathering phase, the presentation phase, and the close. Does that format still work?

Tracy

Yeah, we sometimes say that today you have to be a doctor of selling. A doctor does three phases. First of all, they do a thorough examination. Second of all, they do a diagnosis based on the examination. And third, they offer a prescription and encourage you to take it. In our live sales seminars, where we have thousands of people, we say the three keys are to prospect, which is to find people who can buy and can benefit from what you are selling; to present and show them that what you are selling makes sense to them in a cost effective way; and then it's to follow up and close, which is to get them to take action. So it never changes. It's still the same three in order.

Wright

I've noticed that down through the years in my selling, the close has—I don't define it as I used to. Close was something where I ask for the order, and there was a closing presentation, and all like that. I find that now people buy from me without really having to close.

Tracy

The reason for that is the more thoroughly you diagnose a person's needs, and the more clearly you explain that your product or service is the best thing for him or her all things considered, the easier it is for them to buy and the amount of effort in the close is very small. If the presentation has been poor, or if the qualification process has been poor, this may not be the right client. They may not have the right money. They may not have the right need, and so on. Well, then the closing is very difficult. An old style selling focused all the emphasis on closing, but the new style or the new model of selling is focused on building trust, identifying needs accurately, presenting your product or service specifically to satisfy the needs that have been identified, and then just asking the customer to go ahead.

Wright

What do you think has been the most significant change or addition to the sales process in recent years?

Tracy

Well, one of the things we have to realize in a market society, in which we live, the customer determines everything that we do or don't do. And the biggest change is customers have become more knowledgeable, more sophisticated, more aware, and simultaneously there have been more products and services developed to satisfy them. So sales people have to be more knowledgeable, more thoughtful, and better prepared. They have to know their product or service inside and out. They have to know the alternatives that are available to them. And especially, they have to take time to find out more about the customer before they attempt to advise the customer to buy what they are selling.

Wright

I remember back in the '80s, I used to attend all kinds of sales seminars, and I kept hearing speakers and seminar leaders, workshop leaders say the same thing, that product knowledge was only about 10% of the sales process. And I kept asking myself, "Yes, but which 10." Don't you have to know it all to use the 10 that's necessary to close?

Tracy

Absolutely.

Wright

Why do two sales people with the same education, using the same sales process, selling the same product differ in their level of success?

Tracy

Well, first of all no two people are ever the same. My experience with working with more than five hundred thousand sales people is that the most successful salespeople start a little earlier. They work a little harder. They stay a little later. They invest far more time in learning and preparation. In a recent study, they found that the highest paid sales people spend vastly more time in personal professional development listening to tapes, reading books. My conclusion is that if you are in sales and you drive around listening to the radio, basically you have no future. If you drive around listening to music, you have no future because all the highest paid sales people drive around listening to educational audio programs. That's what gives them the edge. It's almost like they are in constant mental training between calls. Poor sales people start at the last possible moment. The average sales person in America starts, really starts work about 11:00 and begins to wind down about 3:30. The average sales person makes about two calls a day. The average sales person takes long coffee breaks and lunches, leaves early. You know one of the jokes that I say is if you get onto the freeway at 3:30, you find that it is jammed. How can it be jammed? All these people don't get off work until 5:00. Well, one of the reasons it's jammed is all the sales people are on the way home to watch television because they think that after 3:30 nobody wants to talk to them, and before 11:00 people are too busy. So basically, they work far less. Take a complete idiot in selling, who is really ambitious and determined, starts early and works harder, stays later, continually learns to upgrade his skills, sees more people, and so on, they are going to run circles around the genius who starts late, quits early, and only sees a couple of people a day.

Wright

I had several sales mentors when I was younger and they all must have read the same books. Each one of them told me that in a sales situation, the first person to speak loses. Of course, I didn't believe it then and don't believe it now. But how can that be?

Tracy

Well, it's simply not true. I think there may be a misunderstanding, imagine going and sitting in front of a customer and saying nothing. Well, you'd soon be back on the streets because what you've done is you have made every effort to get through to get an appointment, to get face to face with this prospect. Finally, you meet with them and speak with them, and now, basically, you're on stage. Now, sometimes they say that when you ask the closing question, the first person to speak loses.

Wright

Right.

Tracy

And that's probably true. If you ask them, "Do you like what I've shown you so far?" Then just be quiet until you get an answer. "Would you like to go ahead with this?" Just be quiet until you get an answer. There's a saying in professional speaking called, "stepping on your lines." This means you may tell a funny story and people start to laugh and you immediately start on again. So you step on the line and you trip people up. They don't get a chance to laugh.

Wright

Right.

Tracy

So one of the best things you can do is to just ask the question and then wait patiently for an answer even if there is a lot of silence. We say the only pressure you're allowed to use as a professional sales person is the pressure of the silence after you have asked a closing or confirming question.

Wright

I definitely posed the wrong question to you, because actually it was in a closing situation once you give the presentation. However, what bothered me was that the customer loses. I've always thought the customer wins when he buys something if I have discovered his needs.

Tracy

It's poorly phrased. What it means is that if you start talking again, the customer stops thinking about buying and gets distracted.

Wright

Right.

Tracy

So that's why it's so important. Oh by the way, in life it's a very good policy when you ask a question to just wait patiently for the answer. Don't rush in and trip over the line and start talking again before the person has had a chance to respond.

Wright

I've noticed that people, when I ask them questions you know down through the years, of course I've stepped on enough lines in my life, but I've noticed that some people answer very quickly. Others take a long time before they answer. And to consider that silence anything other than thinking about it is kind of dangerous, isn't it?

Tracy

Yes.

Wright

With the entry of internet sales, how is it possible for a customer to assess his needs without a trained sales person discovering needs through examination?

Tracy

Well, I have my own internet business. I do more than a million dollars a year on the internet. It's taken several years to develop it. So I know a little bit about internet business and sales. Here's the basic rule. The internet only works to sell a product that the prospect has already determined he or she is going to buy. In other words, it is not a place where you assess a person's needs unless you are doing something as sophisticated as purchasing a computer from Dell, and even then people who buy a Dell computer using the internet are people who are very knowledgeable about exactly what they want. They are not people who are there to have their needs assessed and to be analyzed and figured out. So the only companies that are successful on the internet are companies that are selling specific fixed products that people have gone there to buy. Amazon is the perfect example. Nobody buys a book from Amazon because Amazon sold it to them. They go to Amazon to buy a book because it's convenient, but they already know the book their going to buy. So, the role of the internet is basically to sell a product where all of the discretion has been taken out of it. It's a specific product at a specific price with specific specifications, and it has to be unconditionally guaranteed. to sell over the internet. So sales people really have little or no role in sales.

Wright

Yeah, I know. I keep forgetting one of the titles of one of your books. I have recommended it to over a thousand people. You wrote it a couple of years ago. It's the one about getting a job and making more money.

Tracy

Yes.

Wright

It's a hardback. It's only about 90 something pages, maybe a hundred pages long, but I'll tell you what, it's probably the most powerful, practical book I have ever read on the subject.

Tracy

Well, thank you.

Wright

So I tell them to go to your website and buy the book that says something about make more money and find a job.

Tracy

Actually, it is Get Paid More And Promoted Faster.

Wright

That's it! That's it! What a great book that was.

Tracy

Well, thank you.

Wright

You know I've read more books and heard more cassettes and CDs and attended more workshops and seminars on customer service than any other single topic. Yet, customer service seems to be at an all-time low. Am I over sensitive, or do we have a problem with customer service in this country?

Tracy

Well, the challenge there, you have to understand that it's very much like saying you know some people are polite and some people are rude. So it differs from person to person. And even within the same restaurant, it differs from person to person in the same business. So, it's very much a personal thing. What we have found, by the way, is that people treat their customers the way the manager treats them. So whenever you go into a place that has great customer service, you'll find that the manager is a good manager, and takes really good care of his people. It's a natural, logical expansion from the manager to the people in the company to the customers. Whenever there is poor customer service, it means you have a poor manager. The manager treats the people poorly, so they just take it out on the first people that they meet. So all over America, and in every single business, there are different levels of customer service. Some are fantastic, some are medium, some are poor, but what we know is that customers today are so demanding that if you do not treat them really well, they will go away and never come back. They will just continue gravitating like moths to a flame. They will continue gravitating toward the companies that treat them the best. That's why the companies that have the best service are the ones that are growing most rapidly.

Wright

I know that you've trained so many people in the last few years because I've watched your career just soar. I'm a real fan, and a lot of my friends have everything taped on TPN that you ever did. So I skipped a question I really wanted to ask you because I'm interested in your feelings about it. The question is, you know, perhaps sales as a vocation is more appealing than it has been in the past; however, it seems that a salesperson does not enjoy the respect and the admiration that a "professional" does. Why do you think that is?

Tracy

Well, there's two answers to that. Earl Nettier once said that there is no such thing as a good job. There are only good people doing that job. So every single job, the person who does it brings honor to the job. Let me give you a quick aside. I was at a California Pizza Kitchen not far from us. One of the people who works there as a porter and a busboy table care is a Mexican immigrant whose name is Manuel Salverago. This guy is hard working. He's got a problem with his back and his leg, so he walks with a limp. He's hard working. He's fast. He is pleasant. He is polite. He recognizes people. He's not even a waiter. He's just a busboy. He's just in motion all the time. You go there and you sit there, and I look for this, you say, "Geez, this is an incredible guy. Look at the way he does that. Look at the way he moves." And he comes up and we talk, and I always say hello to him. And he says hello, he recognizes me. And I said to the manager, "You know that's a remarkable guy there." He says, "Oh, huh, Manuel, he's the most dynamic person in this whole company." He is so respected. He's admired by everybody. He's well paid. Everybody likes him. Why? It's because he brings honor to his work. Now, let's come to sales. In sales, I've learned a very interesting paradox. In sales, it's easy to get in. Anybody can get a sales job. But that is where easy stops. Many people think because it's easy to get in, it's easy to rise. So they get a job, and maybe they have an interview a couple of times, but then they wonder why they are just not rising up like getting into an elevator and pushing a button. After you get the sales job, from then on everything is hard, harder, and harder still. Nothing is easy.

So therefore, everybody who starts off in sales, because it's easy to get in, starts off like a marathon runner way back in the pack, and then the work begins. And you have to work a long time. You know, in order to move to the top of the field, it takes five to seven years to be a master of your craft. Now this is the most remarkable thing, and it's shocking to people. Let's say if you want to be a tennis player, if you want to be a salesperson, if you want to be a lawyer, after you have learned the basic skills, it then takes five to seven years of hard work, continually upgrading your skills, continually practicing to master your craft to get into the top 10%. Now here's a couple of points. If you dedicate yourself to becoming excellent in selling, there's nothing that will stop you from eventually getting into the top 10%. In the top 10% of your field, I don't care what your business is, you're going to be one of the highest paid people in this country. You're going to be respected and esteemed by people around you. You're going to be a major force in your community. You're going to be looked up to and admired. You're going to be taking company sponsored trips. You're going to have a beautiful home and life for your family. But it's going to take you five to seven years of hard work to get there. Now here's the second point. The time's going to pass anyway. It's very important to understand the time is going to pass anyway. Five to seven years from now, five to seven years will have passed. The biggest mistake that people make, and the biggest regret they have, is why didn't I start earlier? Why didn't I start five to seven years ago and just put my head down because the time is going to pass anyway. The only difference is five to seven years from now, are you going to be at the top of your field enjoying a fabulous living, be one of the most respected people in your business, have a beautiful home and a car and a wonderful income, or are you going to be back in the pack struggling away with the 80 to 90% of the majority. But the time is going to pass anyway.

So therefore, it's easy to get into selling, but after that it's like easy to get into a huge marathon. You may have to qualify a little bit, some you don't even have to qualify. You just have to pay the entry fee. But then the race begins, and then it's a long race. That is really hard. It's not easy after that. It's only easy to get into the race, then you have to work. That's why some people make selling an honorable field, and they are the most respected people in their business. And some people just struggle away, and they've got holes in their shoes. They never read, and they never listen to audio programs. They never go to sales seminars. They come in late and they leave early, and they blame all their problems on the company or the competition, and they don't understand why they don't move ahead. But it's purely self-inflicted wounds.

Wright

I've heard a lot about personality profiles in the past few years. There are a lot of companies that have a lot on the market. Do you think one can predict with any accuracy a good person with a sales profile that will be more likely to be successful?

Tracy

Absolutely! We use sales profiles extensively, and we use them with major corporations. I did some work with a Fortune 500 Company recently. I brought in one of my experts who did a personality profile on their entire sales force. They had about eight teams working nationwide. With just the profiles, and there are three profiles, and the first profile is does this person have the personality of a salesperson? The second profile is can this person sell? Do they have the requisite skills? The third skill is will this person sell? Do they have the internal drive? And the third one is the value test. It's very important because there are people who have a great personality, but you put them into a sales situation, they collapse. So they did all three tests. They broke them and categorized them into teams. And then he explained to the senior executives, this is your top team. This is your middle team. This is your bottom team. This is what they do. This is what they say. These are their complaints. These are their successes. And they went back and forth and explained. He never even met these people. He just had them do the test, and they were absolutely astonished. He had absolutely picked out the top performers in every team, the top team in every area; their strengths, weaknesses, what they do, and he said this is your major problem within your sales force nationally. He explained that this is they're very strong on prospecting and getting the first appointment. They are very weak on closing. They are poor at their customer development. It goes on and on, and they were just shaking their heads because all of that stuff they had learned from years of experience. So yes, personality profiles are very, very important. We will never hire a person without doing a basic personality profile on them to find out if they have the personality that we require.

Wright

You know many people, and I would probably fall into this category, look for people as role models and search for successful people to become mentors as they travel the path of becoming better or a more successful salesperson. Is that thinking still useful? If so, who are some of the people that have shaped your business success?

Tracy

Well, I worked with Dr. Albert Schweitzer in Africa many years ago. Schweitzer is famous for having said, "You must teach men at the school of example for they will learn at no other." So role models are critically important for us because we need to see how it is done properly, which is true in every sport. It's true in music. It's true in everything. So what happens with human beings is we gravitate towards what we most admire. If we admire a person, then what we do is we gravitate toward emulating the behaviors of that person. If we admire men and women of courage and integrity, then what we do is we try to exemplify courage and integrity in our own lives. So role models are very important. Mentors are important as well as long as they are role models. A mentor who gives advice, who is also admired by the person receiving the advice, is going to have a major impact on that person's personality. Then the final question with regard to me is I have been positively influenced by hundreds, maybe thousands, of people over the years. You can have a mentor or role model who died two thousand years ago, or whose books you've read, or whose audio programs you've listened too. So you don't have to have direct one-on-one contact with them. Someone can write a fabulous article or a beautiful poem, and you can admire that and respect it and agree with the sentiments in that person. Then that person's views will have an effect on your personality.

Wright

When I first got into sales when I was a young fellow, I used to just take it so seriously, and you know I was probably a drag even to myself. Then I got enrolled, I mean there were records, there weren't any cassettes out yet, of a fellow named Bill Gove in Florida who used to work for 3M.

Tracy

Yeah, I know him very well. He was one of my very dear friends.

Wright

I found out that you can have a great sense of humor and still be a successful salesperson. It's not all that serious. He probably never knew that he was one of my role models, but he certainly was.

Tracy

That's great! He's a great man. He died recently, but Bill Gove was a great man.

Wright

I hated to see him passing. His passing is going to have a great impact especially on the National Association of Speakers.

Tracy

Yes.

Wright

He was really, really admired by and respected widely by that group.

Tracy

Yes.

Wright

Finally, what word of encouragement do you have for anyone in our reading audience that might help them become more successful as they follow their career path of sales and service?

Tracy

Well, the biggest weakness we have in America is what is called the "quick fix" mentality. Everybody wants things fast and easy, and you have to get over that if you want to be successful and happy in your field. You have to realize that success takes a long time, and that you are in a race. So you are going to have to work harder than other people who want to be successful as well. You have to invest more in yourself, in learning and growing. You have to manage your time better. Above all, you have to see more people.

The great rule for success is to spend more time with better prospects, to spend more time with better prospects. The more people you see, the better you get, and the better you get, the more effective you are. The more effective you are, the more sales you make. The more sales you make the more motivated you are to see even more people. So it's what is called a positive feedback loop in psychology. If you constantly upgrade your skills and learn new things, and then try those new things with your prospects and customers, you get feedback, and you get results which motivate you to do even more of it. I'm pretty sure you'll put yourself onto an upward spiral. You must realize that everybody who is at the top today started at the bottom. Everyone who is doing well was once doing poorly. Everybody who is at the top of your field was at one time not in your field at all. What others have done, you can do as well. What others have done, you can do as well if you just learn how and just practice it until you master it.

Wright

What are you working on right now? Are you working on a book? I do want to run people to your website. It's www.briantracy.com. A lot of my friends call me and they say, "I tried to find that Brian Tracy fellow and he doesn't have a website." I say, "Well, you're misspelling it then." But anyway I would like to suggest that people go to your website for products on several different topics that I have enjoyed down through the years. But what are you working on now?

Tracy

Well, I'm just finishing up a new book. It's called *Million Dollar Habits*, and it will be out in December. I just released my latest book which is called, *Change Your Thinking: Change Your Life*, and it's shipping to the bookstores as we speak. I just signed a new contract for a book called *How to Master Your Time* which will be out in march and it's going to be the best book on time management ever written. I am just getting a new contract in the mail for a book that will be out next year called *Getting Rich In America*, which is going to be a powerful book on all the different ways people go from rags to riches.

Wright

The habits book that's coming out, what is it about? Is it a how-to book?

Tracy

Oh yes, it's very practical. It shows 95% of everything that you do in life is governed by your habits, and that successful people have success habits. The habits range from the way they think about themselves to their attitudes toward their goals, setting goals each day, to their attitude toward money, toward work, toward family, relationships, health, business growth, savings and investments, and so on. It's a series of habits that people have that when you practice these habits, which you learn by repetition, you achieve more and more, faster and faster, easier and easier.

The difference in life is that some people have these success habits because they've been taught them or they've developed them, and some people have not yet learned them. The wonderful thing is that they are all learnable. So you can learn to get up a little earlier. You can learn to set priorities on your work. You can learn to write and rewrite your goals. You can learn to save and invest part of what you earn. You can learn to continually upgrade your skills. You can learn to listen better with other people. You can learn the key habits of health, and so on. What I do is I teach this. These are all the habits that are practiced by the happiest, most successful, and best paid people in our society including all self-made millionaires.

Once you develop these habits, there's a rule that everything is hard before it's easy. So developing a habit is hard, but once you develop the habit, it's easy because it's automatic. You just do it. You breathe in, you breathe out. You just follow the habit. This method becomes easy and automatic for you to do what the successful do. You'll make more progress in a week or two or in a year or two than some people make in a lifetime.

Wright

I really appreciate the time you've spent with me. Thank you so much.

About The Author

One of the world's top success motivational speakers, Brian Tracy is the author of may books and audio tape seminars, including *The Psychology of Achievement, The Luck Factor, Breaking the Success Barrier, Thinking Big* and *Success Is a Journey.*

Brian Tracy

www.BrianTracy.com

Chapter 15

JILL LUBLIN

THE INTERVIEW

David E. Wright (Wright)

Today we are talking with Jill Lublin, author of the bestselling books *Guerrilla Publicity* and *Networking Magic*. Jill is a renowned national speaker on the topics of publicity, networking, and marketing. As a strategist and marketing expert, she is the CEO of the consulting firm Promising Promotion, Jill has created successful strategies and techniques that implement bottom line results. Jill is the founder of Good News Media, Inc., a company specializing in positive news. She's also host of the nationally syndicated radio show *Do the Dream* and has created a TV pilot *The Good News*. Jill, welcome to *Marketing Magic*!

Jill Lublin (Lublin)

Thank you, David.

Wright

Jill, what's the difference between public relations and marketing? And more specifically, what is Guerrilla publicity and Guerrilla marketing?

Lublin

If you look at marketing as an overall concept, it's like the tree. There are two branches of the tree: advertising and publicity. So as far as publicity goes it's all about how can you create visibility and credibility without spending a fortune like you would do in advertising. And in Guerrilla, we're all about doing that without spending a lot of money, using instead time and imagination. Those are your two commodities. You use time and imagination. That's Guerrilla. It's getting very creative. It's doing things that stand out. It's standing on street corners with signs like a friend of mine did when she wanted to get a book published. She stood on a busy street corner and said, "Author seeks publisher." That's Guerrilla publicity.

Wright

Your new book is entitled *Networking Magic*. How does networking fit into a successful PR or marketing campaign?

Lublin

Well, the reality is that publicity is all about being visible and networking is about being connected. The more connected and visible you are, your business becomes known and you name becomes known. Who you are is more known; let's put it that way. And certainly networking in these days is one of the keys to success. How do you create more name recognition? If you show up in places, if you belong to organizations, if people know who you are, well, certainly, your publicity is also going to be good. And I think one of the keys to success these days is going back to what I call belly to belly marketing, meaning we've got to see each other again.

Wright

You talk a lot about creating the "Oooh, aah factor" and the "I've heard of you somewhere" syndrome. How can the average person create that kind of buzz about themselves or about their products and services?

Lublin

When you look at the oooh, aah factor, it's what is it about you that makes other people go oooh, and aah? And I think people get too caught up in what it is they're selling or what their products are, and it's actually not about that. What it's about is what is it that you do that serves people, what are you an expert in, and particularly when it comes to media. What they care about is what are you an expert in. Media works that way. That's really key. When you're in a networking event, when you're out and about, the reality is I don't think people really care what you are selling; they want to know how you're going to serve them.

Wright

Let me ask you, Jill, for someone who has spoken and talked to media all over the country for a long time, what is some of the dos and the don'ts to keep in mind?

Lublin

The first thing that media hates is that they hate a story that's too self serving, which actually ties into some of the other things we've spoken about earlier. They also hate press kits that weigh more than the book. In other words, having your press kit is about having a well-written and quick press release. What they love is for you to understand who they are and what they are talking about. For instance, if you're on Oprah it's a very different experience than if you are on the morning news. If you're on the radio show in the morning with the morning guys, it's a different experience than if you're on a talk show in the morning on television. So you have to know the medium that you're on and it's best to know the show and the focus of the show so that you can talk, specifically to how they dance. And you have to know that the media is like a dance. You have to understand the rhythm of which media you're dealing with. So it's really helpful to watch the show and listen to it before you're on it if you have a chance.

Wright

So how do you give a pitch? I think you suggest 30 seconds or less?

Lublin

I do think 30 seconds or less is really key, and the problem with most people is they talk too much, meaning they explain too much of what they are offering. The media is not really known for their patience. And what you've got to be able to do is get to the point really in a laser like way because what you have to know is that every time you talk to a media person it's like an audition. They need to understand are you articulate enough? Can you get to the point fast enough? Do you have a way of being able to say what it is you need to say in a way that their public can understand it? Or as one ABC producer out of San Francisco said to me, "Jill, all I care about is what stops my viewers from changing the channel." Right? So sometimes it's about that. You've got to give them what they need for their readers, viewers, and listeners.

Wright

So is that using sound bytes?

Lublin

Using sound bytes is really good. I like to say, "speak in headlines" because if you'll look at what people read in newspapers, it's the headlines. They often don't even read the whole article. You've got to really learn to capture people's attention speaking in headlines, which can translate also to a sound byte. What is it that's memorable? How can you say something that will stick in peoples' memory so that when it comes to buying something that you sell, they'll think of you?

Wright

So in today's marketplace, it's sometimes hard to separate yourself from the competition. How can someone get past that?

Lublin

Well, the reality is, yes, it's hard to separate yourself from the competition, but the point is focus on what it is that makes you distinct and unique. When it comes to media, I like to say use everything you've got and people often don't even use the obvious. Like if you're a woman, go after women's magazines. If you're African American, go after that press. If you're Hispanic, use the Hispanic press. You can use the ethnic press, the religious press. If you're Christians, use the Christian press. If you are Jewish, use the Jewish press. There are other opportunities that people are really missing that are obvious including your alumni magazines and associations you're a member of, for instance, all have newsletters, and they are so hungry for content. That's great publicity.

Wright

One of the magic formulas to successful publicity and marketing is follow up. What should people keep in mind when following up whether it is with the media, a potential customer, or someone they met at a networking event?

Lublin

Well, in Guerrilla publicity we talk about the rule of seven, and that works well with the media and it's also good with your customers. And that is that you've got to figure on following up about seven times. With the media, we tell you to vary your method of follow up. The first time you may send a press release via e-mail. The second time you may telephone them. The third time maybe you'll send a fax. Then you'll get back on the phone. Then you'll send them e-mail again. Vary the method of communication because media, like your potential customers, likes different kinds of communications. But I've also found in consulting with clients over the years that a lot of times they just don't call you back till the third or fourth time. It's not necessarily a personal thing, it's that people are busy. I find that if you're intentional and serious about your business and people understand that you are that way, meaning they know that you're the kind of person who will follow up, they appreciate that.

Wright

We spoke earlier a bit about networking. What are some of the dos and don'ts of effective networking?

Lublin

Well, certainly networking is all about connecting with people, and I think you know handing out business cards is not necessarily effective networking. And certainly following up from your networking is also key because it is about developing relationships. Sometimes a good relationship can last 30 seconds and sometimes it may last years. Sometimes you'll need a good car mechanic and a person at a networking event will have that for you, and it will be a quick conversation. I like to say, "Be like a butterfly." And I think people sometimes make the mistake that they want to have these deep conversations at networking events. It's actually not the place to get that deep. You want to be able to get wide, and to meet lots of people to make what I call quick connections. And then of course the question is, "How can I help you? What do you need?" And I do think it's important when you go to networking events to be clear about what it is that you need and what your requests are so that you can ask for it. Because I've been to networking events where I'll say to people, "Hey, how can I help you?" and they'll say to me, "I don't know." And I'm thinking, "Well, if you don't know, how can I help you?"

Wright

If you have more of a reserved or shy personality, what advice do you have for these people who want to get out there and network but are hesitant?

Lublin

Well, you know the truth is I think everybody was born a great networker. If you look at children, they negotiate toys; they say, "Oh, I want that. Can I have it?" They make really specific requests. They are really good networkers. And what happens is we decide or somebody tells us that we're not, but I think if we all think back to what we were like as children, that that might help and bring that sense of lighthearted and playfulness into a networking event. And frankly, be yourself. Not everybody is going to be real exuberant, and some people will be more reserved and shy, and that's okay. But I do think it's important to not stand in a corner. Find a nice face that seems open and go talk to that person. Put yourself in a group of people where you can listen for a moment until you're more comfortable. But the important point is don't stand alone and certainly, don't hover in the corner.

Wright

Right. For someone with a small publicity or marketing budget, what advice do you have for these people who want to get their word out, but funds are an issue?

Lublin

Well, certainly I wouldn't recommend that they spend a fortune on publicity depending on what it is they're publicizing, but I think there are certain key things you can do to start making a difference right away. For instance, in every local business journal across the country and in every daily newspaper, there's a section called *The People Section*. This is people in the community who are making announcements. So that is a great place to get free publicity and that costs absolutely nothing. I like to encourage people to use what I call the announcement strategy meaning you make some kind of announcement every 30 to 60 days, and that creates the "I've heard of you somewhere" syndrome, which is a way to keep your name visible without spending a lot of money. You want to encourage reporters to write a story about you. You've got to find what you're an expert in, and the most important question is what problem do you solve? That's what you pitch media is about the problem you solve. And that will guarantee you free publicity where you won't have to spend a fortune.

Wright

Well, what a fascinating conversation. I learned a lot about marketing.

Lublin

Well, thank you, David. That's a good thing because you're very smart about marketing.

Wright

Today we have been talking with Jill Lublin. She is the author of the bestselling books *Guerrilla Publicity* and *Networking Magic*. And having known her for many, many years and knowing a lot of people who use her services, she is consistent and walks her talk. She knows how to market, and I hope our readers can tell that. And I'm sure they will. Thank you so much, Jill, for being with us on *Marketing Magic*.

Lublin

You're welcome. It's been a pleasure to be with you.

About The Author

Jill Lublin, author of the best selling books, Guerrilla Publicity and Networking Magic, is a renowned national speaker on the topics of publicity, networking, and marketing. As the CEO of the strategic consulting firm, Promising Promotion, Jill has created successful marketing strategies and techniques that implement bottom line results. Jill is also founder of GoodNews Media, a company specializing in positive news. She hosts the nationally syndicated radio show, DO the Dream and TV pilot, The Good News.

Jill Lublin

CEO, Promising Promotion

Phone: 415.883.5455

Email: info@promisingpromotion.com

Chapter 16

KEN BANKS, BS, MBA

THE INTERVIEW

David E. Wright (Wright)

Today we are talking to Ken Banks. With over 30 years corporate experience in retail marketing and branding, Ken established KAB Marketing in 2000. His career includes senior market positions with companies such as Proctor & Gamble (Folgers), Dayton- Hudson now Target Corporation, Robinson's Department Stores, Doner Advertising, Eckerd Drugs, Circuit City, Fahlgren Advertising, and PetsMart Stores. Specializing in retail marketing, Ken has been recognized as an authority on retail branding. He has written several articles for many trade publications and has addressed several national and international retail and marketing conferences. A graduate of Wayne State University and the American Graduate School for International Management (Thunderbird), Ken has won many creative awards for his companies and was voted into the Retail Advertising Hall of Fame. Thanks a lot for being with us today, Ken.

Ken Banks (Banks)

It's a pleasure to be with you, David.

Wright

We hear a lot about the importance of branding, but in today's competitive retail market places, isn't price really the deciding factor on where a customer shops?

Banks

Well, there's no doubt that price is certainly a factor, and if you ask 100 customers out there what's the most important factor in choosing a place to shop, price would always come up first. But, I always say that price only gets you on the playing field. You see after you establish what your price perception is...that's when the customer really makes a choice. I think of a painting that I have in my office. It's a picture of a battlefield with the red coats on one side and the white coats on the other with their muskets drawn. Then on each one of them there's a different sign. One says "incredible deals," another says "final markdowns," another shouts "lowest prices," still another "rock bottom prices," and every other sale headline you have ever seen in the Sunday paper. I use that picture as an analogy for today's main streets in cities across the country or the shopping malls with hundreds of stores all battling over who has the best sale prices on any given day. The customer is being sold to death with price promotions. The reality is that the customer really doesn't make the choice solely based on price. It's really based on much more than that; it's based on the relationship they have with one of those stores. You certainly can't get a customer into your store if you have a terrible brand perception. But you definitely cannot keep them loyal solely with a low price perception because tomorrow somebody can knock off your price just as easily as you could have knocked them off the next day and so forth.

What it really takes is a combination of both the price and all the other branding attributes. A good example of that, of course, is Wal-Mart. It's the largest company in the world now, or at least the largest retailer in the world, and they just continue to grow profitably. If you ask anybody around the country: What is Wal-Mart's main theme," they'll always say, "Well, it's always low prices, always." And that's absolutely true and it's been their promise for years! However, if you talk to the people who have built Wal-Mart into the great institution it is today—from Sam Walton all the way up to the key management over the past few years as well as today—you will find out there's a lot more to it than just the prices. It's very interesting to look at the mega-millions Wal-Mart spends in marketing and note the company actually spends a lot less than many other discount stores. The reason for that is because they don't spend as much on sale ads. In fact, Wal-Mart doesn't run *any sale* ads. They run about 12 circulars a year basically saying, "Here's our low prices today on the products you need at this particular time of the year." If it's just before back to school, then it's the most-wanted Back-to-School merchandise. If it's just before the holidays, then it's Holiday merchandise. But beyond that, most of their messages are based on building the relationship and trust that they have with their customers.

Almost every one of the commercials they run features (a) real people, and I mean real people who work in the stores talking about the store and the company, or (b) real customers, not actors, talking about why they shop at the store. In addition, (c) they talk about a lot of other things they do in terms of supporting the community, supporting American manufacturers, supporting the World War II Monument, Children's hospitals, Amber alerts, etc. All these things basically have been established in the mind of the consumer—and I would say more importantly in the *heart* of the consumer—that Wal-Mart is a great place to not only work, but it's certainly a great place to shop. It also reaffirms that in reality it is a pretty good organization to have as your neighbors in town because of all the good things they do. Some research was done not long ago when K-Mart first started having difficulties, and the interesting finding was that many, many customers chose Wal-Mart over K-Mart (which was not surprising based on their sales). However, what was interesting is that many of them had to drive by a K-Mart before they got to the Wal-Mart, so it was more convenient for them to go to K-Mart. And when asked, "Well, why do you do that?" the customers candidly responded, "Because I trust them. They have what I want. They have what they advertise. They don't let me down. I know I can get what I need. I know I'm going to get a good price. And by the way, I'm going to have some people wait on me that really enjoy their job and that's going to make it a pleasant shopping experience. So why should I go to some place (meaning K-mart) that has been consistently disappointing me?" No matter how many celebrities they get to lend their name to their merchandise and advertising it simply not going to work.

Wright

You mentioned convenience as being a critical factor in retailing today, does that mean the retailer should put all their emphasis on building more and more stores so that they're closer to the customer's home, rather than waste money on ads that reach the entire market place?

Banks

Well, convenience really needs to be redefined in today's marketplace. In the old days we'd say convenience means the store was nearby. It could be around the corner. You could get there and get back quickly - certainly that's a factor. But one of the biggest issues in today's world is that as Grey Advertising said a few years ago today's customers are *"caught between a clock and a hard place."* I think if we all think about our own schedules, we could certainly attest to that. We just don't seem to have enough time to do all the things that we want to do, and we certainly don't have time to shop in stores that we don't particularly care to go into and have a disappointing experience. Britt Beemer is a highly respected researcher and one of the Bell Weather monitors of the retail industry (particularly in the home furnishings and electronics and appliances world) wrote a book about the retail marketplace, *Guerilla Marketing.* His company, America's Research Group, did some research looking at how many stores customers shopped for electronics and appliances before they make a purchase. This really points out the importance of convenience in today's retailing.

Back in 1980, they went to an average of three and a half stores per purchase. Or in other words, they went to essentially four stores before they finally made up their minds. By 1995 that was down to just a little bit over two stores. And in 2000 it was a little bit over one store, about 1.3. Estimates today are that it essentially comes down to the fact that they're going to go to one store, and it's the store with whom they really have a relationship and whom they trust. In other words, the one brand that makes the most sense to them with the least potential for disappointment. Well, you might say, what does that have to do with convenience?" It has everything to do with convenience, because the customers say, "I'm going to go to one store where I can get what I want, get it at a good price, and be able to get in and out in a hurry." We've become a nation of *hunters* rather than *gatherers,* meaning that we go into a store, and the faster we can find what we want and get out the better. That's one of the reasons why in almost every city that I go to around the country, we're seeing these big regional malls closing down and in many cases the demolition ball hitting them. They're being replaced with what they call "power malls" or town centers that resemble the old Main Streets of days gone by. And the reason that the customer prefers those types of centers is that they can pull up in front of the store that they want to go to for the product that they want, and get in and out, and continue on with the rest of their life. Compare that to having to walk past 150 other stores that they have no interest in going into, fight a big parking lot to get into one of four doors, and not have a pleasant experience. The customer is really time sensitive.

A good example of a store that understands this is Walgreen's—the most successful drug store chain in America. I think last year Walgreen's opened some 350 more stores on street corners in just about every market in the country. And they didn't build them simply because they decided that they had a lot of real estate or a lot of empty gas stations they could replace. They did it because the customer said, "I don't really even want to have to fight the traffic at that grocery store that are right next door in the strip center. I really want to be able to drive right up to your store. As a matter of fact, if you can make it so I can drive through and just go up to the window and drop off my prescription and pick it up on my way home from work that makes it even better. Walgreen's certainly understood that and responded by building the freestanding stores. Other drug chains have come along and followed suit. But what they did in addition to that, was to be open seven days a week, as well as have some stores be open 24-hours as well. Not so much because they expect to sell a lot of merchandise at two o'clock in the morning, but because what they want to say is "If you need it, we've got it when you want it and you know we're the store for you." The proof is obvious in the bottom line where Walgreen's does twice the sales per store than any other drug chain. But what really makes it all happen? Their former CEO, Dan Jorndt, said a few years ago, "The real reason we're the most convenient is because we can manage our inventories with terrific systems by store so that each store has exactly what the customers who live around that store need and want on a day in and day out basis." Drug stores are based on a needs-driven shopping trip and that comes down to what convenience is all about: "If I can go to the store and get just what I want, then you've made it much more convenient. It's nice to have a good return policy or a rain check policy, but quite frankly, just have what I need, have the brands I need, assure me that I'm getting a good price, and then let me get in and out because I only have about seven minutes to shop your store." (And that's about what the duration of a typical shopping trip is in a drugstore). So at Eckerd we called it—trip assurance; and to provide this you need to do three things. (1) You eliminate the need for comparison-shopping and multiple stops because no one wants to shop. (2) You assure the customers that you have the right product for their needs, and then (3) you assure them that if there is a problem, there's not going to be any hassle satisfying them one way or another. That's what the customer is really looking for today in almost every shopping trip.

Wright

Branding has been around for a long time. Why do you think that there're so few stores that really have effective brand strategies?

Banks

I think the biggest reason more than anything is born out by the fact that if you ask 10 stores to define what branding is, you'll get 10 different answers, because there's a lot of confusion about it. As much as it has been written about, as much as it has been talked about, and as much as it has been touted in the annual reports by CEOs of companies throughout the country, there's not a lot of agreement as to what branding is really all about. I like to go back one step before the branding process and look at a quote from Peter Drucker, who of course is one of the wisest, most respected experts in the business world. Drucker said that "Because the purpose is to create a customer, the business enterprise has two and only two basic functions: *innovation and marketing*. Innovation and marketing produce results. All the rest are costs." I think that defines why branding is so important. If we don't put our money into being innovative and developing stores with what the customer needs today, then constantly look at what they going to need tomorrow and finally find an effective way of communicating the fact in an engaging way, then we don't have much of a chance. So I say that's the key to branding, but when you or I ask a store (or their ad agencies): "What does branding mean to you?" We'll get a lot of different and simplistic answers. I say, "Well, let's first talk about what branding is not." First of all, it's not a new *logo* that you put in your ads or on the store. Second, it's not a catchy new slogan that people will either sing or remember after your name. Third, it's not a new corporate name. We've got a lot of companies that change their name because they think that's going to change what people think of them. It's not the name but what it means to the customer that is important. Fourth, it's not an ad campaign despite what many advertising agencies say when selling themselves as branding experts but in reality just develop a new ad campaign. Believe me, it is much more than that. To be sure a great ad campaign is a critical part of branding, but it is not the brand strategy in and of itself."

And finally it's really not what the *company says* it is at all. It's really what *the customer says it is.* Dr. Leonard Berry at Texas A&M is one of the top retailing academics in the country, and when asked what a brand is, he says, "A brand is not what the company says it is. It's what the customers *think it is.*" He points out that companies with strong brands stand for something that's important to targeted customers, and they've answered the question, "What do we want to be famous for with our customers?" If you think about it, the stores that have gone out of business over the past five or ten years have blamed it on a lot of external factors such as, the economy, a downturn in the industry or terrorist attacks or enumerable other causes. However, if you could probe more deeply and you might ask them, "What were you famous for?" You'd find that most of them weren't famous for anything. They had some stores, opened their doors every day, and they had a lot of stuff in them. So it's a lot more than a mission statement in your company brochures. It really is what the customer feels and believes it is. If you don't have a relationship with your customer, you really don't have a brand, because it is what you stand for and what your customer thinks of you. It is what differentiates you from your competitor, and in the end it is the measure of your success. The strongest brands are those that have a lot of equity in the fact that customers believe in them and have trust in them.

Wright

So having said that, how come some retailers are so successful at branding their stores and others have such a tough go of it?

Banks

I've already mentioned Wal-Mart versus K-Mart, and looking at other major chains it still comes back to the fact that many stores rely primarily on having sales and promotions, while others market themselves in terms of satisfying customer needs. Another example of that is Best Buy and Circuit City. While both are important stores in the consumer electronics and appliances business, about 10 years ago Circuit City was number one in the market and Best Buy was a distant number two. The market shares changed over the past several years and it's just the opposite now. We can attribute it to a lot of things, but basically it was Circuit City's sticking with an attitude that "we have to be the lowest price and to demonstrate this we're going to run a lot of sale ads, and therefore, customers will come to us."

Reality is that the store's price perception was far worse than it's number one competitor. Best Buy, on the other hand, had a positioning strategy that essentially said, "We're going to make shopping easier by giving you a self service store. We're going to have more merchandise in a big box environment so you're going to perceive that, like the warehouse clubs, we have day-in and day-out lower prices. Then we're also going to have people in the stores who are not on commission and who are not driven by selling higher-priced merchandise, and we are going to absolutely make sure that we have a bigger selection so that you can find exactly what you want." They stressed this in just about everything that they did and built it around an effective marketing campaign. The results are right out there. What's interesting is to look at some research completed just the last holiday season that really typifies what happened with sales.

They did a comparison of Best Buy and Circuit City customers, and asked them to rate the stores in 3 areas when answering the question, "Which situation were you most disappointed with in your shopping experience at either Best Buy or Circuit City?" Based on these three factors: one, finding help, the second courtesy, and the third, finding the products they want. Best Buy was perceived as twice as good as Circuit City in terms of satisfying the customer. And the results? You might say, "Well, that may just be the way the customer perceives it, but if you look at both chain's sales over the same period when that the research was in the press, the sales results almost identically reflected the results of the customer surveys. Best Buy's comp sales were nearly twice as good as those at Circuit City.

At the same time, Wal-Mart did about one and a half billion dollars on the day after Thanksgiving. That's almost incomprehensible to an old department store manager-like me. It's amazing that they could do that kind of revenue in one day! What's more fascinating is that it's the result of any big sales circular or event. The same study, which by the way, was done by GfK Custom Research, asked both K-Mart customers and Target customers about finding help and courtesy in the store. They found about 15% of the Target customers were somewhat disappointed in the service they received compared to the 28% of K-Mart's disappointed customers. When rating courtesy, 10%

of Targets customers were disappointed while K-Mart was nearly twice as high at over 18%. I don't have to tell you what happened with the sales.

Of course, Target continues to grow, while, K-Mart has been struggling with bankruptcy and a lot of other performance issues. It really comes down to every day satisfaction for the customers. Alan Weiss, who's a well-known consultant who works with a lot of companies in many industries, has said, "If you're going to succeed in today's tough economy, you got to have three keys to make it. (1) There has to be a market need for your store, meaning you can't just be a store that replicates one that's across the street or at the other end of the mall. You've got to have a unique reason for being. (2) You've got to have the confidence and ability to satisfy that need, and that's so true. There are stores that simply do it well every day, and it starts at the top; but where the ability to satisfy is most critical is at the point of contact for most customers--on the sales floor. (3) Finally, you've got to have a passion for your product or your services. Those retailers that really have a true brand and understand the customers are absolutely passionate about what they do, and they love what they are doing. And the customers, therefore, love shopping there."

Wright

Right. You spend a good portion of your career working for department stores. How come they're having so much trouble growing in sales and traffic?

Banks

It's been interesting watching what's happened to what was once the benchmark of the retail industry. I spent close to eight years working for department stores and after that several more years working with them. I think they failed to keep up with the key factors that most successful retailers consistently possess. I mentioned Leonard Berry at Texas A&M who did some research a few years ago to determine what are the factors that the real successful retailers have in common. It's interesting that they narrowed it down to about four or five of them. Then, if you compare these factors to department stores, there's no question why most chains are struggling. The first one was you had to be *relevant to what the customer needs and wants.* Part of the problem with the department stores is that they really were built on the society in the '40s and '50s when everybody wanted one place to buy a lot of different things and shop on a lot of different floors in their downtown stores. It was an event to go there. However, as department stores expanded, they couldn't capture that "specialness" of that event. If you look at Bloomingdale's or Macy's for example, they do terrific in New York City, but they don't perform quite as well in other markets, especially in major malls. The same holds true for almost every major department store in any given city. I grew up in Detroit and Hudson's was not just a department store, it was part of your life. In Minneapolis, Dayton's was like that. And in Cincinnati it was Shillitos, or in Columbus with Lazarus. All these were part of life in their hometown. But they've lost that as they've grown and expanded—or were gobbled up by a major chain. The big chains have to be able to get that consistency in all their stores and they've failed to meet customer expectations.

I think the second thing department stores have been missing is the factor of providing value to the customers.

You notice I didn't say that the stores needed to just provide good prices, because, as we know, price is only a part of the value. It's the value of the service and the products they are selling; it's the value of the shopping experience, and more importantly it's the value of the people in the stores and how they take care of the customer. You really have to provide the sense of "OK, if I'm getting a good price, am I sacrificing anything?" or "If I'm getting great service, am I paying a premium for that?" You've got to keep it in the context that more and more department stores over the years still tried to provide the service they used to provide, but in doing so they couldn't—or wouldn't-provide the *value*. They thought they could make up for it by having a monthly clearance sale here and a big storewide sale there. However, the two just didn't mix. You've got to have a happy blend of service, assortment, and pricing, and the successful stores certainly continue to do that. And I don't mean just the discount stores, but specialty stores like Coach, whose stores sell great leather goods and definitely not at a low price. They're consistently doing well because their people and their customers see a value in the service and selection. Stores like Jos. A. Bank for men's wear and in a totally different category, the Container Store in Dallas. These are stores whose customers just absolutely love to visit.

Then it comes down to that other factor of *convenience*, the department stores fail to make the whole experience an easy one. As a matter of fact, it hasn't been an *enjoyable* shopping experience (the fourth factor) to go to a department store either.

However, I think the biggest factor that department stores are missing is being able to keep the professionalism and the personalized service that they once had with the people or associates in the stores. The department stores were really successful due to the service they provided, and they might have underestimated the value of their sales staff. Their once loyal customers say, "We weren't necessarily as loyal to the store as we were to the people that worked there." The bottom line is that when they lost the passion of the people in the store, they've lost a lot in terms of sales and profitability.

Wright

Well, what steps should the stores' marketing department take, to make sure that the brand is understood as well inside the organization as it is outside in the marketplace?

Banks

It doesn't happen by accident. I have developed, with my partner Terri Kabachnick, a program we call *Total Brand Integration® (TBI)*. My specialty is brand strategy. Terri's is getting the right people in retail organizations. We called it TBI because I have been talking throughout my career about how important an effective marketing strategy is in terms of establishing the brand with the customer. On the other hand, Terri has spent a lot of time working with companies assessing and analyzing how to get the right people to live up to that brand strategy. In developing Total Brand Integration®, we established 5 key steps to getting your brand totally integrated in to all levels of the organization. The first one is you've got to understand what the brand strategy is.

It's interesting that we executives in marketing develop these brand strategies and we put a lot of work and a lot of research into implementing them; however, we often don't do as good a job in making sure everybody within the organization understands what that brand strategy is. As important as research with the customer is, it's also very important to understand how relevant that brand strategy is *to the people in the stores*. It's extremely important to do research with every level of the store—not just the people on the sales floor but the management, the district managers, the operations vice presidents, and for that matter the entire headquarters team as well. You have to really understand where you exist in their minds and *hearts*. It's also essential that you understand your competitive position in very simple terms. You need to draw a perceptual map of where your store is relative to your competition. If the factors are on service and prices, you want to see where you stand on that map relative to your competition, then determine where you should be or want to be, and set up a plan to get there.

The *second* step we talked about is understanding the personalities of our people as well as we understand our customers. We do a lot of demographic and psychographic research in terms of almost drawing a picture of our target customer, but what you have to do beyond that is to do the same study with the people who work in your stores. Understanding who the customer is keeps you from trying to go after a target that is neither profitable nor loyal to your brand. In the same way you really have to target the right attributes with the people in the stores. The type of person, for example, who would work well in a TGI Friday's, is not necessarily the same one that would work in a Morton's or a Palm restaurant, although they are all restaurants they are distinctly different personalities. By the way, the kind of person who would work well in a McDonalds is not going to be the same one who would work effectively in that Friday's either. Restaurants provide a good example as we base the overall experience on the service we receive.

The retail stores are rated in the same way. The kind of people that you want and need to have in your stores is critical. When I was at PetsMart, for example, one of the key criteria of people we hired (not just in the stores but throughout the whole organization) was to determine if in fact whether they liked or do they own pets? Because if they did, then they can relate to a customer who treats their dog or their cat as a member of the family. The way to do that is to determine that they share the same feelings as well. You have to make a contract with the customer where you must marry the truth of the brands with the heart of the brand. I learned this when I was working with Publicist, one of the world's largest advertising agencies, who had developed this idea of the consumer contract. That is taking the truth of the brand, which are the facts of the store—for example in my PetsMart illustration we were a big-box store with an unbelievable selection of products as well as services, all conveniently located. The selection and services had to be coupled with the heart of the brand, which is that intangible relationship with the customer. We were saying that we're going to have people working in the stores who absolutely understood pets are part of the family because they felt the same about their pets! By marrying those two attributes and putting them not only into our advertising but also into the very people who took care of our customers, we felt that we had a consumer contract that required us to perform every day with every transaction.

The *third* part of this *total brand integration* is to define and research the people as well as the customer's since they are needed to bring the brand to life. Thoroughly understand those people through a number of scientific assessment tools that are available to us. You need to determine what type of people should be in your stores. What are the attributes and behaviors of the best people you currently have in your stores? Finally, which of ones don't perform very well? What are their attributes and behaviors? Once you identify these poor performer characteristics, you make sure that you and your managers don't hire to the standards that are below those who really perform well. It's amazing what you can find out through simple assessments and comparing them. You then know what, as we call it, the DNA is of the most successful performers in your stores. When you do that, you can make the choice of getting the kind of people who really relate to the customers and who live up to your brand everyday.

Fourth, you have to communicate your strategy effectively to your people. They must understand who the target customer is and why they are the most profitable visitors to the store. These are the customers to whom you must give the most attention. You can't expect the store or corporate staff to understand this by simply sending out a videotape or memo. You have to educate and explain—and you have to do it consistently.

Fifth, and finally, you have to align the hiring standards to meet the type of people who can succeed in your store and in your culture. Most importantly you have hire people who enjoy your business and who can thrive in your environment. If they don't like what they're doing, the customer is the first to know.

Wright

You talk about the importance of the people in the stores getting the brand strategy, but we all know that one of the biggest challenges is just getting people to reliably man the store. Isn't this just an HR issue that has nothing to do with the branding or marketing activity?

Banks

That's one of the biggest challenges that we all face in retail today, and I think we tend to build the silos within the organization when we don't want other departments interfering with what we determine as our responsibilities. I can honestly say that I've been there and done that more often than I'd like to admit. We get so tied up with our own departments that in a typical organization, the marketing people will say, (and I admit to having said this myself) "Look, I'll take care of the marketing. You take care of whatever it is you do!" Well, on the same token, the human resources department and training departments are saying, "We'll take care of hiring of people and training them. You take care of doing whatever you do and leave people up to us." The real successful stores aren't like that anymore, and by that I mean the marketing department must, in conjunction with the whole organization, develop this brand strategy. When we developed the brand strategy at PetsMart, for example, it wasn't me that developed it. It was a team effort. We called it our brand strategy team, and it represented everybody and every function in the organization from not only from marketing but also from operations, merchandising, human resources, I.S., and the veterinary professional services. We all sat down and developed it together, so we all took ownership of it. And then, together, we defined not only what our message should be and what are the important factors, but we also determined what our stores should look like, and what should the people in the stores look like—what kind of people do we want in there waiting on our customers? By doing that, we established the criteria for the kind of people that were going to be successful in our stores and we also established what kind of training they were going to need in order to take care of our customers. It really made a lot more sense to do it that way. We have to get around the idea that branding is a marketing-only function. It is a total company function. You really have to follow the five steps in our *totalbrandintegration®* process. Make sure that the strategies are aligned throughout the organization and that every part of the store organization lives up to it. This has to start absolutely with the top of the organization with the CEO and then everybody has to buy into it. Once you do that, then you can align the kind of people that you bring into the organization or in some cases the kind of people that you let go out of an organization. The ones who stay must be in tune with what the whole brand strategy is all about. You really have to have the passion for the brand and this is how you generate that passion.

Wright

So you get the right kind of people and then all you have to do is put on a big sale and the customers will beat a path to your door, right?

Banks

Oh, I wish it were that easy! First, you have to keep everlastingly at it. It's not something where the retailer will develop the brand strategy and the record a message from the CEO. They'll put it on a video or on an in-store communications and send it out to the stores and say, "From this day forward we will now be living up to the brand in this way." It doesn't happen that way, unfortunately, because the business changes and the customer change. I think of what David LDellassandro, the CEO of John Hancock, has said. He believes that: "The brand building efforts are a form of leadership. You really have to show your internal audience where you want them to go." And that, I think, is the key of making the brand successful. Of course, we often say, "Well, gee, if you just get the brand strategy together, everything will work." Well, it's got to really start at the top. The CEO must be the Brand Champion. McDonalds, for example, just a couple of years ago was having significant troubles as evidenced by their stock prices and their sales. Even in the *Wall Street Journal* there was a headline that said, "Rude Employees Are Costing McDonalds Corporation Millions of Dollars in Lost Sales." The CEO of the company at the time said, "You know, our research shows 11% of our customers are dissatisfied with the service experience they have when they come in—so dissatisfied that they write a complaint to the restaurant." After evaluating this information, they determined it was probably costing the company $675 million dollars in sales a year. That's taking this whole idea of branding to heart by saying it's more than just having a smiling face serving-less-than perfect hamburgers. People really had to believe in McDonald's where they worked and the kind of job it was. Now, the new management at McDonalds has realized that over the last year and a half or so, because not only are they producing a better product, but also they're producing better people. They have better standards of cleanliness and operations in the store. They're starting to reflect this in the revenue and profits, which continue to improve.

The same thing holds true in the conventional retail stores. Those stores that really do well live up to it every day. I mentioned the Container Store, a chain of specialty stores based in Dallas, Texas. Their whole focus is that the people who they hire must live up to their brand every day, and their brand is to offer solutions to help make your house and your life more organized. The people in the stores *absolutely* say, "I just love working at this place!" Then you ask the customers and the customers say the same thing. "I love shopping here because their people love working here." So it's this combination of the two. Once you have that kind of loyalty, you can go out and aggressively market it. The message you give to the customer has to be the message that you live at the point of connection. We talk a lot about CRM, or customer relationship management, as being one of the keys to business right now. And when you think about that, well, where does that relationship start? It starts when the customer walks in to the store and interacts with one of the people on the sales floor. If the store sales associates don't get it, all the other parts of the organization and everything else that you've done just falls flat. Why? Because that's the place where you plug in the brand to the customer, and it's essential in doing it right there every time.

Wright

It sounds pretty comprehensive this brand strategy concept. Tell me, who is ultimately responsible for making it all happen?

Banks

As I indicated earlier, it absolutely starts at the top. The CEO's who are dedicated to making the brand live and understand what branding is all about are the ones who are responsible for a successful operation today. Over the years we've tended to say that branding is a marketing function. Well, if marketing truly is what Peter Drucker said it is—the key to the business of growing the business, of generating the profits, etc.—then why do many senior officers in many stores fail to get involved with the branding process? Oh, they may buy into it in an executive committee meeting, but how many of them really live up to it day in and day out? How many are truly Brand Champions? I believe it was Michael Gould, CEO of Bloomingdale's—a store which certainly has a great brand who said, "Our brand standards are met every day and unless everyone from me to the person in the store is not living up to those standards, then we don't have a chance of succeeding with our customers." If you look at some of the successful stores out there, and it's not just the Wal-Marts of the world, they confirm what Gould said. It's the companies like Motherhood Maternity and Joseph A. Bank and Chico's and other great companies. It really starts with the CEOs at these companies who have set the standard for what the brand is going to be about, and they make sure that everybody on their team is consistently saying the same things through that strategy.

While internal communications or internal marketing are critical, it really starts at the top. You have to set up a structure for what branding is all about—it's about the success of the company. "Whose job is it?" The CEO, as I said, has to be the *brand champion*, if you will. And then it goes to the marketing departments who have to be *the brand evangelist*. Marketing has to communicate this strategy and find the effective ways of communicating it not only externally but internally as well. And then it gets to the management of the stores or the district managers, and they have to be the brand *apostles* who are taking that word out to the stores. They have to be able to recite and live the strategy just as well as the CEO, and they have to make sure that they set the standards day in and day out for the stores. When they do that, then you've got the people in the stores who make it their way of life. They represent that brand strategy to the customer with every shopping trip. It sounds pretty easy, but it's a never-ending job. I think if I had to say one thing about the branding thing is it's not an ad or a campaign, it's *a way of life*. Once a company realizes that, it becomes natural.

I keep going back to Wal-Mart because they are so successful and I have had many friends in their organization. Wal-Mart understands that what they stand for is a way of life with them in everything they do. I remember being at a conference with one of the senior marketing executives at Wal-Mart, and we were meeting at the Hyatt or a Westin Hotel, and after dinner I said, "Well, see you for breakfast. I'll meet you downstairs." He said, "Sorry, we're not staying here. We're staying at the Best Western down the street." I said, "Oh, really? Couldn't you get in?" He responded, "No, we have a philosophy at our company that we really believe in keeping our costs low so we can pass them on to the customer, and it's not just at store level. We keep our travel expenses down wherever we can. So, you know I'm going to stay at the Best Western. If I can save on our operating expenses, we'll save the customer in the long run."

It's really becoming more than a strategy. My friend, B.J. Bueno has written a book called, *Cult Branding*. If you think about it, branding really becomes kind of a cult when the brand becomes something that the loyal customer is almost obsessed with. Think about Starbucks or Southwest Airlines...

Wright

Well, what a great conversation. I've learned a lot here today about branding.

Banks

Well, good. You know it's amazing. I put all this "stuff" into notes and we get to talking about it and I'm already on the next point before we finish the first one because there's so much to developing a great branding strategy. However, you can see there's a common thread through the whole thing—and that's people. Customers and associates.

Wright

Yes.

Banks

And you know what I try to do is to simplify it by saying, branding starts at the top and you must make sure that it gets communicated to every level in the organization.

Wright

Today we've been talking to Ken Banks whose firm focuses on helping retailers, media, organizations, and advertisers develop brand strategies and programs to position themselves with today's customers. He continues to be in demand for speaking engagements on branding in a variety of marketing and advertising topics at major meetings and conferences around the country. Ken, thank you so much for being with us today. It's been very enjoyable and I've learned a lot.

Banks

It's been my pleasure and I absolutely love to talk about branding and about retailing, so it was a great experience for me as well.

About The Author

With over 30 years experience in retail marketing and branding, Ken Banks established KAB Marketing in 2000. Ken focuses on helping retailers, media organizations, and advertisers develop brand strategies and programs to better position themselves with today's customers. He is in demand for speaking engagements on branding and marketing nationally and internationally.

Ken's career includes senior marketing positions with companies such as Procter & Gamble (Folger's), Dayton-Hudson (now Target Corp.), Robinson's, Doner Advertising, Eckerd Drugs, Circuit City, Fahlgren Advertising, and PetsMart Stores. Ken has been recognized as an authority on retail branding. He has authored several trade articles on retail branding.

A graduate of Wayne State University and the American Graduate School for International Management (Thunderbird), Ken has won many creative awards for his companies and was elected into the Retail Advertising Hall of Fame.

Ken Banks, BS, MBA

KAB Marketing

10810 72nd Street N, Suite 207

Largo, Florida 33777

Phone: 727.515.1932

Email: Ken@KenBanks.com

www.KenBanksMarketing.com

Chapter 17

Bob Pritchard

THE INTERVIEW

David E. Wright (Wright)

Today we are talking to Bob Pritchard. Bob is the CEO of international marketing power house Marketforce One, Inc., with head offices in Los Angeles and offices in Europe and Australia. Bob is the recipient of the Academy Award of Marketing Business, the "International Marketer of the Year." He is a consultant and/or speaker to 87 Fortune 500 companies and speaks to around 100 major organizations a year in the United States, Europe, and Australia. He is the author of six best selling books, including *Kick Ass Marketing, 15 Keys to Guaranteed Business Success,* and *Complex Marketing Made Simple*. Bob Pritchard, welcome to *Marketing Magic*!

Bob Pritchard (Pritchard)

Thank you very much.

Wright

You've enjoyed great success for your clients based on the premise that the product, price, satisfied customers, and brand awareness are all totally irrelevant to successful marketing in this new highly competitive marketplace. So what makes these former pillars of marketing and sales no longer relevant?

Pritchard

I think what differentiates Marketforce One and the reason we've had so much success is that the research we've done here, in Europe, and in Australia shows that 87% of all marketing is based on either product or price. It is indirectly about satisfied customers or focuses on just getting brand awareness. And what triggered my initial thoughts about this was an article I read in *Time* magazine about four or five years ago where Bob Kuperman, the CEO of Chiat Day, which is a five billion dollar advertising agency, said that their research indicated that 95% of brand advertising today doesn't work. So I had a deeper look and found that Levis in the U.K. did a similar study which said 90-odd percent didn't work. Samuelson Talbot in Australia did a similar research with similar results. I thought, "*Okay, 87% of advertising uses these four pillars as the primary basis of the message and 95% of this advertising doesn't work, so there must be a correlation somewhere.*" So when we started rationalizing it, we realized that if you consider any product or service, very few companies have got a unique product, most products have become commoditized. Consider the simple well known brands, Coke and Pepsi or Eveready and Duracell or Ford and General Motors. Most products have a comparable competitive product. And if a company does happen to come up with something totally unique, then the competitors are going to replicate it very quickly.

Wright

Right.

Pritchard

So, we went further and found that an old Harvard Business School study that showed 92% of consumers find like products interchangeable, so even if people prefer a Duracell, when they can't buy a Duracell, they'll take an Eveready—doesn't make very much difference. So it seemed to me that if your marketing, advertising and promotion is based on the product or service itself, and competitors are selling pretty much exactly the same product, you are not differentiating yourself at all. And so that's wasted marketing and advertising dollars because you are really marketing the whole category of products or services as far as the consumers recall is concerned. Then when they buy, if they don't buy yours, they'll buy the competitors.

Then we considered the price issue and interestingly we found that while most companies come to us and say, *"In our business, price is critical."* And we say, *"No, it's not, you are just conditioned to think it is."* Their immediate response is, *"Well, our business is unique. You don't understand."* But then we found that, according to research, 87% of people in the U.S. don't buy based on price solely. While price is in the top three to five reasons it is the primary issue only 13% of the time. Other things are also really important considerations, things like service, reliability, trust and those sorts of issues. So when you look at peoples' considerations when they actually buy, in the majority of cases the importance of price is considerably less than most businesses perceive. For example, I spoke in Detroit to a motor manufacturer and they said, *"The motor industry is so price competitive."* Well, if that was true, and people bought cars based on price, Los Angeles would be full of Hyundais and Kias. The overwhelming majority of people are not driving around in low cost cars. They're driving BMWs and Mercedes, and Saturns. Certainly not the least expensive car.

I spoke to the apparel manufacturers and they said exactly the same thing, "The apparel industry is driven by price." So we looked at clothing. When people are going out somewhere, how many of them race down to Target and buy the cheapest shirt they can buy? When they go to the supermarket, how many buy generic products? They buy the most popular products. I don't buy based on price, and I'm sure you don't buy based on price either.

Wright

Right.

Pritchard

When you look at 87% of the population, they don't buy based on price either. Yet somehow we've got ourselves absolutely convinced that all our customers are interested in is price. The reality is that if you don't give your customers a clear and convincing choice, if you don't differentiate the benefits of your product or service really clearly from your competitors, they will see several products that are very similar and of course, buy based on price. That's just logical.

But if you clearly differentiate your product and you give customers a real reason, or even a perceived reason to buy your product, then they'll buy your product over the competitor's, irrespective of the price. Now I'm not saying that you can charge double or triple or anything like that, but research shows that you can charge 13 to 17% more than your competitors and still not lose the business if you've clearly differentiated yourself positively. So price isn't important to getting satisfied customers.

Harvard Business School research also shows that 62% of all satisfied customers don't repurchase from the source that they were satisfied with. When we looked at why that is, after quite some research we found that people, when they go and buy something, believe, quite rightly, that they're entitled to be satisfied. That's one of the elements they are buying. You are not going to get somebody back to buy again by just giving them something they're entitled to. We found that for people to come back and repurchase, you have really got to knock their socks off. They have to walk out of your store or from doing business with you, whether they have purchased a service or a product, saying, *"Wow! That was fantastic! I really enjoyed that experience! Those people were so helpful. They gave me excellent information. I really trust what they've told me."* It is interesting that studies have shown that while customer service has improved over 300% in a decade, customer satisfaction is at an all time low. People want a lot more than most companies are giving, and we found that when customers experience that "wow" factor, they'll come back, but if you just satisfy them, they're never going to come back! We have also found that many companies believe they are giving service way beyond what is expected, but customers don't see it that way and believe that they are entitled to that level of service. Then companies are amazed when they don't get the repeat business.

Another factor is that in the main, people don't trust corporations or the media. The last research that I saw, I think it was Gallop, said that over 90% of people trust their family or friends, but only 17% of people trust corporations and I think the media did even worse than that, governments even worse again. So most people do not believe advertising or a company's propaganda, but they really believe word of mouth. You need your customer's friends and families to go around saying, *"Wow! That was a great experience I had with those people."* You'll get great word of mouth and that will translate into sales, then into loyalty, lower marketing costs, higher profits, greater ROI. We have demonstrated conclusively, over and over again, that when it comes to product, price and satisfied customers, none of those count unless you really have differentiated your product or service benefits clearly and unless you "knock the customers socks off."

When it comes to brand awareness today, there's so much clutter out there. I mean there's this enormous proliferation of media vehicles. Every surface on the planet's got ads on it. The customer is getting more and more and more cynical. They've got less and less time to relate to any advertising and mostly they're distracted at the time they are exposed to the message. They are running to an appointment, trying not to hit anyone on the freeway, putting the kids to bed or they're doing something else. So even the really "pointy" ads don't have the impact that they used to, and the fluffy, meaningless brand awareness advertising has even less. And while the average person sees around 3,000 ads a day, they can only remember and describe between two and five of those 3,000. So with 3,000 companies out there trying to buy brand awareness, and with only two to five of them working—and you can bet that the majority if not all of the two to five being recalled are the Cokes or others with big research, testing and frequency budgets—what hope does the average advertiser have? So if you're not a big guy, and most likely even if you are, you're just getting lost in the rush. It became apparent to us at Marketforce One that trying to buy brand awareness wasn't going to work either. When you look back at the .com experience, they spent tens of billions of dollars getting brand awareness, and where are they? They've all gone broke. Everybody knew who they were, but people weren't buying off them. It is apparent when you look at the performance of most well known companies that just because people know who you are, it doesn't guarantee a sale.

So we decided, almost a decade ago, that we needed to go to corporations and say to them, "Stop advertising your products; stop being price driven; stop telling people how many satisfied customers you've got; and stop brand advertising / awareness type ads because they don't work now and as we progress into a more and more competitive world and more commoditization they are going to work even less." And that's paid dividends. We are saying to businesses, "You know you have to do a lot more for your customers today," and so as I touch wood, it's working really well.

Wright

If product, price, satisfied customers, and brand awareness are no longer important, then what is?

Pritchard

I think the most important thing today is to build what we call brand equity. It's having people really respect you and your brand, who you are, what you stand for and your customer ethic and this results in very powerful word of mouth. Your brand equity is the combination of a whole lot of things, it's a combination of the personal experience you have with the product when the product works really well for you, it's the word of mouth, the "buzz" in the community, it's what your friends, relations and people that you speak to tell you about it, it's the image you get from media exposure and advertising, its whether you are perceived as caring about the environment and the community. The few very successful advertising companies, like for example Johnson's Baby Powder, they don't sell the product, what they sell is a great mother-child relationship. They are always selling that warm loving mother-child relationship. All of their competitors are out there telling you how super absorbent they are. Well, if you get a choice between something that holds an extra half cup of water and a loving relationship with your child, you're going to take the relationship every time. You don't see Johnson's out there saying, *"Hey, we're really absorbent"* and all of that stuff that everybody else is doing. They're out there saying, *"We're a product that you can always trust and rely on, we've been around a long, long time, we will help you to build a wonderful relationship with your child, we help you do the right thing, we've got the same beliefs and interests as you, we're on the same wave length that you're on."* And that continues to build the equity in the product, year after year, generation after generation.

Your corporate reputation certainly helps you if you're a good corporate citizen and you're perceived to be caring about the community. I think that's becoming a more and more important element among all of those things that add to brand equity. But it really is a combination of all of these things that create the resultant brand equity value. I think about Coca-Cola. They have got a market capitalization of around about 185 billion dollars. Yet their physical assets are only worth 15 billion. The 170 billion dollar difference is the equity they have in their brand. Now, Coke's got a 99% brand awareness around the world, Pepsi's got a 99% brand awareness around the world, but if you were going to put both Pepsi and Coke on the auction block tomorrow, I would venture that Coke would bring a much, much larger return than Pepsi would. Yet their products are almost identical, so the difference is the equity that Coke has built up in its brand.

Now how do you get the message across to the marketplace? First of all, you need to know what business you're in. It's sounds like a ridiculous question, but we find that a lot of companies that we go into really don't know what business they're in. For example, a company that's selling window frames is not really in the window frame business because people don't say, *"Today, I've got to buy a window frame."* They say, *"Wouldn't it be comforting to have a view of the kids at the pool?"* So the customer is actually buying a view. Now if the company's selling window frames, there is actually a disconnect between the buyer and the seller. In a competitive market, the company is unlikely to be as successful as if they were selling the same thing that the customer was buying, and the customer is buying a view. We've actually got a client who used to sell window frames, and as soon as we switched the advertising from window frames to *"Buy a view, watch your children while they're in the swimming pool,"* their sales went up dramatically. We didn't have to spend any more money on advertising, we did nothing different except sell the same thing the customer was buying, we got rid of that disconnect.

I recently recorded some training DVDs for Pfizer Pharmaceuticals and they had undertaken a study to determine the maximum number of product benefits that can be promoted to a potential buyer in a simple message form that will trigger the optimum result. That number is three. Once you offered more than three, the sales performance diminished. Obviously, if you are selling the same thing the customer is buying, and if you are hammering three really good benefits, then you greatly increase your chances of obtaining a sale.

The other thing that is important to realize is that people make the decision to buy emotionally. Every single decision you make, you make emotionally. You'll only buy something or do something if it's actually of benefit to you or if it makes you feel better in some way. People make their decision emotionally and then justify it pragmatically, so we found that by selling emotional benefits and then justifying them pragmatically, you get the person to move through the process from, *"Yes, that makes me feel better," to "I really am interested."* Then, in combination that gives you high brand equity, and of course, once you've got equity, once people respect your brand and like your brand, they'll buy it over and over and over again. It makes it much more difficult for a competitor to get your business. You solve the clutter issue, you are no longer competing on a level playing field. You get strong loyalty. You get a lot more word of mouth because people are proud of what they are buying. This word of mouth produces further sales, and when somebody wants to buy your products, you can usually get a higher price for it than you can if you are trying to sell it head to head against a competitor. It makes a huge difference in your ability to get into a position to make a sale, and the ease of getting a sale.

So, the things that are important today—selling emotionally, making sure that you've got a no disconnect between what you are selling and what the customer is buying, hammering three emotional points with pragmatic justification, adding value, giving customer service beyond what is expected and being a good corporate citizen–builds the equity and that leads to strong word of mouth and more sales.

Wright

So how important is advertising in today's highly fragmented media market place?

Pritchard

I think advertising is still very important, but using advertising in a highly targeted way, not in the mass market sense that I think is still far too prevalent today. Today we've really got to know our customers. For example, one of our clients is in the Caravanning and RV industry. You can look at the market and say, *"The RV and caravan market is seniors who have retired and love to travel, meet people and tour the country, and people who have a young family, want an economical family holiday with lots of quality time doing things among nature."* But in fact, we've actually segmented that market into 14 different buyers, so there are 14 different types of people that go into that caravan RV market. And those 14 segments are different, they buy for different reasons. Of course there's a lot of overlap too, but in the majority of cases their primary motivation is different and they get their information from different sources. Therefore the message that you need to motivate them to buy is often slightly, or even vastly different. So are the media and communication mediums that you need to use to reach them.

Today you need to know your market precisely, know exactly who they are, where to reach them, know their hot buttons, and know precisely what communication vehicles to use. Some of those people that are caravan nuts or RV nuts will read the RV and caravan publications, others won't. You'll have to get at them in a different way. So once you know precisely who they are, then you use advertising of some sort, whether it be through targeted publications, direct or through technology such as SMS or internet through PR, sponsorship or sales promotions to reach them. Irrespective of whatever tool you use, its still really advertising in the broad sense. Advertising is as important as it ever was, but you need to know your market precisely, highly segment it, and hit people between the eyes. I'm not a great believer in the mass market approach at all because I think it's too hard to get results these days.

Wright

Right. You argue that the most critical element in successful marketing of a product or a service today is differentiating your product from your competitors, so how do you achieve that?

Pritchard

When you understand people, they don't buy the product when they're confronted with four or five products that are all seemingly not much different. They buy the difference between the products. They buy the benefits to them that one product offers, or is perceived to offer, that another doesn't. And so you've got to differentiate. You've got to focus on what you can readily communicate as being the difference between you and your competitor. To give a really simple example, the fast food industry is unbelievably competitive and there's very little difference between lots and lots of fast food outlets. If you consider pizza, there are pizza stores everywhere, every suburb's got a dozen pizza shops. Then Domino's differentiated themselves by identifying the primary motivation for people, or a good segment of the market, who buy a home delivered pizza. People want the delivery quickly. So Domino's *"30 minutes or it's free"* blitzed the rest of the market and their growth in that period of time was extraordinary. They didn't promise people a great pizza, they didn't promise them a hot pizza, they didn't promise them a cheap pizza, they didn't promise them extra pepperoni, they didn't do any of that. They just said, *"If you're looking for food that's fast, we're it!"* And so if you're sitting there watching Monday night football with half a dozen friends and you want something to eat, or if you're sitting at home with the kids, and the kids say, *"We're hungry,"* you immediately think *"I want something fast."* Domino's *"30 minutes or it's free"* means it's going to be quick. They really differentiated themselves from their competitors and blitzed them. It didn't have anything to do with the product itself. They just found the primary motivation behind a sizable segment of the populations reason to buy. I remember a few years ago, as will most people who are a little bit older, like me, there was a Unilever product called Blue Omo, a washing powder, that was released all over the world. Unilever differentiated Blue Omo by saying, *"Blue Omo washes whiter than white."* Of course, the strap line "whiter than white" really doesn't make any sense.

But what it does say is, "We're going to wash your clothes as clean as clean as clean as clean as they can get." So would you rather buy just a regular washing powder or do you want to buy the one that gets your clothes ultra clean? Blue Omo became the number one washing powder everywhere in the world. As you know, if you walk down the supermarket aisle, there are literally dozens of washing powders all made by the same handful of companies. But Blue Omo blitzed it because they created a difference that the consumer identified with. Wheaties, for as long as I can remember has been *"The Breakfast of Champions"* and has been a market leader. Yet there are all those breakfast cereals out there, but if you want the one the champions eat, the one where the champions are on the packet, buy Wheaties.

Wright

Right.

Pritchard

What General Mills has done is simply found a way to differentiate themselves. They're not out there talking about using the best quality wheat, or any of that stuff. All they're saying is the champions eat our product. Mom assumes that if it is good enough for the champions and for Olympic Gold medalists, it is probably good... and my child also needs the healthy stuff that champions need! Avis, *"We try harder."* How many people have rented an Avis car because Avis tries harder. It suggests that I'm going to get that extra bit of help or service if I rent an Avis car. Avis addresses the wide belief that all rental car companies are pretty much the same, that none of them really care; they all give you the minimum level of service and nobody's really in a hurry to help you. But this strap line creates a difference, the possibility that Avis maybe does care that little bit more and maybe they're going to try that little bit harder, so I'll give them a shot.

All this is clear evidence to me that people don't buy the product, they buy the difference between your product and the competitor's product. So you need to find what that is, whether it's real, perceived or even desired, and hammer it home.

Wright

With the dramatic change in the way business is done today, what is the real role of marketing and how important is it in a company?

Pritchard

Well, I think marketing is *the* most important part of a business. You'd expect me as a marketer to say that, but I think marketing is *the* most important thing in a company because everything begins with a sale. You can have the best technical team in the world. You can have the best accountant. You can have people who are the best at investing your money and hedging international currency. But if you don't sell somebody something, every one of these people is out of a job. Marketing is what drives sales; and therefore, *the* most important thing in a corporation. However, in the past 15 years in particular the financial people in companies have really taken control. Boards of Directors, these days are usually financial people. All of the major executives in corporations are financial people. Corporations have experienced a disconnect in my opinion, between what is important long term from a marketing perspective and the demands of the stockholders.

I gave a presentation a couple of years ago to the Association of Corporate Treasurers, which is the corporate treasurers from all the major companies, and what I talked about was how do we bridge this disconnect between the attitudes of marketing people and the attitudes of financial people. Financial people, particularly in public companies, are looking for a result every quarter. The major changes in the marketplace in the past decade have demanded a significantly different approach be taken to marketing which has made it impossible to continually get a short term result and build the long term marketing health of the company. Marketers must build long term loyalty through developing customer relationships and using customer relationship management to really understand our customers. This marketing approach takes time and you certainly can't do it in a quarter, it takes years. So we've got this disconnect where we've got our financial people out there saying, *"We need quarterly results. We've got to keep these stock prices up. We've got to produce good figures."* And you've got marketing people saying, "Yeah, okay. I've got to balance getting a quick quarterly result through maximizing quarterly sales with building long term relationships and ensuring that we've got customers there in the future." More importantly, in the future, clients need to have more say in what companies produce, how they do business, (provide just in time production and deliveries etc depending on the business) and those who don't have these customer relationships run the risk of long term failure. In many companies we find that there's a real problem between marketing people and financial people as to what direction needs to be. This spells long term disaster.

We also take the view that marketing today is not just advertising, promotion, public relations and the other disciplines that it used to be. We believe that marketing is every single action that takes place in a company that either directly or indirectly impacts a customer or a potential customer. It doesn't matter what it is. I don't care if it's a phone call to the receptionist or a service call two years after the initial purchase. That's marketing today because in this highly competitive environment you need every contact with a potential customer to be a 'wow'. To me it's all marketing. I believe when somebody walks into your foyer and meets the receptionist and makes an inquiry, that's marketing. When somebody clicks on your website, that's marketing. It doesn't matter. When somebody delivers the package you bought to your home, that's marketing. When somebody provides a service call, that's marketing. Because they're all the things that affect your brand equity and your ultimate future. They're all the things that are going to determine whether you've got a really good relationship with your customers, whether you've got great word of mouth, whether you've got loyalty. All of those things are going to depend on the relationships that you build, every contact is going to contribute to that. So we believe that every single thing that impacts a customer or a potential customer one way or another is marketing.

Last week in Europe I worked with a private, family owned Swedish company with annual sales of many billions of U.S. dollars, primarily controlled by one person. They have a flat management structure and an open door management policy. The CEO is always totally in touch with the marketplace and because they are privately owned they can act, or react, very quickly and they are extremely flexible. Anybody can talk to the boss pretty much at any time. They can make decisions very quickly because they don't have the layers of structure that encumber most public companies, yet they are a large organization with some 15,000 employees. But most importantly, while they need to make an annual profit, because that's how you stay in business, they're not being pressured by stockholders to increase the quarterly profit and maintain stock price. They have a medium and long term marketing strategy that is designed for the long term health of the company, not the short term health of the stockholders. They actually did take part of the company public and ended up buying it back because they found that as a public company they had much less flexibility. Therefore, they were more vulnerable to attack from the competition than they were when they were totally privately owned.

Wright

Right.

Pritchard

Corporations are going to have to adjust because the world's getting more and more competitive. Brand equity and building long term meaningful relationships with customers is going to become more and more important. So therefore, it's going to be more and more important for corporations to be more flexible and farsighted in their marketing and that means a lesser emphasis on the quarterly results.

Wright

Well, CRM or customer relationship management is a big buzz word today. Could you tell our readers what CRM is and is it important?

Pritchard

CRM is very important, well it's critical, but not necessarily in the form it takes now. What happened a few years ago when CRM became the big buzz word, a lot of people who had technology products suddenly adapted them to be CRM tools. But most of them weren't really CRM tools, they were just made to fit. And CRM's being used to streamline systems, provide the systems for offshore call centers and primarily to cut costs and cut heads, particularly in the United States. And so they've become a nice easy efficient cost cutting vehicle. However, cost cutting did not lead to great relationships with customers. I was the keynote speaker at the World CRM Congress in Paris last year talking about how CRM should be used today. Corporation after corporation stood up and said CRM was just not working, it had not improved customer feedback or customer 'intelligence' and had not improved customer relationships. Most had managed to cut costs but in fact decreased what their customers think of them. Their customers are tired of talking to machines, being put on hold, getting programmed responses and they're tired of talking to somebody that's

25,000 miles away who doesn't have the faintest idea what's going on. Their customers find it very frustrating.

If you go into www.complaints.com and the many similar websites that air grievances from angry customers, all of these delays, all the put on holds and talking to people who are 25,000 miles away has really hurt a lot of companies. One upset customer can now tell tens of thousands of people throughout the world in a matter of seconds. And so CRM, while it's important, should be about understanding our customers better. It's about getting to know customers. One of the things I did at this conference was to collect all of the brochures by companies selling CRM solutions that were on display in the Expo, and I added up the number of different reasons that were given to buy their products. In total there were 236 reasons to buy the various pieces of software. And of those 236, only 51 were about improving customer-company relationships. The rest of them were all about cutting costs. Now, if CRM is really about customer relationship management, surely the major reasons for installing it or for adopting it is to improve relationships. But it hasn't been. It's been about cutting costs. Accordingly, I believe that most companies that have bought 'off the shelf' CRM products have suffered because of it.

We certainly we need to know much more about our customers. We need to understand their lifestyles. We need to know what makes them tick. With the technology we've got today, we can data mine and through cross referencing find out enormous amounts about our customers and the most effective way to reach and motivate them. But you can't achieve it with stock standard CRM product. It just doesn't work.

Wright

Marketing is often referred to as an inexact science, particularly by financial people who currently yield most of the power in corporations. Just how inexact a science is marketing?

Pritchard

Well, I think marketing is about as exact a science as you can get. We work with a highly skilled technology company called Internetrix, and we've been working with them for a long time. We have determined ways to measure just about anything. We can measure the marketing effectiveness of how a company handles people walking in off the street and talking to a receptionist. We can measure the effectiveness of how phone calls into a company are handled from an eventual sales/relationship perspective. We can track every action on a web site and then trace it back to what's happened out in the marketplace. So I believe you can actually measure every facet of marketing today. Yet still you get people saying *"We can't do sponsorship because we can't measure its effectiveness."* If the sponsorship is created correctly, created to sell product and not just give brand awareness, of course you can measure the results. If you can't, don't do it. That's the other thing. We're great believers in selling people stuff. Business is about making a profit. Business is about selling people things. We are not fans of fluffy 'brand awareness' advertising. We believe it is a waste of money.

Wright

Right.

Pritchard

We believe that all marketing endeavors need to be geared up towards selling somebody something, even if the message is soft, kind and gentle and doesn't look like a sell, there needs to be a calculated close in there, rather than this soft, washy brand awareness, and having a good feeling about your message which is simply wallpaper and has people glaze over. We have found that by putting a lot of thought into how you structure every element of the marketing strategy, working with a commercially minded technology company, and then, with the knowledge that you've built up, working closely with the corporation, we can track absolutely everything. We've got a program where we can track everything down to a bathroom light going out at a remote office 500 miles away. And it can show in real time as a red alert on the CEO's pc, his laptop or on his mobile phone while he is lying on the beach in the Bahamas. Technology today can track everything, making marketing an extremely measurable science.

We must measure every marketing dollar spent. It seems crazy to me that somebody has to go and get three signatures to buy a box of paper clips and yet can go and spend any amount of money on a marketing promotion, direct mail program or whatever, and not know what the result is. And that happens all the time. Typical conversation. *"How did your direct mail work?" "Well, we think it was pretty good."* What do they mean by they think it was pretty good? They should know. Most business people wouldn't do anything else without being able to measure it and find what result they got for their spend, yet many marketers get away with murder. Any marketing manager worth their salt when they're getting a budget approved, needs to say, *"I want $76,500.00 for a direct mail campaign, this is who we're going to target and why, tests have shown that we're going to get these results, and at the top end of the scale we're going to get a return on the investment of x, and at the bottom of the scale we're going to get a return on the investment of y. Thirty days after the program is completed, I'll give you the ROI figures."* If a marketing manager can't do that today, then they should be working flipping hamburgers.

Wright

You're right! You are one of the most successful business speakers in the world. Tell me why should a corporation hire a business speaker? Can you really make a difference or is it simply entertainment or information that attendees forget after they go back to their office?

Pritchard

I think there are three types of business speakers. There's the business speaker who gives a lot of information. There's the business speaker who's entertaining. And there's the business speaker who has managed to combine both of those things. It has been proven that the business speaker who's been able to combine the high quality information with the entertainment and the motivation for the attendees to go and implement it, is critical to a corporation. Corporations need an outside look at what they are doing. People working for companies who hire consultants often say, *"Why would they use you when we have got an army of our own excellent marketing people?"* The reason is that an outside marketer can look at the company in a different light, and it's amazing the things you see that they mightn't see. You also have the advantage of working in other industries and therefore being able to take some of the expertise these industries have developed and apply it to their industry. I also get to consistently work on platforms with some of the best experts in the world and some of this expertise also rubs off. So a business speaker who researches the industry, knows what the current situation is, knows the challenges they're facing, knows what their competitors are doing, looks at the opportunities, and looks at the threats to the industry, will give them a different perspective. When I speak to a group I want to challenge them in an entertaining way, and I want to get them to think differently about their business and their issues. Often, company personnel get jaded hearing a message from their own people and a powerful speaker can reinforce the message in a fresh new way. I deliver the message with a bunch of really poignant stories that are funny, entertaining, get people to laugh, but have a real message to them so people relate and remember. I have people come up to me who I worked for 10 years ago, and they will say, *"You know I'm still telling my sales team that story because it's funny and it really gets the message across."*

Certainly, researching and custom writing every presentation is a lot more work, and companies pay a bit more for the speaker, but they get a far more effective speaker and much better results. We all get testimonials immediately after our presentations saying we were wonderful and funny and made the earth move. But the real testimonials are the ones you get six months later which say you really made a difference. They're the ones that count. The good speakers can make a real difference to a corporation. A speaker needs not only great content, but has to be able to motivate the people to change. I need to get the audience to say, *"I'm going into the office tomorrow, and I'm going to re-look at that issue, and I'm going to re-look at the way I do business, and I'm going to change."* And if you can do that, you're worth the money. A good speaker doesn't have to change the corporation very much, or change the attitude of the sales team very much, or change the attitude of the marketing people very much but that change magnified through the whole sales force pays for the speaker in the first five minutes of the next day. So I think we're very important.

Wright

Well, what an interesting conversation. I've really learned a lot here today, and I want you to know how much I appreciate you taking all of this time. I know you're busy and you're all over the world doing what you do.

Pritchard

I'm loving it.

Wright

And I just appreciate that we finally got together and I appreciate the time you've spent with me.

Pritchard

Thank you very much. I've really enjoyed it.

Wright

Today we have been talking to Bob Pritchard who is the CEO of international marketing power house Marketforce One, Incorporated. He is headquartered in Los Angeles, but as we have found out today, he travels all over Europe, Australia, and of course, all over the United States. You might want to check out amazon.com for his best selling books. Bob, I just really want to thank you again for spending all of this time on *Marketing Magic*.

Pritchard

Thanks very, very much.

About The Author

Bob Pritchard, CEO of international marketing powerhouse Marketforce One, Inc. has been developing business and marketing strategies for cutting edge businesses for 30 years. His unique experience has won him numerous major awards including the highly prestigious "International Marketer of the Year" award. His business and marketing insights have led to him presenting to over 1,000 corporations, including nearly 100 Fortune 500 companies.

Bob Pritchard
The Summit
22353 Sweet Willow Lane
Woodland Hills, California 91367
Phone: 818.346.0005
Email: bob@bobpritchard.com
www.bobpritchard.com

Chapter 18

RICHARD TYLER

THE INTERVIEW

David E. Wright (Wright)

Today we are talking to Richard Tyler. Richard is the CEO of Richard Tyler International, Inc., an organization that is one of the top training and consulting firms in the world. Mr. Tyler's success in sales, management, leadership, customer service, and quality improvement, and his reputation for powerful educational methods and motivational techniques have made him one of the most sought after consultants, lecturers, and teachers. Mr. Tyler shares his philosophies with millions of individuals each year through keynote speaking, syndicated writing, radio, television, seminars, books, tapes, and CDs. Mr. Tyler's book, *Smart Business Strategies, the Guide to Small Business Marketing Excellence*, has been hailed as one of the best books ever written for small business marketing. His *Power Learning Series* of business books and his *Conversations On* books are a great success. His philosophies have been featured in *Entrepreneur Magazine* and *Sales and Marketing Management Magazine* as well as in hundreds of articles and interviews. Mr. Tyler is the founder of Leadership for Tomorrow™, an organization dedicated to educating young adults to the importance of self esteem, goal setting, and lifelong success. Mr. Tyler is a member of the *National*

Speakers Association, the *International Platform Association*, the *American Society for Training and Development*, and the *Society for Human Resource Management*. Mr. Tyler has served on the *Houston National Speakers Association* Board of Directors. For 14 consecutive years Mr. Tyler has been listed in Who's Who in Professional Speaking. Mr. Tyler is an Advisory Board Member and past Chairman of the *"Be An Angel Fund, Inc."* which helps multiply handicapped and profoundly deaf children to have a better life. Richard Tyler, welcome to *Marketing Magic*.

Richard Tyler (Tyler)

Thank you, David.

Wright

Richard, you have seen and advised thousands of small businesses throughout your career. What do you see as the biggest challenges for the entrepreneur today?

Tyler

Today's customers are savvier than ever before. Technology has touched every aspect of our lives from the way we do business to the way we communicate with clients. Entrepreneurs can no longer simply rely on the integrity of a business or the quality of a product to achieve the desired results. Certainly, reaching excellence requires so much more. It takes a willingness to be receptive to new opportunities and a drive to go the distance in promoting your business.

Achieving excellence takes a willingness to look deep into your business and a commitment to doing the work necessary to differentiate your products or services from the competition. It then takes an extraordinary commitment to communicating with your customers the message that sets you apart from everyone else. Many call this marketing. I like to think of it as connecting with your customer, which in the end is the desired result of marketing. Think of it this way, if a company's marketing efforts are not connecting with their customers, then all the company is doing is wasting money while at the same time losing business!

Wright

Great point! So how would you begin advising an entrepreneur who isn't sure where to begin the marketing process?

Tyler

We always start with a clear understanding of what commitment means. As far as I'm concerned, there are some very clear, practical ways to launch a marketing strategy, but to achieve excellence requires this commitment—no matter how uncomfortable, no matter how difficult, no matter how stressful—to do whatever it takes within moral and ethical boundaries to achieve your goals. Simply making this commitment will set you apart from most of your competition.

The entrepreneur just starting out faces many challenges—not the least of which is how to best communicate the company's message. Those who have been a part of a large corporation know that big companies often have very big marketing budgets. They have in-house marketing departments and often spend a significant amount of money on outside expertise. In contrast, most new, small-business owners simply do not have the internal expertise or the financial resources to retain outside professional marketing assistance. It's the irony of entrepreneurship. When you most need professional help, you're least likely able to afford it.

We tell people all the time, "Don't despair. People just like you are launching and managing successful small businesses every day, and only a very slim percentage of those people are marketing experts. By understanding what the successful businesses are doing right and redirecting your efforts accordingly, you too can achieve marketing excellence."

Wright

Okay. Assuming the entrepreneur is committed to achieving excellence, what's next?

Tyler

We teach that there are really five key points to consider when you embrace the process of achieving marketing excellence: *Clarify, Learn the Basics, Pay Attention to the Details, Learn from Your Customers* and *Think Long Term.* Before we have a discussion about the marketing details of a particular business, we focus on these five keys. Understanding them provides the right perspective on beginning the journey to marketing excellence. Once an entrepreneur understands these key foundational components, he or she will not only recognize this as the place to begin, but he or she will see it as the right place to visit frequently just to make sure the company's marketing efforts are on track.

Wright

You said the first step was to clarify. Tell us how this works.

Tyler

If you expect to achieve marketing excellence, you must consistently and effectively communicate your company's core message. To do that, you need to *have* a core message. I've had people tell me, "That's obvious, we're an *ABC* company" only to be corrected by a fellow employee who says, "No we're not, we're an *XYZ* company!" And so goes the classic "who are we *really*?" discussion. It's a discussion that is common, but not common enough.

If you are to effectively connect with your customers, you must first clarify your message. Many companies will labor for years without ever really defining who they are until there is a crisis (usually financial). Then they realize they've been focusing on the wrong things for too long.

Clarifying is often most difficult for young companies. There is a natural reluctance to define the scope of the business too narrowly. This is understandable because often while the company is getting established, it needs business and can't always afford to be too picky about how it employs its resources. You might be surprised at how some of the most well-known companies started out. For example, did you know that the founders of Sony started the company without even having a product in mind to create? All they knew for sure is that they wanted to improve lives by applying technology to consumer products. So before they ever came close to manufacturing the products we associate with the Sony brand today, the company made (and failed to succeed with) a rice cooker and a tape recorder before just getting by with a simple heating pad product.

The lesson most of us understand intuitively is that maintaining some flexibility is very important. After all, a dogmatic fixation on a particular niche, product or market has been the downfall of many companies. Just look at Kodak. Once the undisputed heavyweight of the film industry, Kodak failed to recognize and adjust to the introduction of digital-camera technology until they started losing very significant market share. While the ability to be nimble enough to quickly react to changes in the market is very important, it shouldn't keep the entrepreneur from clearly defining the product or service, the customer, or the market as he or she understands it today.

Even if your current "heating-pad business" is destined to build the most earth-changing invention ten years from now, you must be able to clearly define in two or three sentences who you are and what you do *today*. Some call this "the elevator speech," the presentation you could complete in the time it takes to ride up or down a few floors on an elevator. It's a good exercise to do this with several people in your company. Have them summarize for you in a couple of sentences what your company is all about. I predict those who do this will find a few surprises. The Clarification process should be used to clearly define the company's message and should be revisited every six months. This will be extremely valuable as you begin addressing your specific marketing efforts.

Wright

So once the message is crafted, I suspect it's time to start communicating it, but isn't this where a lot of formal marketing training is required?

Tyler

I don't think so. Achieving marketing excellence does not mean that you have to become a professional marketing organization—you just have to be willing to learn enough to make a substantial contribution to the marketing of your business. You may recall hearing the sage advice about the best two times to plant a tree? Answer: "Twenty years ago and today." The same advice is true for marketing. It doesn't really matter where your business is in its life cycle; the time to learn—or *relearn*—the basics is *today*! This becomes particularly important when you're faced with increased competition. Allow me to share a true story about a couple of small business owners who understand this point well.

David and his sister Julia own a small franchised retail store in a small town not far from a large city. They have owned the store for ten years and have built a nice living by consistently achieving increased sales from year to year. Not long before the store's tenth anniversary, however, the two discovered that a large chain-store operation had plans to move closer to their area. They even heard from others who operate small businesses that when this big retail chain comes to town, small operations end up closing because of the competitive pressure.

Although David and Julia are not marketing professionals, they decided that they were not going to wait for the competition to show up before they took action. About six months before their tenth anniversary, they decided to launch a promotional marketing campaign that would culminate in a grand celebration on their anniversary date.

For each of the four months leading up to the tenth anniversary, David and Julia organized an event designed to make every person in the town aware of their store, its location, its product mix—essentially what it was all about. The brother and sister duo decided that a well-informed, loyal customer was their best defense against any competition and they set out to make a big splash and get noticed. They held events at the store, talked their vendors into giving away free merchandise and invited civic and youth organizations to participate in organizing the events. They brought in "door-buster" merchandise for each event—like a television or microwave for two dollars—and placed ads in the local paper to let their customers know. They held competitions, sponsored parades and got the whole town talking and anticipating the next event.

By the time the anniversary day arrived, the whole town was buzzing. This tiny store had *hundreds* of people lined up outside waiting to get in on the day the store turned ten. The store sold more merchandise in that one day than it typically sold in one month. The impact was astounding—and it was not due to some sophisticated, professional marketing and advertising strategy. It was the result of two people who decided they needed to communicate their product in a way that connected with their customers and made them remember—now *that's* marketing!

We strongly encourage our clients to take the time to learn the basics of marketing; to understand the tools available to them so that even if they decide never to personally perform the details (the marketing plan, the ad design, copyrighting, etc.) they can better work with those who do to get exactly what their business needs. A friend of mine who runs a marketing firm says he believes companies that outsource their marketing and advertising function because they don't understand it are making a big mistake. He believes the reason to outsource is when you don't have the specific expertise on staff or when you decide it's best for your business to employ internal resources in other ways.

Simply outsourcing something you don't understand will end up being an exercise in frustration to you and your outsource partner. When you understand the basics of marketing, you can do some of it yourself or at the very least you will be able to communicate more intelligently with the professionals who will do it for you. There are many resources that will provide you with the information you need.

In fact, it's the need for such a resource that led me to write my first book, *Smart Business Strategies—The Guide to Small Business Marketing.*

Once you understand what marketing and advertising is about and what it is designed to do and *not* do, you can effectively hire an outside professional to help move your business years ahead of where it would otherwise be.

Wright

So what you're saying is that even if you aren't always performing the details, you can't ignore them, right?

Tyler

That's exactly right. "Don't sweat the details" may be good advice for some other part of your life, but not when it comes to marketing your business. If the business professional doesn't do so already, he or she must think of marketing this way: Every detail of every interaction matters. Every step you take to sell your product or service is critically important. Every word you say or write leaves an impression. And of course the same rule applies when it comes to the actions of your employees. Every public impression made by you and those that represent your company *is* marketing. Simply put, if you want to achieve marketing excellence, you must not overlook the details that are sending messages about you every day. It may be easy to agree with that statement, but I believe it is one of the most under appreciated principles of marketing today. Unfortunately, the impact of ignoring the details that make up your public impression can be devastating.

Take a minute to think of a company with whom you no longer do business. Chances are you can remember why you stopped doing business with them. And chances are it was the result of just one or two interactions. It could have been a rude clerk, an employee's unwillingness to take the time to understand your wants or needs, the failure to correct a simple product defect, etc. Unfortunately, all it takes is one or two negative experiences to drive us away from a particular company. Even after having many years of positive experiences, we will most remember the last impression.

Wright

So how can a company tell if it has an impression problem?

Tyler

Well, believe it or not, this can be one of the easiest and least expensive investments an entrepreneur can make to improve his or her chances of long-term success. Here is what we tell our clients: Find three people who know your business well. They might be long-time customers, business associates, or board members, anyone who you can trust to shoot straight and provide you with sincere feedback. Tell them something like this: "Jack, I respect your opinion a great deal which is why I've come to you. I am working on improving the marketing of my business and I feel it is important to start with understanding how we come across to our customers. You're very familiar with our business; you've shopped our store for many years now. I need to know what you see as potential problems. Please understand that I'm looking for sincere feedback and nothing is off limits. If it makes you too uncomfortable to tell me exactly what *you* think, tell me what have you heard others say."

You may well get the standard polite answer, "Gee, Jill, I think you folks are doing a fantastic job over there at ABC, I don't know anything I'd change," or something to that effect. But if you are serious about reaching excellence, you'll keep probing by saying something like this:

"Thanks Jack, I appreciate that. But I know that we can all improve something. If you had to give us two things to improve, what would they be? Remember, I came to you because I have great respect for your opinion and I know I can count on you to shoot straight with me."

By continuing to probe and being sincere about wanting real feedback, you might get a response something like this: "Well Jill, there is one thing I've noticed. It might not be a big thing, but lately I've noticed that when I go into your store in the evening, I am rarely ever greeted by an employee and the store looks rather disheveled. It's a shame, really because it's not the impression I get when I shop during the day. Last week, I even heard some customers talking about how they probably wouldn't be coming back because they couldn't get someone to help them. . . ." –you get the picture.

This simple exercise can be extremely valuable. And for those who plan to get the most from it, we have two rules:

Rule 1: Be ready for the feedback and don't get defensive. My advice is to write down the comments, show genuine appreciation for them and then revisit them later. It's hard to be objective in the face of someone calling your baby ugly, but in this case, it's *absolutely necessary*.

Rule 2: If you don't get real constructive feedback (the kind that's often tough to hear at first), keep looking for someone to provide it. No doubt you'll be able to find plenty of people to tell you how great your company is. But that's not going to help you understand where your opportunities are. Some of the greatest leaders of our time kept someone close who would provide open feedback—these leaders clearly understood the value in that kind of relationship.

This process should include all components—large and small—that people associate with your brand. This includes the way people are greeted when calling or visiting your company, the general attitude of your employees, the look and feel of your office/store facilities, your logo design, ad copy, sales literature, stationery, business cards, your training strategies, your work habits, and so on. In short, everything you say, do and produce is a reflection, a mirror image of your business. Those are details that matter. By creating a system to manage the details of your business, you will be establishing a critical component necessary to achieving marketing excellence.

Wright

Richard, you mentioned that a company's customers can be a key source of information. On the surface that seems easy to see—but in reality, you've found it's an untapped source, isn't that right?

Tyler

That's exactly right. It's amazing to me how infrequently business owners or managers take time to learn from their customers. It's easy to fall into the trap of thinking that we know what our customers want—we're the experts, right? Well, no. We're *not* the experts. Our customers do provide feedback everyday; they either invest in or don't invest in what we're offering. But we can't rely on that as our sole indicator about how well we're doing in meeting their wants and needs because if we do, we're missing way too much. Responding only after we start to see lagging sales, is responding too late. We can all be much more involved in getting to know our customers; finding out what they like and don't like; what they respond to and don't respond to; what are their habits, their frustrations and challenges.

It is precisely this kind of detailed attention to the customer that enabled EMC, a data storage provider, to effectively take on IBM in the early 1990s. Back when IBM owned the data storage market and all other companies in that business were barely "also-rans," EMC decided to do something radical; talk to the customer. And not just any customer, the professional responsible for managing and using the technology they had to offer. IBM had become so big and dominant that the company effectively ignored the data storage market in most ways except to collect the 70%+ gross margins they were extracting from their 76% share of the market. They offered a robust, one-size-fits-all solution that was not exactly what the customer wanted, but it was almost always what the customer accepted. After all, everyone understood that you wouldn't get fired for choosing IBM. So, by default, IBM was the safe choice, and almost everyone just accepted that.

But then along came EMC, a company that wasn't even on the radar in the data storage market. EMC listened to the customer and decided they could compete with IBM by developing a product they believed was a better solution. Their dedication to truly understanding the customer and their commitment to innovation combined with a clever marketing strategy lead to a tenfold increase in sales in just about five years. EMC rapidly stole market share from IBM and became the clear market leader. The key to this amazing success was, of course that EMC started the process by learning from the customer.

Regardless of your business, your customer has a lot to tell you. If you set up a process within your company to collect customer feedback on a regular basis, you will give yourself a huge advantage when it comes to planning and executing your marketing strategy.

Wright

Is setting up such a process to get this customer feedback difficult? Where should one begin?

Tyler

Well, certainly with what you already know and are already doing. We suggest gathering members of your team and discussing what you know about your customers. Make sure you distinguish between what you know and what you think you know. This is where a lot of companies get into trouble. They build entire strategic plans around false assumptions. But understand that this is very easy to do. When an assumption about your customer makes logical sense, who will question it? If the assumption is wrong and it's not questioned, then decisions are made on the basis of misinformation—it happens everyday; probably even in your company.

When you challenge assumptions with your team members and give them permission to question everything, I predict you will discover there is still a great deal more to learn about your customer. Get your team involved in coming up with new ways to learn more about your customer, new ways to involve your customer in improving your business and new ways to serve and delight your customer.

One of the best things about the process of building stronger relationships with your customers is that it often doesn't even require introducing new products or sophisticated services. The simplest efforts—staying open one extra hour so commuters have a little more time to stop by your store, setting up a special client webpage to facilitate a faster review of work in progress, an occasional phone call to get customer feedback—are so many times the most powerful. In fact, many of the most successful products on the market today are the direct result of customer feedback. So our advice is to be careful about assumptions and focus more attention on learning from your customer.

Wright

What is your experience with how well small businesspeople plan?

Tyler

Business owners and managers certainly don't start up and run a business just so they can watch it fail in a few months. Yet, I am always curious why they plan that way. Just ask any entrepreneur to tell you how much of his or her day is spent thinking longer term than the next 30 or 60 days. Most will tell you that it is very little. This is really one of the most challenging components of running a business; how do we plan for the future when we're not even sure what's happening next week?

There is a lot of truth in the old saying, "Fail to plan and plan to fail." It's particularly accurate when it comes to marketing your business. If you fail to plan your marketing strategy, you are taking a big risk with your money. In fact, you would be much better off not marketing at all because in most cases, you would just be wasting a lot of money. Allow me to illustrate.

I have a friend in the marketing business. He had a cosmetic dentist for a client. The client had a successful practice and had a background that would allow him to develop and market some new products for his industry. He called my friend to talk about marketing. At their initial meeting, the dentist struggled to articulate his goals for his business. He couldn't clearly define his target audience or even the direction he wanted to take some of the products he was developing. He didn't have a handle on his short-term or long-term growth plans. Nevertheless, he enthusiastically told my friend that the previous week he agreed to run a series of commercials on a local cable station. Surprised, my friend asked the dentist what the spots would say, when they would run and what he was hoping to achieve with this marketing effort. The dentist simply told him, "I don't know. I just thought I'd give it a try and see what happens." It should be no surprise that this dentist wasted thousands of dollars because he simply did not understand the critical importance of a well-designed marketing plan.

Wright

Are you suggesting that every business needs to have a sophisticated marketing plan before getting started?

Tyler

No, no. Please don't misunderstand my point here. I am *not* saying that you need to have a sophisticated marketing plan before you can effectively market your business. I am saying that you need to have a good idea about where you want your business to be one year, three years and five years from now. We all want our businesses to be here for the long term. We just need to regularly remind ourselves that the long term is made up of a whole lot of short terms, and what we do in the short term determines whether we even get to *have* a long term.

The focus on thinking long term is paramount when considering marketing for two main reasons:

First, if you don't think long term, then you will be tempted to market your business without a plan. And if you don't market with a plan, I assure you, you will waste money.

Second, even with a plan, if you don't think long term you will most likely not stay committed to your plan. And if you don't stay committed to your plan, you will throw it away before it has a chance to pay you big returns on your investment. I've seen it happen so many times that it has become a cliché.

Let's back up to number one: "*If you don't think long term then you will be tempted to market your business without a plan.*" In other words, if you're only considering making your sales goal this month, then you will make marketing decisions that are too short-term and most likely, ineffective (and by the way, making the decision to *not* do any marketing is making a marketing decision). Let's see how this might work. Say you are thinking short term and you decide that you need to run an ad in the local newspaper to stimulate enough sales to make this month's numbers. If you're in a mid-size or large market, you could easily pay thousands of dollars for the ad. Without any other marketing support, you're pinning a lot of hope on the effectiveness of one ad to create enough sales' margin to pay for the ad and still make the month's goals.

Let's say this newspaper ad is part of a two-year marketing strategy. If you are placing an ad ten times in the newspaper, you have negotiating power and can use that to substantially reduce the required investment necessary to run the ad this month (sometimes paying a fraction of what it would have cost you to run the ad only once). That means you not only save money, but you now have additional budget to say, run some radio spots or hold special events to reach so many more people during the same time period. Don't you think that tripling the reach of your message for a lower investment is a better marketing decision?

It is so important to point out that marketing is not about creating that one perfect strike. That one-time perfect print, radio or TV ad that automatically compels everyone exposed to it to buy your service or product. Marketing is creating a plan that reaches the people most likely to be interested in your product or service with a message that best tells them how the product or service is going to satisfy a want or need they have. It takes time, a careful plan and patience to achieve that. Without a plan, your decisions will likely be short-sighted and not cost-effective.

Wright

That certainly makes sense. Now, let's look at your second point about thinking long term. What exactly do you mean when you say, "*Even with a plan, if you don't think long term you will most likely not stay committed to your plan*"?

Tyler

As I pointed out previously, an effective plan will take time to show its effectiveness. It is rather rare for a consumer to buy on his or her first exposure to a product or service. Every successful marketer understands this well: it typically takes multiple impressions for a person to become a customer. There are many reasons for this, but it is enough to say that human nature makes us a skeptical bunch. The more times I see a product, or company, or brand, the more I get used to it. The more I get used to it, the more I'll consider it when I have the need for that product or service. If I have a need *and* I am reminded of the company who can satisfy that need *and* I'm comfortable with that product or service, then I become a customer. You can begin to see how this works.

Unfortunately, many companies who do not see an immediate positive impact of a particular marketing strategy abandon the effort—just before the potential customer was ready to invest. The tragedy is that the company built equity with that potential customer and then walked away from it. I am sure you can think of some companies that have done that.

Thinking long term about marketing is easier after you have gone through the first four steps that we have already covered. By clarifying who you are, taking the time to learn some basics of marketing, carefully considering the details of the impression you leave with your customers and absorbing regular feedback from those customers, you will have set the kind of foundation that makes planning the long term much more realistic and much more effective.

Yes, there is so much more to be learned about the fine details and the strategy of marketing; and there always will be. Just remember that every investment you make in learning more about your company and your customers is an investment in marketing. And the amount of effort you put into those investments is directly proportional to the success of your overall marketing effort. I believe entrepreneurs must invest heavily in the foundational steps we have outlined in our discussion if they are serious about achieving marketing excellence. In fact, *now* is an excellent time to get started!

Wright

Today we've been talking to Richard Tyler. Thank you so much, Richard, for being with us today on *Marketing Magic.*

About The Author

Richard Tyler is the CEO of **Richard Tyler International, Inc.™** an organization named one of the top training and consulting firms in the world. Mr. Tyler's success in sales, management, leadership, quality improvement and customer service and his reputation for powerful educational methods and motivational techniques, has made him one of the most sought after consultants, lecturers, teachers and success coaches. Mr. Tyler shares his philosophies with millions of individuals each year through keynote speaking, syndicated writing, radio, television, seminars, books, compact discs and tapes.

Mr. Tyler's book *SMART BUSINESS STRATEGIES™, The Guide to Small Business Marketing EXCELLENCE* has been hailed as one of the best books ever written for small-business marketing. His successful books include; *Leadership Defined, Real World Customer Service Strategies That Work, Real World Human Resource Strategies That Work, Real World Teambuilding Strategies That Work, Conversations on Success, Conversations on Customer Service & Sales, Conversations on Health & Wellness, Conversations on Faith,* and *Marketing Magic.* His philosophies have been featured in *Entrepreneur Magazine®* as well as in hundreds of articles and interviews.

Mr. Tyler is the founder of the Leadership for Tomorrow™ an organization dedicated to educating young adults in the importance of self-esteem, goal setting and life-long success. He serves on the Advisory Board and is past Board Chairperson to Be An Angel Fund, a non-profit organization helping multiply handicapped children and profoundly deaf children to have a better life.

Richard Tyler

Richard Tyler International, Inc.™

P.O. BOX 630249

Houston, Texas 77263-0249

Phone: 713.974.7214

Email: RichardTyler@RichardTyler.com

WEBSITES

www.RichardTylerInternational.com

www.RichardTyler.com

www.SalesImmersion.biz

www.TylerTraining.com

www.ExcellenceEdge.com

www.DiscEducation.com

BOOK WEBSITES

www.LeadershipDefined.biz

www.ConversationsOn.biz

www.RealWorldStrategies.biz

www.MarketingMagicBook.biz